#Driven

COREY MINOR SMITH

ISBN-13: 978-0-578-44400-0
ISBN-10: 0-578-44400-3

#Driven

Dajon,
  Keep excelling!
Corey
5/2/2019

Author's Note

This is a work of nonfiction based on real life events and conversations from my memory of how they transpired at the time. This work is not written to represent word-for-word transcripts. Rather, it is presented from the best of my knowledge and recollection. In order to maintain anonymity, in some instances, I have changed the names of certain individuals.

Foreword

By

Les Brown
International Motivational Speaker and Author

There is a moment in life when you will experience a paradigm shift in your innermost being. Perhaps you have been there…it's the moment when you have to choose if the moment will define you, or whether you will define the moment. Life happens to you. It happens to everyone. The question that remains is, *what will you allow life to produce in you?* Corey Minor Smith has an intriguing tale of perseverance through overwhelming adversity. Her story begins with very humble beginnings. Somehow, being raised in multiple households, having two unstable parents, and a series of challenges didn't give Corey an excuse to abandon her dreams. Instead, she became relentless; she chose to take the road less traveled and trailed her way to success.

Corey Minor Smith is a classic example of the fact that it doesn't matter what happens to you in life; rather, it's what happens *in* you. Corey chose not to be another statistic or victim of circumstance. In this book, she provides you with her journey of going beyond the problems of life and becoming unstoppable. Undoubtedly, you will see yourself in these pages and recognize that you too can overcome any problem that stands in the pathway of your greatness. Today, Corey Minor Smith has accomplished her goals of completing undergraduate, graduate, and legal studies, and is pursuing her lifelong dreams.

As you read these pages, you will be inspired to look at your life and determine how the next chapter will be written. Corey Minor Smith is living proof that life doesn't determine your destination. It is up to you to determine how your story will unfold. Prepare yourself for an inspirational ride that will compel you to overcome setbacks, develop mental resiliency, and manifest your greatness!

Prologue

M any see success as a straight and narrow line from the start to the finish. Others realize that once they reach it, success is a series of swirls, circles, restarts, and multiple finishes. My life is not easy to follow; just like the series of swirls, circles, restarts, and multiple finishes. It's confusing for me to think back and remember which state, school, or household I was in at any given time in my life. But, there are some key points in my life that serve as landmarks that are not easily removed or forgotten.

A high school teacher introduced me to a phrase that has stuck with me throughout my adult life…"Undesirable circumstances." We all have undesirable circumstances in our lives. They are events in life that can hold us back. They are the negatives that can discourage a person from living the way God intends for them to live. Undesirable circumstances may be those things that we are ashamed of, or that people talk negatively about to others. Undesirable circumstances are my landmarks that have not been easily removed or forgotten in my life.

It was not until I heard Football Hall of Famer Shannon Sharpe's speech during his induction into the National Professional Football Hall of Fame, that I could fully articulate my drive to succeed in life. The undesirable circumstances in my life fueled my desire to succeed. My eyes filled with tears as he described a five-alarm fire that he felt inside. I often wondered what prevented me from staying on the wrong path.

What inspiration did I have that led me to want to live a productive, goal-oriented, achievement-filled life? What continued to encourage me to press forward despite the pain, emotional hurt, and obstacles that

1

continued to block my path?

In high school, I was involved in every possible organization available, and I tried to get the best grades that I could. Grandma Bluchelle used to say that I was trying to keep busy so that I did not have to think about the things that happened in my life. One of my best friends, Camela, used to tell me that I was overcompensating for the *lack* in my life.

I CAN ONLY THINK OF GOD, family, and friends who prayed with me, and for me, when I did not know to pray for myself. I also think of Shannon Sharpe's description of a five-alarm fire. One of his coaches asked why he trained when others did not…why he practiced when others went out to eat. His response was, "I had a five-alarm fire inside that I could never explain…all I knew was that I did not want to go back to Glenville. I did not want to eat cold oatmeal anymore. I did not want to eat possum, squirrel, or turtle anymore." Shannon's words resonated in my heart. My eyes filled with tears with each word he emphasized. He wanted more. That desire for more drove him to be the best football player he could be.

Despite my undesirable circumstances, I wanted more. I did not want to ever open a cabinet or refrigerator and not see food inside. No more drugs, drinking, or taking the car. Like Shannon said in his speech, my children will not live one day, let alone one hour, in the life I had as a child. My undesirable circumstances continuously fuel the inferno inside me that gives me my burning desire to want more, do more, and achieve more. Whatever your goals are, do not allow undesirable circumstances to be excuses for you to fail; instead, allow them to be reasons for you to excel. I encourage you to be Continuously Motivated to Succeed ("CMS") by applying the five CMS principles in your life today:

Faith, Motivation, Determination, Preparation, and Action.

Faith

Chapter One

Family

My Mom held my small four-year-old hand in hers as *she* made *our* way down the narrow aisle. I was not making *my* way down the aisle; I was in haul as a child my size and age would be. My cousin Jason followed behind me. Being even younger than I, Jason was being the silly boy that he was. It did not take much to distract his attention to anything and everything around him except where he was going at the moment. He kept bumping into the back of me; and finally, he pushed into me hard enough that it forced my head to ram into my Mom's behind. Mom stopped and her head turned. She gave both of us a look that said, *you two had better behave.* We both knew what her look meant without her even having to say a word.

Being rambunctious kids, we were often subject to the sting of a belt, a wooden spoon, a house shoe, or anything else within Mom's reach. Nothing was off limits when it came to her putting us in our place. We did not quite comprehend the age-old thinking of, *you don't embarrass yourself or your parents in front of white folks,* but we thoroughly understood the concept of getting our behinds spanked. That was a message that only the school of hard knocks could instill.

As we passed row after row of seats—some filled with passengers, while others were empty with large seatbelts waiting to wrap themselves around a warm body—it felt as if all eyes were on me as we moved down the aisle. The inside of the plane seemed cramped and restrictive, yet vast and mysterious at the same time. The wonder of being able to soar through the sky on a big bus baffled me, and my eyes showed my bewilderment.

We were following a stewardess—that was the title of flight attendants back then. I quickly took my eyes off of the small vertical windows lining the sides of the plane, and refocused on where I was walking. My eyes fastened on a neatly pressed blue jacket with a matching mid-length skirt, as the stewardess led us to our seats.

This adventure was the beginning of my travels on airplanes and other modes of transportation to childhood living arrangements from city to city, houses to homes, and school to schools, while bouncing between the two parental households that were raising me. After that first flight with my Mom, I ended up traveling the airways by myself. I flew from one state to another to have extended visits with my unwed parents. I never lived with either of my parents long enough to fully establish an attentive, caring parent/child relationship. My life was challenging as a child with unwed, separated parents. The fact that my parents lived in different states left me always wishing I could live in one place. I longed for my bedroom to always be in the same place, and to have the same set of friends that lived near me. That never happened. Mom lived in Ohio and Texas, and Dad lived in California.

During my time in Ohio—a rust-belt blue-collar state, white-flight was near the end by the mid-'70s to early '80s, and factory jobs and layoff notices were synonymous. The rise in crime became evident, and people on the corners sold drugs and sexual favors. With jobs dwindling, there were fewer tax dollars supporting schools, and less police presence was seen in the area. All of that can be related to the street entities starting to become societal problems that were quickly getting out of hand.

I often wonder if any part of my parents' problems was simply the ills of society that kept us from being the stereotypical nuclear TV family. Before my parents' permanent separation, they tried to do things the *family* way; they worked hard to stay together and do the best that they could for me. They were teenagers when I was born; Mom was seventeen, and Dad was nineteen. Having a child enter one's life while at those tender ages can slow down, or stop one's educational plans. Emotional maturity of young parents can often be a problem as well. In some cases, young parents, while still struggling to "find themselves" are ill equipped mentally to raise a child. For sure, the amount of income they are able to earn changes the day-to-day existence of what they are able to provide in the way of housing, neighborhood choices, clothing, food, transportation, and schooling for their child.

During that first airplane ride with my Mom, we were on our way to join Dad in sunny California and start a new life as a family...*again*. Mom and I had already moved at least four times since I was born. My Dad shared a house with his brother—my Uncle Louis—and my uncle's wife Pat, and their son Jason. Both of my parents had their comfort zones - security blankets of staying connected to their high school friends. Mom, at any given time, talked on the phone with her girlfriend Roxanne. Most of Mom's friends from Canton, Ohio called her "Shee Shee." Mom's name is Geneva, but people call her G.G. Her close friends turned G.G. into Shee Shee; a nickname that only they knew how to say with just the right amount of sass and emphasis.

Dad's claim to fame was his high school football career. He was known as "Herm" to his friends. Grandma Bluchelle called him Herman Robert. Whenever he comes home to Canton, Dad's closest friends refer to him as "Bo Hick." Mom and Dad's other names did not matter to me when I did not have either of them around to say goodnight to me at night before the lights went out.

Unfortunately, not long after living in California, Mom and I moved out. My parents argued a lot, and struggled day to day with how to have a loving relationship. I do not know what issues attacked their relationship. As a child, I often wondered if I was the reason they could not get along. My parents' arguments often got ugly. Objects were thrown and verbal assaults were slung with the same ease that loving gestures are given in picture-perfect homes. My Mom stated loudly on a routine basis that she wanted Dad to get out of the house and leave her alone. However, in reality, it was "his house," a fact that he routinely shouted back just as loudly; so eventually, Mom and I moved to the downstairs section of a duplex. It was only one street away from Dad's place, but we still were moving away, and the family was not together in the traditional sense as had been the goal when we moved there.

Our new place was not much, but it was enough for Mom to call it hers. A converted garage created a large bedroom that led into a kitchen. Down a small narrow hallway was our tiny bathroom, and further down the hall was our quaint living room. Dad was over all the time. He taught me how to ride my *Pink Panther* bike while we lived there. We were not living under the same roof, but it was the closest we ever came to being a family.

Once, Mom had a guest over. It was a white man who came to watch the premiere of *Roots* with us. Dad came over and frantically blew his horn because he could not pull his car into the driveway as he normally could. I could tell Mom's guest was a bit nervous hearing the horn blaring, and a male voice outside yelling about a car being in the driveway. Mom explained to the man that all the noise from outside was coming from my Dad.

After Dad parked his car, he came inside and rushed toward the man. He introduced himself with a very firm handshake. Dad was not rude to the man, but he definitely made it clear that he would always be a presence in Mom's life: a fact that he made clear every chance he got. I guess things got to the point where being one street away was not far enough from Dad for Mom.

Eventually, we moved back to Canton, Ohio. Sometimes people move because they know the rent is going to increase at the end of their lease. That was the case with us on more than a few occasions. Other times, we left because we were behind on our rent, so we would move out in the middle of the night to avoid being seen by the landlord.

Moving around was commonplace during my childhood. Until my senior year in high school, I never knew how strange it was to move around so much. My teachers would ask when I had learned certain things, and I would have to reflect on which school taught me, instead of what grade I was in when I learned something. To my amazement, I attended fourteen schools: two preschools, eight elementary schools, three middle/junior high schools, and two high schools…all between three different states.

I have often been asked, "Was one of your parents in the military?" I would always jokingly respond that whenever I was tired of staying with one parent, I would move to live with the other. The truth is it was probably the other way around. When one of my parents got exhausted from the responsibility of raising me, it was time to go live with the other parent.

I became a professional traveler as a child. I knew the procedures of flying alone like the back of my hand. The stewardesses catered to me from gate to gate, and they were always helpful in making sure that I got to the right person once I reached my destination. When I would go live with Dad, he would drive to San Francisco to pick me up and drop me back off at the airport. My stepmother, Carol, was usually too emotional to go with us to the airport when it was time for me to go back home to Mom. Carol always preferred not to be around when it was time for people to leave. With teary eyes, she would give me a hug the night before, and would be gone the next morning before we left for the airport. San Francisco is about an hour away from South Vallejo where Dad lived, and usually he would have a friend ride with us to the airport. Back then, family and friends could walk all the way through the terminal with a traveler. For me, as a young traveler, that was great because Dad would stay with me until the stewardess assisted me to my seat. It made saying goodbye easier.

Once my flight arrived at whatever state Mom was living in at the time, the stewardess would come to my seat and ask me to wait until everyone else had departed the plane. Then she would walk me off the plane and take me to Mom who was always waiting for me at the gate. With Mom, I usually traveled into Houston Intercontinental, which was always at least an hour or more from where she lived in Houston. I landed in Hobby airport a couple of times because sometimes the flights were cheaper. When flying to Ohio, I usually flew into Cleveland or Akron/Canton airport, whichever one offered a cheaper flight. It was nice to have Mom waiting for me as soon as I exited the plane.

The stewardesses always gave me "wings" before handing me off to either parent. I traveled so much as a young child that I had a collection of wings from Delta Airlines. Grandma Bluchelle kept a lot of stuff; she was a hoarder of memories. After she passed away, we cleaned her house and I found a pair of my "wings" in one of her chest of drawers. It brought back fond memories of my travels.

Once, I flew to California from Ohio and I sat in first class. It was quite different than my coach flights. First class was spacious with leather seats and menus to order dinner. Next to me sat a very kind older white man dressed in a business suit. He had a head full of salt and pepper colored hair, a round face, and perfect teeth. I could not take my eyes off his teeth when he smiled at me, which he did a lot during the flight.

After taking off, the stewardess came to our row to take our dinner orders. I remember that she had a bright smile, and gave what seemed to be an extra kind presentation of our options for dinner. I guess it was part of flying in first class, and her responsibility to make sure all those on board felt like they were flying the *friendly skies*. While she waited in the aisle next to our row, the man leaned in toward me to ask what I liked to eat as he held out the menu for me to look over with him. He patiently described the food options as he pointed to each meal on the menu. The stewardess told me that I could have whichever meal I wanted. The man continued to review my options with me, and then we gave both of our orders to the stewardess. Thinking about what I would eat later at Dad's house, I ordered chicken, vegetables, and rice, because Carol made rice with every meal, so it seemed like the right choice to make. When our meals came, mine was hot and tasty. I do not think anyone would say that about most airline food nowadays. That trip set the stage for many more flights to come.

Chapter Two

Transient

Traveling back and forth, from house to house with different doors and paint schemes, the concept of home became blurred while living between my parents' households. The non-scientific climate change of moving from the Midwest to Texas and California, along with the diverseness of each neighborhood or lack thereof, meant a new school was often met by me with a wide eyed—*what next?* I was always "the new girl."

DeLores Pressley, an international motivational speaker, once interviewed me on *Joy 1520 AM*—a local radio station owned by CAP III in Canton, Ohio—shortly after I started my career at the Stark County Prosecutor's Office. While often listening to her soft, friendly voice on the radio during my daily drive to work, I remember saying to myself, *I must meet that woman.* When we did meet, I quickly became aware that the radio hid her inner and outer beauty; her personality unfolded in multiple ways as I got to know her.

DeLores is a beautiful woman who I later learned started a plus-size modeling company after being rejected many times in the mainstream modeling world. She later went on to be featured in *Glamour*, on *NBC*, *ABC*, and on national radio and television shows, like *Oprah*, in addition to hosting her own TV and internet radio shows. DeLores is a mover and a shaker in her own right. The more I got to know her, the more she motivated me.

However, the day she interviewed me, I believe my story motivated her. DeLores started off the interview with routine questions, but went further and continued to ask questions in a way that encouraged a relaxed, engaging conversation. As she listened to the names of the schools I had

11

attended, and the states that I had lived in, DeLores gave me an amazing gaze of wonderment. She seemed puzzled. The room felt as if there were questions marks painted on the walls, the desk, and on the microphone. She hung on to every word I said, and then interrupted me as I continued to list the schools.

"I know that you are finished…you went to all those schools and more?" she asked.

I nodded my head. "Yes."

The way Delores asked the question, reminded me that I had been on a journey. I kept a mental diary of so much of my childhood lifestyle and information down to a fine detail. We stared at each other in disbelief. The number of addresses I had over the years would probably triple in number if I were actually able to list them all. My life began with living with both of my parents. Over time, my situation changed to having at least eight different households, encompassing three different states, with different people helping to shape me into the person I am now.

Chapter Three

Dad

Once Mom and I moved back to Ohio from California, I missed my Dad. I was used to seeing him almost daily; despite everything that was wrong, or despite what should have been better in our lives. I'm sure I fell into the same feelings a lot of young girls have about their fathers. Dad was my world at times. He was my Superman: my defender and a true hero in my eyes. At least that's what I wanted to believe. It sounded like a great idea to me at the time, so it had to be right. *Me and my daddy!* I thought to myself.

I spoke with Dad regularly on the phone. He sent money every so often so that Mom could buy the things I needed. It might seem a bit strange, but when a child becomes aware of *occasional* money coming from a parent, sometimes it might score higher than the parent that is there full-time.

On rare occasions, Dad would make surprise visits to Canton. I was so excited to see him whenever he came to town. I could tell it irritated Mom when I ran and jumped into his arms. My Superman. His *Old Spice* scent, his tight dark skin, and his sly smile, all won me over to be silly putty in his arms. By the time Dad would spin me around and throw me in the air, I was all giggles. He would be all smiles, and Mom would stand there stern-faced with her arms crossed. When Dad made eye contact with Mom, his smile slowly turned solemn as he put me back down.

The letdown concerning my relationship with Dad was that he was not around for the day-to-day responsibility of raising me. Dad did not live in Canton. He lived in California, and he did not have all the daily responsibilities of raising me that my Mom had. He did not provide for me on a consistent basis. Mom said he did not provide for me as he should have, and that he only sent $50 a month, if that. She said she struggled to take care of me on her own. I could hear bitterness in her voice every time she mentioned how hard it was for her to make ends meet with little financial help from him. I'm sure my excitement when he would give tokens of monetary affection made her even more angry. Nevertheless, I was excited when he gave me things, just like any child would be when they received the gift they waited all year long for and got to open it on Christmas day.

I was excited to know that I would have that special feeling every day when I went to live with Dad in South Vallejo, California. The way we were together during visits was going to be magnified into a happily ever after, at least in my mind, once I moved to live with him in California. However, when I arrived at Dad's house, a woman came out the front door to greet me. She looked vaguely familiar, but I was not sure who she was. I thought she looked like the same lady whose house Dad and I went to for a birthday party when mom and I lived with him before we moved back to Canton. As the woman got a little closer, the shape of her face, her figure, and the way she was dressed, let me know I was familiar with her.

That's Ms. Carol! But...what is she doing at Dad's house? I thought to myself as I tried hard not to look surprised. Hesitatingly, I reached out to receive a hug from her outstretched arms. As if in slow motion, my mind did a rewind back to the time when Dad took me to a birthday party for Carol's daughter. I knew Carol and Dad were good friends, but Dad had left out a small detail before my arrival. He never told me that Carol and her daughter Misty were living with him! I had no idea. I do not know if my Mom knew about Dad's living arrangement, but I was shocked. It was supposed to be just my Dad and me! I was disappointed. The fairytale of living a close-knit life alone with my Daddy—just the two of us—was crowded with two other people.

The silly kid disappointment that I had on arrival quickly dissipated. Soon, I found myself having fun playing with Misty and with Carol's nieces—Colleen and Annie. All three of them ran outside to greet me just as I accepted Carol's hug. The mind of a child is resilient: once the three kids my age showed up and I began to have fun, I forgot all about the disappointment that was overwhelming me just moments before. Kids forget everything else when they are having fun. A real boogieman could come up to them, and as long as kids are having a good time, they do not care. Fun is all that matters.

Misty, Annie, and Colleen were my tour guides around the neighborhood, and Carol showed me Vallejo. Old Vallejo was a quaint place when I was a child. It's a waterfront port city northeast of Oakland, California, and is located in the North Bay region of the San Francisco Bay Area. When I was a child, Vallejo was populated with a range of races and cultures. Even to this day, Vallejo might be one of the most diverse small cities in the United States.

As part of my grand tour, we went to Bud's Burger on Sonoma Boulevard to get cheeseburgers, fries, and drinks. It was a tiny place, but people gathered around to order what I thought had to be the best burger ever at the time. The place was so small that it was almost like being in a house kitchen and a breakfast nook all in one, with the added fixture of a cash register thrown in the middle. There were a few seats in the restaurant, but they were mostly just a place for people to wait to pick up their food and not necessarily for dine-in use. Bud's quickly became one of my favorite places to eat when I started to earn an allowance. For a few dollars, I could get the biggest, juiciest, cheeseburger with steaming hot, crispy golden brown fries, and a pop. I loved the cheesecake at Jack in the Box, and nothing could compare to Nation's milkshakes, and Pioneer Chicken's chicken sandwiches; but Bud's was my favorite.

Over time, I visited Carol's friends and family, and I adapted to Misty, Annie, and Colleen's way of life. Colleen and I were both nine, but I beat her by a few months. Annie was seven, and Misty was six. I often look back on all the people I met in California, from the adults to children, and I feel blessed in the fact that I was accepted and made a part of an extended family. Only child syndrome; good or bad, I had an upside to now have what I could call sisters. I felt blessed for sure.

When I first met Annie and Colleen, they lived with their mother, Loretta, who was Carol's sister, and with their Grandma Annie, who was Carol's mother. The two adult women and the two children all lived in a motel. Until then, I did not know people actually lived in motels. The motel where they lived had rooms that could be rented on a long-term basis. Annie and Colleen showed me around and even taught me how to reach into the pop machine and get the pop to fall out without paying for it. Then we'd run up the stairs hoping no one saw us. The motel became a playground of sorts for us. We played along the corridors, knocking on all the doors on one floor, and then quickly scrambling down the stairs to another floor before anyone could catch us.

We worked up big appetites with all the little devious activities that we would get into before making our way to Grandma Annie's room. Waiting for us when we got there was rice with sugar and milk, and we would eat every bit put in front of us before heading back outside to play until Carol was ready to go home.

Grandma Annie was a cook at a school for German Shepherds that were bred and trained to be guide dogs for the blind. Sometimes after a day of mischief, we'd find hand-cut French fries, rice, soy chicken, and most anything else we wanted for a snack, waiting for us on any given day at any given time. We played all day without a care in the world until the end of the day. When bath time rolled around, we doubled up in a bubble bath together and played some more. After getting out of the tub, we played until we fell asleep.

The four of us were practically inseparable. As kids do, we learned a lot from each other, some of which were maybe not the most sanitary of things to pick up. I learned my fair share from them, including how to preserve my chewing gum and save it to chew the next day. We would take a break from chewing gum by simply putting it in the refrigerator. We had a reserved spot in the refrigerator specifically for that purpose, and we stuck the gum there. It was usually there when I returned to get it the next day. Sometimes I forgot the exact spot or color of my gum. When that happened, and I could not remember which one was mine, I would just grab one that was close to the spot where I thought I left mine, or pick one which was the color I thought I remembered mine being. We were cousins; so there was no concern of germs or cooties if I grabbed a piece of gum that was not mine.

When Grandma Annie, Loretta, Colleen, and Annie moved from the motel to Benicia Road, I was surprised to learn that Misty's dad lived there too. *What?* Yes, Misty's father who was married to Misty's mother Carol, who was now kind of my stepmother…well, the bottom line is that Carol's ex-husband lived with his ex-mother-in-law. If that sounds confusing, imagine how confusing it was to me at the age of ten.

We visited Grandma Annie's daily, and Misty's dad was always there. I guess it was nice for Misty because she got to see her father and interact with him on a daily basis. But it was awkward for me; I was merely the daughter of the "other man." Misty's father was not my father, and I was uncomfortable around him at first. I recalled how my Dad had reacted when mom had a male friend over to her apartment. I wondered if my Dad would still have that reaction now. I also wondered if Misty's dad would not like me since his former wife was now with Dad.

It is a drama soup box; not knowing which way to see things, or how to react as a child, or even an adult, when it comes to blended families that consist of old and new additions. Former and new relationships, and the connections between them co-mingling, can bring about never-ending and reoccurring problems. Children can end up being pawns in retaliation and spite. It is a huge sigh of relief when blended families have peace, and a welcoming mature way of accepting all involved.

Misty's dad was tall with a very dark complexion. The parts of his eyes that are supposed to be white were light beige. Only his teeth appeared to be white. He always spoke soft and fast. He sounded like *Super Fly* from the old Blaxploitation film I watched one night on cable when I was home alone while Mom went out.

"Hey, how ya' doin, behbeh girl?" he would say as he lifted Misty up in his arms, making her just as tall as he was. I looked up wishing he would pick me up too. My Dad was warm, but Misty's dad was genuinely affectionate and playful with her. He kissed her on her cheek, and his bright teeth seemed to fill the room with light as he smiled gently from ear-to-ear while putting her down. Because he was tall, it seemed to take forever before her feet were back on the ground.

My stepmother Carol and her family are Hawaiian. Before meeting her family, I expected to see "Hawaiian" looking people like the hula dancers on *Hawaii Five-O* with Jack Lord. Even though Carol and her family are from Hawaii, they are mixed with black. Therefore, no one in Carol's immediate family looked Hawaiian, except for her sister Louise, and her niece Annie. Louise lived in Sacramento and it was always a treat to go to see Louise's children, Ben and Kelly.

I remember looking through Louise's record collection once while we were visiting at her house, and seeing her on the cover of two of the records. Louise was a singer and very beautiful. Her husband was handsome, and he reminded me of a shorter version of Tom Selleck due to his dark hair and thick mustache. They had a tiny dog who they named Tippy. Whenever Tippy was excited, he ran around the house or the backyard patio nonstop. You could hear him coming because his paw nails made a tipping sound with every step he made on hard surfaces. Their yard was large and perfectly landscaped with trees and bamboo, rockers, a canopy covered patio, and a Jacuzzi tub. To us, the Jacuzzi was a full-sized swimming pool. Misty and I would play in the Jacuzzi until our fingers and toes were wrinkled like raisins.

We spent Easter in Sacramento one year. Louise and Kelly made cookies for all of us and gave them to us when we arrived. Misty, Annie, and Colleen had specially designed and personalized Easter cookies with their names on them. My cookies were not personalized with my name on them like the cookies for the other girls; my cookies just had designs on them.

After passing out the cookies to us, Louise and Kelly jokingly whispered to Carol, "We could not remember her name" as they smiled in my direction. I did not understand how they could not remember my name when we visited them so many times. They could have called Carol and asked her my name if they had forgotten it. That would have been easy to do. The absence of having my cookies personalized made me a little sad. I felt left out as the others giggled and talked about how pretty their Easter cookies were. Louise and Kelly did not mean to leave me out or make me feel *different*, but different is exactly what I felt. Blended extended families can, and will, have their moments of pain, even when most of the other moments are joyous. But then again, regular old families can have the same problems.

Ben and Kelly seemed to be the favorite grandkids in Carol's family. Whenever they came to visit us in South Vallejo, they did not have to go to church. It seemed that they could do what they wanted because they were *Ben and Kelly*. Misty, Annie, Colleen, and I *had* to go to church. I guess because Ben and Kelly were not required to go to church when they were at their home, it was no different when they were in South Vallejo. Although we all wanted to stay home and play with Ben and Kelly, the rest of us had to go to church. We hoped they would still be at Grandma Annie's when we returned so we could play with them when the Bible Baptist bus dropped us off.

The bus picked us up for church and dropped us off at home after church. On the bus, we sang songs all the way to church. With each stop, more children got on board and joined right in with the singing. My favorite song was, "The B-I-B-L-E." My favorite verse is, "The B-I-B-L-E, yes that's the book for me. I will stand up tall on the Word of God… the B-I-B-L-E."

Bible Baptist gave me a strong spiritual foundation. Each Sunday was exciting to me because I loved to learn Bible verses. It became my goal to learn the verses, get them correct, and earn prizes the following Sunday at church. Almost every Sunday, I went up to altar call to get "saved." One Sunday, the children's church leader told me that I only needed to get saved one time. I told him that I thought Jesus left my heart, so I kept going up to the altar to get Him back.

He said, "Once Jesus comes into your heart, He does not leave."

I missed children's church once I became older and had to attend church in the main sanctuary. I did not like the regular church service as much as I liked children's church, because I did not understand what the sermons were about. I could not relate to anything I heard. I began to appreciate children's church more, and wanted to go back there and win prizes for memorizing and reciting information.

Even as an adult, I still have a strong appreciation for children's church in my heart. I wanted my kids to enjoy church with the same excitement that I had as a child. I wanted them to develop a personal relationship with God. I wanted them to enjoy learning about God. When my children were young, I was a children's church instructor. I created games, lessons, and activities that presented the Word of God in a fun, interactive way based on the things I remembered from Bible Baptist.

One thing I will always remember is memorizing John 3:16. *For God so loved the world. He gave his only begotten Son. That whosoever believes in Him shall not perish, but have everlasting life.*

Even today, I see myself as a child at Bible Baptist reciting that verse to my children's church teacher.

Start children off on the way they should go, and even when they are old they will not turn from it. Proverbs 22:6.

I also remember the Bible studies I hosted at my Dad's house. I loved to make brownies as our snack for Bible study. The lesson I remember the most was the one on faith. The teen bible study leader explained faith with the example of sitting in a chair.

He explained, "We sit in a chair not knowing if it is broken or if it will hold us. But each time we go to sit down, we don't check it and examine the legs for sturdiness or test it before we sit down. We just sit down, believing it will hold us." He continued while pointing at the chair I was in, "Believing that a chair will hold us is like having faith in God. We just believe He is there with us, and for us, and will not let us fall."

That is why we labor and strive, because we have put our hope in the living God, who is the Savior of all people, and especially of those who believe. 1 Timothy 4:10.

After getting to know Carol's family and having Misty as a sister, I felt comfortable with my new environment and my new school. Patterson Elementary was not really "new" to me. It is where I started school when I first lived in South Vallejo with Mom and Dad. I had attended Grant preschool, Beverly Hills preschool, and started Kindergarten at Patterson before Mom and I moved back to Canton. In Canton, I attended Lake Cable, Summit, and Madge Youtz Elementary schools before moving back to South Vallejo. Six schools later, and only in the second grade, I lived with Dad, Carol, and Misty and was enrolled in Patterson again.

After excelling on a few school projects, I was selected to test for a gifted student program. I went to a small room with a man that reminded me of Mr. Rogers from *Mr. Rogers' Neighborhood* on PBS. He was dressed in a short sleeve plaid shirt with a dark-colored tie, tight-fitting slacks, and shiny black shoes. A button-down cardigan sweater draped over the back of his chair where he sat after we entered the room. If he put it on while getting ready to leave the room, my vision of Mr. Rogers would have been complete. I was not selected for the program, but as a second grader, I was placed in a split class and I was assigned third-grade work. I continued that program in third grade, completing fourth-grade work. My school life was going great, but home life was another story.

At Dad's house, the tension grew as time went on. When Mom called, Carol said things in the background while I was on the phone with Mom. With my naiveté, I told Mom what Carol said, and then attempted to tell Carol what Mom said. Dad tried to act as the mediator to avoid any instigation of the feud by blocking my relay of messages. Adults sometimes make kids grow up too fast, and sway their opinion of others without letting children make up their own mind. They do this by the drama they put the children through when there is jealousy or hate involved on any level.

I later learned as an adult that there was more to the story behind the relationship between Dad and Carol that caused the tension between her and Mom. Carol, Mom, and Dad had all worked together at a convenience store before Dad became a truck driver for the same company. Dad was also the best man in Carol's wedding to Misty's dad. At the time, Carol liked Dad even though she was married, and he was in a relationship with Mom. Mom knew it. *Best man, huh?*

When I asked Dad about Carol being the same woman whose house we had gone to for the birthday party, he told me that Carol liked him then. Dad said she always wanted to be with him, but because she had a child by her first husband, her family strongly encouraged her to marry Misty's dad and lose whatever feelings she had for Dad. Carol and her husband were still married in the beginning of her living with Dad. Once their divorce was final, Carol and Dad got married. *Blended family!* Carol and her daughter Misty, and me and Dad. *Life can be truly stranger than fiction*; an old saying that fit my childhood when it came to the actions of the adults in my life.

In addition to the tension between Mom and Carol, I dealt with Mom disliking Dad for his lack of providing for me when I was with her. Mom always told me that Dad did not love me like he did Misty. I did not know how to feel about hearing her say that. I did not know whether it was true or not. When I went to live with Dad, I did not have much of a relationship with him. He was always on the road as a truck driver. He did not drive long distance runs, but he was usually gone before I woke up to go to school, and he did not come back home until I was already in bed.

I often thought to myself, *Maybe Mom is right. Maybe he doesn't care. Why is he always gone?*

I questioned him about it one day. "Tell me that Mom was your girlfriend," I said. He did not answer me. "How were you involved in my life? Were you there during Mom's pregnancy? Were you there when I was born?"

After each question, he said, "No."

I wished that I had not asked the questions. Once he said that he was not there when I was born, I felt the muscles throughout my body tighten as my teeth clenched. I heard Mom's words ringing in my head: *He doesn't love you. He doesn't care about you. He loves Misty more than you.*

I demanded that he say that my mom was his girlfriend. "If you don't say it, then I'm not your daughter!" I shouted as if trying to talk over Mom's voice in my head.

He would not say it. I was enraged. I folded my arms and pouted as I sat in the back seat in Carol's cream-colored, two-door Nova. It was the only thing I could think to do to show how angry I was. I sat in the back seat and refused to talk to him during the drive. I did not speak to him for the rest of the day.

* * * * *

At the end of third grade, arrangements were made for me to go to Houston to live with Mom. I stayed with her throughout fourth grade and through part of the seventh grade. After that, I returned to South Vallejo and was even closer with Kelly than I had been before. Although I was upset about the Easter cookie incident, I liked Kelly and really enjoyed being around her. During one visit, Kelly took me along with her and her friend for a ride around Sacramento, and then to a park to play in the sprinklers. I was concerned about going because I did not want to mess up my hair. I had a Jheri curl at the time. Yes, I was that child who you did not want to have her head touch anything around you, because my hair might have stained everything with an oily substance.

"Don't worry, we have some activator," Kelly said.

"You do?!" I was shocked and surprised. I thought only black people used Jheri curl activator.

Kelly used activator for her perm hairstyle to have the "wet" look too. Some people with Kelly's hair texture use mousse or styling gel to have the "wet" look; but Kelly and her friend used Jheri curl activator. We drove around, went to the park, and played in the sprinklers. When I returned to her house, I showered, washed my hair, and used Kelly's activator. This seemed to create a different kind of relationship between me and Kelly. I felt that she related to me even though she was Hawaiian and I was black. Somehow the Jheri curl activator, R&B, and rap music, connected us.

I felt so comfortable and included whenever I was with Kelly, that is until one day when I overheard Carol talking to her sister Loretta. Loretta was telling Carol that Kelly's father did not want her to date black guys. I took the comment personally. I wondered what he thought was wrong with black guys. I wondered if he had a problem with Carol being with Dad. *How does he feel about me?* I questioned. All of the questions running through my head about Kelly's dad did not change my relationship with her. I still felt connected to her, no matter what her father thought about black people.

Kelly was different than her father in my eyes. She shared everything with me and even gave me the clothes she did not want anymore. She told me, "I know you will take care of these," as she handed me my first pair of Vidal Sassoon jeans.

I felt proud and pleased to accept clothes from Kelly, although they were usually too big. I just tucked the shirts in tight, and I used my skills from that year's seventh grade home economics class to tailor the pants to fit. I turned the jeans inside out, put them on, and pinned away the amount needed from the inseam to make the jeans fit…or at least fit better. After pinning the pants all the way down to my ankles, I carefully removed the jeans to avoid sticking myself with the straight pins. I usually sat in my bedroom on my pink day bed and listened to my Walkman with a tape of MC Lyte while I sewed each pant leg by hand.

Each stitch became more and more painful as I had to use more pressure to push the needle through the thick two-layer denim. The music in my Walkman did not relieve the pain in my fingers. The music did not stop the bleeding when my thimble slipped off and the needle stabbed me. But sometimes, once I was done, the fit was just right, and the pain was worth it. Other times, I did not start far enough to the crotch area which left an open gap, exposing the original stitching before the jeans fit along my thigh and down the rest of the leg. Even worse, there were times where the pinned line was not so straight; that led to the seam being too tight, and then loose, only to be too tight at the knee, not tight enough at the calf, and so tight at the ankle that I could not get my foot through without a fight.

The things we do to be in style and cute starts early.

I wanted to dress nice, but after a while, I did not want the hand-me-down jeans anymore. In addition to the clothes Kelly gave me, it meant giving up clothes my friend Jasmine gave me. I liked the clothes from Jasmine. Her mom ordered from *Spiegel* catalogs. Kelly's clothes were usually name brand too; like Levi's, Jordache, or Sassoon. But they were not worth the pain. I also did not want to buy pants that were too big just because they were on sale for five or ten dollars. I even wore shoes that were two different sizes, just to dress nice. Annie and I had the same shoes, but her shoes were a half size bigger than mine. When the sole of my left shoe split in half, Annie gave me her left shoe so that I could still have shoes to wear with slacks.

Times were tough, but with all of my new family and friends, I managed to stay above water, style wise.

I later met another side of Carol's family that followed Hawaiian culture and "looked" Hawaiian. While Annie, Louise, and her family were all beautiful with a light tan complexion and long dark hair, there was Imani who was even more beautiful. Imani had more of the Hawaiian traits than the rest of the family. When she first met someone, she kissed the person on both cheeks and gave a big, tight hug. I loved going with Imani and her family to hula classes or luaus in the park. It seemed that Imani and her family were better off financially than others in Carol's family. They lived in a better neighborhood, dressed nicer, and had a better-looking car and home. I once overheard a few conversations among some of Carol's family members about how they thought that Imani and her family thought they were better than the rest of the family. To me, it appeared that Imani's family made a good living by selling their Hawaiian culture with their hula classes, hula competitions, and luaus.

Even though I enjoyed the hula classes, I felt like I was immersed in Hawaiian culture when I was given the name Kuuipo and thought that I picked up on what Carol called, *speaking Portuguese*. Speaking Portuguese essentially meant that she added a "dagah" to every word, like, "I gotdagah godagah todagah dadagah stordagah. Translation: "I got to go to the store." I practiced and practiced until she told me that I could speak acceptable Portuguese. I thought it was their Hawaiian language. Even after living in California for over thirty years, Carol still speaks in broken English with a strong accent.

Chapter Four

Never Was Daddy's Little Girl

W hen I returned to live with Dad when I was in the seventh grade, my view of him changed dramatically. My feelings were mixed with anger and wonderment of, *why are you the way you are, and how do you feel about me as your daughter?*

As children, we need our parents to guide us and protect us with the grace of God, of wisdom and love. As children, we can be taken advantage of by our lack of comprehension.

Just think of all that we see and hear in the world today. It is often said nowadays, "These children today grow up too fast." Yes, today's children are not as naïve as the children of my childhood. I'm sure each generation states the same thing about the newer generation; but nonetheless, children are not adults, and adults need to protect children as they grow into adults and save them from harm's way.

I felt Dad did not protect me, defend me, or support me in a difficult situation. For a period of time at Dad's house, Carol's stepfather stayed with us. He was quite the talker, and he talked to us kids all the time. He was funny and engaging. One afternoon while he lay in his bed, I was over at the doorway listening to him. He had always talked to both Misty and me in every room in the house, and the bedroom was no different. I had never felt uncomfortable being in the bedroom with him before. As he was speaking, I mentioned that I was cold. While smiling, he lifted the covers up and away from his body and responded by saying that I could get in the bed with him. As a child, I did not know that he was speaking inappropriately to me.

I naively responded, "Ok." To me, he was *Grandpa*. I thought that I would just lie next to Grandpa and get warm. I did not think anything was inappropriate about that.

Right when I was going to get in the bed with him, he just laughed and pulled the covers back toward him and said, "I'm just kidding."

I was confused by his laugh. I did not understand why I could not get in bed with him to get warm. *Why is he laughing like that?* I wondered to myself as I continued to stare at him. I stood there confused while he acted amused.

I soon found out the reason why he laughed the way he did. *Grandpa* revealed his intentions as we were in the living room one day. He was talking to me as Misty was engrossed in the television, and Carol was in the kitchen. Near the end of the conversation, Grandpa reached for me and held me in a way I knew was wrong. I felt almost trapped. Initially, he gave me a hug that felt normal to be given by anyone, but then, his hands left my back and grabbed my butt. It was no accidental touch. He grabbed my butt with both of his old, frail hands and squeezed.

At my age, I had been told as most children are told, "No one ever touches your private parts." A child may be short on a few insights, such as, maybe having little or no sex education, but everyone knew about *Stranger Danger.* Even with the most basic of street smarts, most children will recognize an inappropriate touch. I did.

Broad daylight. The room went dark in my eyes with anger and fear. I pulled away, and he stumbled to keep his balance. I ran out of the house and went to a friend's house. I left Misty to enjoy her TV program. I did not tell anyone what happened. However, later I spoke to my friends, and they all said I should tell on him, and I did.

When Dad came home from work, I told him what Grandpa did. Dad said, "Show me what he did." My dad's tone was not caring, as if to say, *Is that all that happened? You're fine. Move on.*

Nowadays, I think about the incident, and I think that Dad might have known that Grandpa was a dirty ole' man. My friends were nearby waiting to see what they thought should happen as I told Dad, and all he did was smirk and implore me to show him how Grandpa grabbed me.

Embarrassed, I felt that I looked foolish in front of my friends who might have been there in part to support me, or who only wanted to see the aftermath of the drama.

"What?!" I said, angered and dismayed. "I am not going to do to you what he did to me! I am not going to show you!" I yelled. "He did what I said he did, and I'm not going to show you!"

I started to cry, ran to my room, and slammed the door. I cried more and more thinking that Dad did not believe me. I could not believe that Dad wanted me to show him, rather than have that man explain himself; or better yet, to get out of our house, or for my Dad to beat him up.

That incident influenced my teen years to come. I let the words of my Mom ring in the disappointment louder and more thundering as I grew older.

He doesn't love you…he doesn't care about you.

After that incident, I felt disconnected from Dad. I found myself starting to connect with my friends more. For years to come, I felt like hanging in the streets more, and wanted to stay away from home at all costs. Soon, I found myself wrapped up in stealing cars and drinking; anything so that I would be out of the house except to eat and sleep. I sought friends who were like me; the ones that looked for love and attention and who thought the streets were the place to find it. Drinking, hanging out, and selling drugs became very attractive to me.

Chapter Five

Drug Raid

L ife had normalized for me by the time I was nine. I had been exposed to a lot of things that were wrong in life, but to me…they were normal. I had a child's mind and mentality concerning how I viewed the things that I saw. Some would call that time in my life a *tender age* based on the number of my years. However, children seem to find a way to normalize what they see and hear. If, by chance, AK-47 rifles are going off all the time and if that is what a child is around on a regular basis, that child may begin to consider that environment as being normal. They begin to rationalize that environment as just being the way of the world.

One day when I was lived with my Mom, I remember telling one of her friends how to freebase. I rattled off the process without a care in the world, and doing so seemed normal to me. While having a conversation during a casual walk through our apartment complex on the south side of Houston from her apartment to my Mom's apartment, I gave a matter of fact play-by-play account on freebasing cocaine. My Mom's friend watched me, from time to time, while Mom was at work, so the two of us were together a lot. With the knowledge that I recited to her, I can only imagine that she was confused as to whether I was the same child that she had seen earlier that day playing with the other kids my age. The knowledge I dropped on her was not something most would think a child my age would know with such precision. I explained to her how, while I was in California, I saw people cooking drugs on the stove, and taking the substance over to the kitchen table to smoke from a glass pipe.

To this day, the image of someone freebasing is still very vivid in my mind. There I was, in the living room, watching people walk back and forth from the stove to the kitchen table. We had wood saloon shutters for the kitchen door—like the kind that were in saloons in old western movies—that swung back and forth when you entered or exited. There was a small gap between the shutters, and each time someone walked through, it was like a camera snapping a picture. The picture stayed in my mind, and on that day, while back with my Mom's friend, I just described what I saw, but my conversation was not that of a child. Unbeknownst to me, I had knowledge of something my tender eyes should not have ever seen.

I do not know how the topic came up between me and Mom's friend, and I thought nothing of it when saying what I said to her. But Mom thought a whole lot about it when she became aware of what I had witnessed. Mom was horrified to know that I had even observed such things during my "visit" in California. So, to say the least, I did not go back…at least not that summer.

When I returned to Dad's house during spring break of my seventh-grade year, there were always people at his house…people like Tim. Tim did not have any of his front teeth. They all were missing. He was skinny and wore old, outstretched raggedy T-shirts and jeans with holes in the knees. Tim lived with his elderly parents in Beverly Hills, a neighborhood that was the product of *white-flight*. Beverly Hills is a suburb of South Vallejo, not Los Angeles.

Tim was what you would call, *less than manly*. He was very squeamish about little things. I remember he would get upset because Carol allowed me to drive when we went to pick him up. He acted as though he was terrified for his life when I drove. I was twelve at the time, and I was driving a stick shift car. I may have been young, but I was a quick learner, and I drove like anyone else who had enough skills to pass the driving test.

Tim screamed and hollered in the backseat, "She can't drive this car! Why are you letting her drive this car?!"

He screamed, and a bit of his saliva shot out of his mouth and on to my cheek. When his saliva landed on me, it felt like it was burning through my skin. I thought the burning sensation coming from his spit was due to it being toxic from all the drugs Tim used at my Dad's house. Or, it could have been from the drugs I suspected he used at his elderly parents' home in their basement while they were upstairs sitting, wrapped up in afghans, watching *The Lone Ranger*.

Tim was among many that I saw do drugs at Dad's house. I also saw people smoking weed all the time at my friends' houses, as well as at Dad's house. People smoked marijuana in front of me and Misty all the time when I lived in South Vallejo. It was commonplace. They smoked it in the car, in our house, at friends' houses, in the park…almost every place that I frequented back then. Our age never seemed to be of any concern for the adults around us. What we witnessed never seemed to bother any of them when they were getting high. Seeing people smoking from a bong seemed natural to me. On any given day, I would see Teresa—my friend Felicia's Aunt—sitting at the kitchen table picking the stems and seeds out of the marijuana in order to make "nickel" and "dime" bags. Teresa would carry on a full conversation with herself with the same enthusiasm and detail as if someone else were part of the conversation besides herself.

"See you have to take this stuff out. I could make the bag appear heavier and sell it, but if I do, I could fuck up my clientele, and then they won't want to buy from me. Gotta have that Indo."

Indo was a popular word in the '80s used to describe marijuana that had a strong potency. Teresa often talked about how good her supply was, and she bragged on how both women and men liked her. The latter was not hard to believe. She was pretty with light brown eyes, smooth cocoa skin, and a beautiful physique. But usually her shape was hidden under large T-shirts and baggy sweatpants. She rarely wore makeup; just jeans, T-shirts, and a beanie on her head. She never really had her hair done. She gave definition to the term, *au naturel*. Teresa dated Rick and had a son with him. Rick was "the man." He was one of the biggest drug dealers in South Vallejo, and the source of Teresa's good Indo supply. When he was not selling drugs, he was in prison.

Even though I saw weed nearly every day, and knew what it looked like, I actually believed Teresa when she said, "Here…try this. It's natural," as she handed me what looked like a joint.

At first I stood and stared at her without reaching for the joint.

"Here…it's good for you," she continued while handing the joint in my direction. I took it in my hand and looked at the smoke coming from one end. The other end was damp from being in her mouth.

I continued to stare at the joint in my hand. My mind was in a state of trying to process that what was between my fingertips was not the foul smelling weed that I saw smoked all the time by the adults around me, but instead was something "natural…something good for me."

Pinching the top of the thinly rolled joint between my index finger and my thumb, I put it up to my lips and sucked the smoke into my mouth with one deep inhale. I mimicked what I had seen those around me do with ease. The smoke filled my mouth and swarmed like bees racing out of a hive straight to the back of my throat. *Aggghhhh…*Immediately, I started coughing uncontrollably. I was choking. I could not stop choking, coughing, and harsh-like barking. My throat felt like it was on fire and my eyes began to burn.

"You ok?" Teresa asked.

The smoke continued to choke me. Tears welled up in my eyes. I bent down at the waist trying to catch my breath, and I continued to cough into my fist. My other hand held the joint up high in the air as I tried to hand it back to Teresa. My coughs overwhelmed me and Teresa got up and took the joint from my outstretched hand.

Why did she tell me it was natural and good for me? I thought. I do not know why I did not know it was weed. I saw weed nearly every day. I knew what it looked like. I knew how it smelled. Yet, I believed Teresa when she tried to convince me that it was not weed.

Maybe she told me that it was natural because it was pure weed, rather than a Gremmie, I thought. Gremmies were becoming more popular in the '80s too. Gremmies were joints that were laced with cocaine. Whatever kind of joint it was, I knew one thing about it…I did not want to try to smoke weed ever again.

Like marijuana, drugs and crime were the norm in South Vallejo. Another norm in South Vallejo was that teens liked listening to music and watching music videos. My friends and I were no exception. After coming home from school, we spent the rest of the day trying to learn the dance routines of Salt–N-Pepa, Janet Jackson, or my favorite group—New Edition. Trying to get the moves just right was a small sense of normalcy for us. Outside of the drugs, my life was great as a kid.

One night, however, life was not so great. I was lying on my pink daybed enjoying my favorite rap artist—MC Lyte on my Walkman. Suddenly, I heard…*BOOOOMMM!!!* A man dressed in all black from head to toe busted through my bedroom door with a big gun yelling, "Don't move!" Don't move!"

Letting the gun he had drawn guide him, he scanned the room and began searching it. I started screaming. More men in black with big black guns came into my room. I screamed louder. I did not know what was going on or who the men were. Soon after coming in my room, they led me out of my room, down the hallway, and into the living room where there were more men dressed in black and holding big black guns. The men directed me to go in the kitchen. I did as I was told. When I got there, Misty, Colleen, and Annie were already in the kitchen… guarded by men in black with big, black guns.

Drug raid!

There I was, but a child, and I was in a drug raid. Until that moment, I thought my life was normal. I thought I was in the middle of life and it was fine and cool just as it was. I started to realize more about my life at the time…I could have been in the middle of getting up for a snack out of the fridge. I could have been in the middle of sitting on the toilet or showering. I could have been in the middle of holding one of the *supposed* "natural" joints from Theresa. I could have been doing a lot of things; but there I was… guarded by men with big guns in my Dad's kitchen.

Yes, a drug raid had awakened my senses about my existence.

I looked around the room past the men with the guns, and I saw Carol's sister, Loretta, standing on the other side of the kitchen next to the stove. Dad had gone to the store, and I did not know where Carol was. I looked in Loretta's direction as if to ask her what was going on. As soon as we made eye contact, she looked down toward the ground. Deception and shame framed her gaze.

Our house was not raided for the weed I had seen nearly every day. Our house was raided for crack cocaine. Once I understood what was going on, I wanted to tell the men in black about other people who had drugs in their houses.

"Why are you here?" I yelled. "You need to be where there are drug dealers!"

I wanted to yell out the names of everyone I knew of who sold drugs.

"Why my house?" I asked.

Like I said, a drug raid woke up my existence.

No matter how angry I was that my house was raided, I was more concerned that there were so many others whose houses I thought should have been raided instead of mine. But my thoughts meant nothing. The men in black with big guns did not care if I was mad. They did not go to raid any other houses. They waited for Dad.

Unsuspecting, Dad walked through the front door with grocery bags in his hands. The bags flew across the room as two officers snatched him just as he stepped into the house. They threw him up against the wall. One officer smashed the left side of Dad's face into the wall so hard that I thought it would go straight through to the other side. Two other officers went over to handcuff him. They took him to the ground just as other officers moved me away from the western style shutter doors and further into the kitchen. I could not see any more.

I just heard Dad asking, "Man…why y'all gotta be so rough?"

Once Dad was handcuffed and taken out of the house, the officers left the kitchen. I went back to the shutters to see what I could see. Two officers came from Dad's room, and the other officers shuffled through our house. They Stormtrooper style stepped over the piles of the mess they made. When they finally left, I looked throughout the house. The officers had busted the waterbed in Dad and Carol's room. Clothes were all over the floor from the closets. The drawers were emptied, and clothes, socks, and underwear were thrown about.

My Dad was taken away, and no one explained anything to me. I later learned bits and pieces about what happened to Dad from rumors on the streets, things said at school, and from what Felicia's grandma heard on a police scanner. Allegedly, Loretta was a paid informant and she had helped arrange Dad's arrest. When Dad went to the store, she called the cops so that they could be there when Dad returned. I discovered that night, for the first time, that my Dad sold drugs out of our house with me inside.

I could not believe it. Dad had a well-paying job as a truck driver for a big company in the area. We were actually going to celebrate his twelve-year anniversary with the company the following month. Dad was going to receive an award from the company where he started as a store clerk and later became a driver. After the raid, it was all gone. He no longer had a truck-driving career…no benefits…no nothing. Soon, we faced losing the house to foreclosure and the cars to repossession. Worst of all, Dad went to jail.

I could not understand the whole situation. *Why was Dad selling drugs? When did he have time to sell drugs when he was always at work?*

As a child, none of it made sense in my head and I was not able to connect all the dots. I asked questions of everyone around me, but they did not, or could not, answer my questions.

I asked, "How does Dad's job know about this if his name was not in the newspaper?"

"They just do," Carol said.

I had other questions, but no one answered them either. Dad and Carol did not want me to talk to my family in Ohio. They tried to prevent me from telling Grandma Bluchelle or Aunt Niambi about the drug raid, or the fact that Dad was in jail.

The phone was cut off at the house. When I called Grandma Bluchelle and Aunt Niambi from a pay phone, Dad and Carol found out. They grilled me with questions about why I had called Ohio, and they wanted to know what I had said to them on the phone. I did not understand why they were questioning me so much. I just wanted to talk to Grandma Bluchelle like I always had. I did not understand why they wanted to keep me from talking to her.

When we went to visit Dad in jail, I could not stand to look at him in the county jumpsuit. I did not like the fact that he would not explain to me why he was in there. He left me with Carol and Misty, and he did not tell me why. In protest, I turned my back to him for most of the visit. Carol was offended. She did not talk to me during the ride back to South Vallejo, or for the rest of the day for that matter. I did not care. I did not like the fact that neither of them would be honest with me. I was hurting. I was lost and confused, and Dad and Carol only seemed to understand their situation, and not mine as a child. For a long time, I had witnessed things that a child should not see, and they did nothing to prevent that; and now when they should explain things in a way that I could understand them on my level, they would not. The fact that I was a child seemed to only be a factor depending on how much it affected them, more so than how it affected me.

Many years later as an adult, I asked Dad about the details of the raid. He told me that he only served twenty-eight days of a six-month sentence. However, that was just the beginning of Dad's frequent arrests and time in jail. After that first arrest, he was never *legitimately* gainfully employed again.

* * * * *

Although being raised alongside his stepdaughter, and in the care of his wife Carol, Dad was absent from my life in many ways. From the events of that day of the raid, and the time I felt Dad did not stand up for me when Carol's stepdad hugged me inappropriately, I felt my *little girl spirit* pulling away from Dad. It was years later before I personally felt some sort of reconnection with my Dad. I talked to him a lot after I graduated from law school. I know it made him happy to know I called on him for advice or when I just needed to talk to him. He also helped talk me through times of dealing with Mom's illness. However, when I was thirty-seven, I learned the truth about how Dad really felt about me and Mom moving from South Vallejo when I was five.

Usually, Dad stays at my house when he visits me in Canton, and he spends a lot of time hanging out with others while staying with me. During his visit one summer, I was happy that he came to my house to visit. I looked forward to the time we could spend together and talk. It was late one night and although I usually go to bed pretty early, I was still up that night working on cases. Surprisingly, Dad came in the living room where I was sitting on the couch. I stopped working, and we sat in the living room and talked. I was glad that Dad and I were finally alone and could have a moment just to talk. I wanted to tell him about my feelings regarding my pending divorce, and I wanted his opinion on the whole situation. The conversation somehow turned away from talking about my separation from my husband and toward the separation of him and Mom.

"Yeah, yo' mom shudna' left. I told her not to leave, but she left," he said. "I told her if she stayed, I would take care of her, but she still wanted to leave."

I listened intently. I had never heard his side of the story before.

He went on to say, "I told God that if I got with another woman and she had a child, I was gonna take care of that child like it was mine."

I looked at him puzzled. "So…you knew that Mom and I were struggling?" I asked.

"Yep," he stated matter of factly. "She shuldna left," he said in a cocky tone as if he dared anyone to challenge him.

"You knew there were times that I did not eat?" I asked in disbelief. It dawned on me that things did not have to be the way they were.

"I know that it was hard for you and your mom, but she shuldna left," he said with no remorse.

"Do you know how many households I lived in?" I asked, choking from the tightness in my throat, and ready to curse any tear that dared to fall from my eyes as I thought of his seemingly arrogant disregard for my feelings.

"Nope, but I know it's gonna be in your book," he said through a mischievous laugh.

"But, I am your daughter…I am your only child," I said, no longer able to hold the tears that streamed down my face.

Dad looked at me as he shrugged his shoulders and repeated, "I know, but like I said…she shuldna left."

"Ok, Dad. I've heard enough. I'm going to bed. Good night."

I went straight to my room and closed the door. As soon as my head hit the pillow, I cried uncontrollably until I fell asleep. The next morning, I talked to Dad again. I thought, *Perhaps he does not know that he hurt my feelings. Perhaps he did not mean what he said. How could a man say those things to his only child? How could he not have any remorse?*

I told him that the things he said hurt my feelings and that I cried myself to sleep.

"I was just telling you the truth. You want to know the truth, don't ya'?" he said without any regret.

I dropped the conversation at that point. There was no need in hashing things out any further.

Even though my dad still stays at my house whenever he comes to Canton, since that time, I only talk to him on holidays, or sometimes on other special occasions.

Dad attempted to apologize a few years later. He came to Canton for my cousin Juba's wedding. During the ride home, my younger cousin—whom we affectionately call L—talked about his parents and a lot of emotional distress he endured because of the consequences of their behavior. L then started to talk about all my achievements and he directed his anger toward my Dad. L listed every accomplishment that I had reached in my life.

Dad interrupted, "I'm proud of her…"

"You can't take credit for nothin' she has accomplished. What did you do to help her get where she is?! How you gon' talk like you did something to take credit for?"

It was intense in the car to say the least, but no one could go anywhere. We were stuck in the tension that was trapped in the car like someone walking through mud and suddenly realizing that it is cement. No more words were exchanged as we traveled down the highway heading back to

Canton from Akron. Later that night, Dad came downstairs where I was working in my home office. As I sat at my desk typing, he knelt on one knee and braced himself on the back of my chair with one arm.

Then he fixed the words to release from his mouth, "I'm sorr…"

I cut him off. "How could you? How could you do that to your only child? How does a man treat his only child, his only daughter, the way you have treated me?"

I did not allow Dad to apologize. To this day, I do not know if I want to hear an apology from him, or if I will ever accept one if it comes.

Chapter Six

Mom

After kindergarten, and the official separation of my parents, Mom and I left California heading back to Ohio. A *Mayflower* eighteen-wheel truck moved our belongings across country while we rode the *Greyhound* bus. If I could add up all of the miles I travelled due to moving, a map would be saturated with markings. If I had traveler mile points to receive coupons to purchase items, I'd have a garage sale to rid myself of all the stuff I could have purchased with those traveler mile points. It seemed that every time I turned around, I was on the road again.

The *Greyhound* made several stops day and night along our trip heading to Ohio. We stopped at a bus station in the middle of the night, and I was finally able to get something to eat. Mom had brought one of the bowls from our kitchen back in South Vallejo with her, and she had cereal in her purse. When the bus stopped, she bought a small carton of milk so that I could eat before it was time to get back on the bus. Unfortunately, by the time we waited in line for the milk, I only had time for a few bites of the cereal before it was time to board again. I ate while we walked. Before I could finish my bowl of cereal, Mom took the bowl out of my hands and put it on a nearby ledge. We rushed to the bus when the announcer made the final call for travelers to Ohio. It took a long time to get to Canton from South Vallejo.

Once we arrived in Canton, we stayed with Tricia—one of Mom's childhood friends, until Mom got on her feet. While living with Tricia and her family, I attended Lake Cable Elementary. Now that I am more familiar with the economic and social divide in Canton, I know that Lake Cable is a predominately white area and on the upper level of the socio-economic scale. However, as a child, I did not know the financial differences between me and the other students; but I did know that I was the only black child in my class, and one of about three in the whole school.

We stayed with Tricia and her husband in their small two-bedroom apartment. Mom and I were in one room, and Tricia and her husband were in the other. Tricia was pregnant with their first child. We were there for about two months and we left just in time for them to prepare the second bedroom before their baby arrived.

Mom found a decent paying job and an apartment in the City of Canton. It did not take long for her to have the apartment fully furnished and decorated. The one bedroom apartment was the lower level of an upstairs/downstairs duplex. Mom had a way of turning any place into her own in an artistic way. One design she created with the help of my Grandma Vickie, was the silhouette of a palm tree on a mirrored background. Mom had originally made the silhouette to decorate a wall at my Dad's house, but she ended up keeping it for herself when we moved out of his house. Both Mom and Grandma Vickie had artistic skills. Once they came up with a concept, Grandma Vickie would sketch the layout and design, and Mom would finalize the decorative piece. She cut out Grandma Vickie's design and mounted it on the mirror that she custom cut to fit a door or wall wherever we lived at the time. The location for the mirror was usually selected in an area in the living room that had enough space to add a wicker chair that, as Mom used to say, was "made for a queen." Her favorite was usually the kind of wicker chair that had a large fan back and headrest with Captain Chair arms and a coned base. To this day, when I see pictures from proms and concerts with couples or groups of people from back in the 80s with that type of wicker chair as the theme, I still laugh because it brings back memories.

Next to the queen's chair sat a two-foot statue of a smiling Buddha on a pedestal. I never saw Mom worship or pray to the smiling Buddha. I do not think that was the purpose of her having it. I think she just liked the way the statue looked. It made you want to smile every time you looked at it. The smiling Buddha traveled with us throughout Canton.

Mom always looked like a queen when she sat in her wicker chair. She had honey blond hair, and soft, clear, honey-tone skin. She only stood about 5'2" in height, but she commanded attention in a room like a 6'0"

Beverly Johnson supermodel.

A man that went to school with Mom and Dad once told me, "You look good, but you ain't got nothing on your momma from back in the day."

Due to our sometimes unscheduled/spontaneous moves, the custom designed wall décor would remain with the apartment that we left. Every move meant the process had to start all over again with the concept, design, drawing, cutout, and mounting, until Mom got tired of the look as time, fashion, and style changed. My Grandma Vickie did not need to create the sketch anymore; and soon after that, Mom did not care about the wicker chair anymore either.

Mom sometimes allowed me to have the one bedroom in the apartment, and she would sleep on the couch in the living room instead. We were in our own place even though I had to transfer schools again. This time, I attended Summit Elementary School. Mom took me to register for school. The administrator asked several questions, including some about Dad and his whereabouts. She wanted to know whether he was allowed to pick me up from school.

I remember Mom chuckling as she responded, "He may show up" before explaining that Dad lived in California. I do not recall much about Summit Elementary except that I was not there long.

One day I went to my room to look for my shoes because Mom and I were going out to eat with one of her friends. As I reached under the bed, I heard a loud crash. I rolled under the bed for safety. Mom screamed my name, and I scurried from under the bed. To my surprise, a huge section of the ceiling had fallen down and landed right next to me. My Mom heard the sound and yelled out my name. A huge hole was above me, and dust was falling all around me. Mom ran into the bedroom. She thought I made the dresser fall or something like that. I remember the look of terror and relief in her eyes as she rushed over to hug me and reassure herself that I was all right.

We moved again. Lucky for us, Mom usually found decent places to live, even with her limited income.

After the first apartment in Canton, Mom found an affordable two-bedroom place for us. It was a side-by-side duplex on the other end of town. The move meant a new school for me. I ended up attending Madge Youtz Elementary. Even though I was only in the first grade, I dressed myself, made breakfast, and went off to school on my own with the other neighborhood kids. I was a *latchkey* kid. Usually Mom had gone to work before I woke up for school, and she was not there when I returned home. I would make myself something to eat, do my homework, watch TV, and I spent time at the Northeast Community Center after school until Mom came home from work. I was young, but it was just the two of us, so I had to grow up quick.

I had relatives in the apartment complex near the school, and I was able to make friends quickly. That made moving a lot easier. Most of the kids in that neighborhood were boys. They treated me like a little sister, and they acted like they were my bodyguards. As an only child, I liked to think of them as the older brothers I never had. They always looked out for me and made sure that I was okay.

I had fun with the twin boys that lived next door. I was so impressed with them because they taught themselves how to do backflips. For every backflip they did, I ran in my house and got cookies from the cookie jar to give to them. I spent a lot of time at their house. They had a huge family with multiple sets of twins. I was invited right into their family like an adopted sister. I learned how to play Spades, Old Maid, and War. We listened to music together and often played board games. The time spent next door distracted me from how much time Mom was not at home. I also enjoyed running around, climbing trees, playing dodge or kickball, or participating in the activities at the Northeast Community Center. Even in the second grade, I cooked, cleaned, did my homework, and tended to myself while Mom was at work. That neighborhood was nice. I liked the kids I played with and I was doing well in school. Life was again normal; or at least normal for me.

Then, one morning I heard...*CRASH!!!! BANG!!! THUD!!!*

The loud sound of breaking glass pierced through the house. It was early in the morning, and I was getting ready for school when I heard the door to Mom's room rumble and finally open as if someone was frantically trying to get out. I looked out my bedroom door to see what made the noise. I saw a tall, caramel brown man run down the hall in his white underwear briefs. He ran down the stairs, skipping two to three steps at a time.

I heard a big *THUMP!!!* I did not know where the man had gone, but I heard a woman's voice screaming outside for "Thomas" to come out of the house.

"I know you're in there," she screamed.

When I went downstairs, I saw broken glass all over the living room floor. It was a jigsaw puzzle of glass ready to rip skin if someone walked on it. I looked up to see that the large two-paned window was shattered. The morning breeze gently blew the curtains into the house. They seemed to dance back and forth. Any other time, it would have been beautiful if the windows were open for a summer breeze, but this time, it was an ugly breeze that was blowing in. At that moment, I noticed Mom's plants were overturned on the living room floor.

Mom spent a lot of time taking care of her plants. They were her pride and joy. The living room was a jungle, or one might even call it a botanical garden of green. It seemed that she repotted her plants every weekend. She poured special water with eggshells in the container into the flowerpots on a regularly scheduled basis. But all the nurturing she did could not bring the plants back to their peaceful positions on the windowsill. The window glass was shattered, and there was a huge brick in the midst of the shattered glass on the living room floor. The woman continued to scream for "Thomas" to come out. No matter how much she screamed, "Thomas" did not come out. After no response, the woman sped out of our driveway and down the street. I saw the tire marks in the driveway when I left for school later that morning.

Mom finally appeared after the woman drove away. Her hair was neatly wrapped under a silk hair scarf. She slowly pulled the belt straps from the sides of her robe toward the front, and firmly tied the belt along her lower abdomen. When I looked up at her face, I saw tears flowing. She reached up to dry the tears, as if to catch them before they fell from her chin. She told me not to worry about anything that I saw or heard, and to hurry up and get to school before I was late.

I started to ask if she wanted me to help clean up, but she told me again to, "Just go to school."

I walked to school alone that day because I left later than usual. All the way to school, I wondered, *who is Thomas, and why was that lady yelling outside our house?*

When I returned home from school, my Grandma Vickie was there with Mom. All the glass was cleaned up from the floor, but the window was still missing. I overheard the conversation that took place in the dining room between mother and daughter about being involved with a married man. They sat at the table with the mirrored palm tree in the background.

From what I gathered during their conversation, Thomas' wife knew he was involved with Mom. She had found out where we lived, and came to the house to let Mom and Thomas know that she knew what was going on. No one ever discussed the situation with me. I actually never thought about it again until high school when I learned that one of my gymnastic teammates was Thomas' daughter, and it was her mom who had thrown the brick through our window years earlier. It was interesting how the connection came up.

One day my teammate mentioned her dad's name and said that he was a twin. Because I had overheard different conversations Mom had about Thomas, I remembered that he was a twin, and I realized that his name was the same one that my teammate mentioned. When she said her mother's name, I knew that her dad was "Thomas," the man that I saw running down the hall and skipping down the stairs of our house that early morning. Thomas' daughter and I were very good friends throughout high school, but I never told her about the morning her dad was at my house.

After I completed the first grade and started the second grade, Mom decided to move to Houston, Texas. Houston was supposed to have better job opportunities. However, this time, the move did not include me going with her. Instead, I went to live with Dad in South Vallejo, California, and Mom moved to Houston without me. I visited Mom the summer after third grade. She lived in a small, one-bedroom apartment in a complex of about one hundred units in a predominately-Black neighborhood on the south side of Houston. Mom picked me up from the airport and took me to her apartment. The apartment smelled like gas.

"I've been having trouble with my stove," she told me.

She showed me where I would sleep on a small couch up against the wall in her living room. This time, she had the bedroom, and I slept on the couch with the decorative throw pillows. She went to her room and came back out with an album. She handed it to me. I could not believe my eyes. It was a New Edition album. Mom bought my very first New Edition album. New Edition became my favorite group, and Ralph was my favorite member. I listened to the album most days when I was alone and Mom was at work. Houston was hot, and I did not like the heat at all. Mom drove a light blue station wagon that did not have air conditioning. I did not like that either. I would rather stay in the house than go with her anywhere in that station wagon on a hot, humid day.

Mom had two jobs; one at Wendy's, the other at 7-11. She left Canton, Ohio, where she worked one job at US Chemical, to move to Houston to work two jobs and live in a place that was no better than the duplex where we had lived in Canton. I could not understand her logic, but that was her choice. She told me that she did not want me to be bored while I was visiting her; nor did she want me to sit up in the apartment alone all day while she went to work.

"I would like you to enjoy your time here, Corey."

The following morning, Mom drove me across town to spend time with my cousin Perry, while she went to work.

During that scorching hot summer, Perry and I were home alone while both of our moms worked during the day to provide for us. We played with other kids in his apartment complex and went swimming a lot. The Houston heat was brutal, and going swimming was about the only way to get me out of the air-conditioned apartment. Neither of us knew how to swim, but we still had fun. One thing I liked about Houston was that almost every apartment complex we lived in had a swimming pool.

Staying in Houston with Mom meant another new school for me. The new school was the exact opposite of Lake Cable Elementary. I went from being the only black student in my class at Lake Cable, to being one of many at my new school. There were only about four white students in the entire school. I cannot recall my teacher's name, but I will never forget the lessons I learned from him. He would not allow students to come to class unprepared, with combs in their hair, or with their clothes disheveled. I know for sure he would not allow sagging pants if that would have been the style back then like it is now.

He instilled a sense of pride in each of us, and insisted that we have pride in one another. He taught us how to behave like young ladies and gentlemen. He required us to walk together as a group to the cafeteria for breakfast and lunch. Instead of racing each other to get in line to get our food and then sitting down to eat like we were starving...our teacher mandated that we walk to the food area in a single-file line. He made us walk in a calm and orderly fashion, get our food, stand at our place at the table with our hands behind our backs, and wait for each student from our class to get his/her lunch and come to the table. After everyone came to the table, we all sat down together, said grace, and began eating as if we were taught every rule of fine dining etiquette.

It reminded me of the rules at Dad's house when I lived with him the first time. Back then, we had to eat at the kitchen table together and could not watch TV or turn on the radio during our meal. We said our grace and were encouraged to make a "happy plate," which meant we ate all the food on our plates. We could not eat with our elbows on the table. When we finished eating, we had to ask, "May I be excused from the table?" and wait to be excused before getting up to put our dishes in the sink or going outside to play with friends. All the manners and rules at Dad's house seemed to be destroyed with the rest of the house during the drug raid.

When I lived with Mom, she came home from work stressed, and she fussed as soon as she came in the door. My reply was always, "Well, hello to you too, Mom." Seeing how Mom struggled, I appreciated her willingness to do whatever she had to do just to suffice. But I wanted more than just to suffice, and I set forth to live another way when I got older. I was determined to go to college and get a job I felt good about, one that would allow me to earn a decent wage, to have things I enjoyed and, to give freely.

By the time I was in third grade, I knew I wanted a family. When I was in South Vallejo, Misty and I sat in the backseat of the car while Dad and Carol sat in the front. That vision was a family to me: a mother, father, and kids. I wanted family traditions like when Carol, Misty, and I went to pick Dad up from work on Christmas Eve so that we could all be together before the stroke of midnight on Christmas day. To me, that was a family. I wanted a family.

That year, I decided to stay in California. I did not like the idea of being in a single parent home with Mom. I wanted a mother and a father at home like I had when living with Dad and Carol. The image of a family affected me throughout my life. The desire to have *that* image was something I could not shake.

I remember a time when Dad, Mom, and I were supposed to have a family photo shoot together; the kind of pictures that are taken at department stores with the phony background of clouds or a fake fence in a field. I looked forward to taking the picture, but at the last minute, Dad changed his mind and did not go to the studio with us. Mom and I took the picture without him. It always bothered me that Dad was not in the picture. As imperfect as my Dad was, he was still my Dad, and I loved him. I always loved the thought of a family, and I was willing to put myself in that position no matter what, then and later in life.

During my marriage, I would not take a picture with my children without their dad. If he was not available, or did not want to be in the picture, my sons took the picture together without either of their parents in it.

When I was in the fifth grade, Mom married a Nigerian man named Charles. Charles had the look of the '80s pop music artist, Billie Ocean. He was nice to me. He was protective of me. He was a father figure to me. I do not know where Mom met him, or how long they knew each other. All I remember is that I spent time away with Roxanne and Perry, and when I came home, I was told that Mom and Charles were getting married. We moved into a two-bedroom apartment. I had my own room. I had stability. I had a family. I even had a pet; a dog named Pepper. My family image was complete.

I enjoyed listening to Charles and his brother, Brema, reminisce about Nigeria. They taught me words in their native language. Charles showed me how to make Fu Fu, and a sauce with just enough spice so that it was not too hot for me. Fu Fu is an African dish eaten with a very spicy sauce and dough. Charles made the dough out of Bisquick and water. I am sure it was made with something more authentic in Nigeria, but that's what Charles used when he made it for us.

We rolled the Bisquick dough into small balls. With each dough ball, I was taught to dip it into a bowl of spicy Fu Fu sauce. I did not really like the dough balls. I asked if there was a substitute. Thinking back on how Carol made rice with everything, I asked Charles if I could eat the sauce with rice instead, and if he would not mind taking it a little easy on the spice. I wanted to eat the meal as it was prepared, but the spice was just too hot for me. I thought I was spending time with a father figure, and that he was into teaching me and sharing things with me; but soon, it appeared that he was not there to be with my Mom.

I was happy. I finally had a family when I went to Mom's house. I remember filling out forms at Smith Elementary in the fifth grade and being happy that I could write the same last name for Mom and my stepfather, Charles. To me, that was a pretty acceptable family setup. I even told Mom and Charles that I wanted him to adopt me so that I could have his last name too. That discussion was short-lived. What appeared to be an acceptable family setup did not last long.

In the middle of my sixth-grade year, one day Charles left us. He said that he was going away to go to school. He never said which school he was going to, where it was, or how long he would be there. He did not even say that he planned to come home during breaks. He just said he was leaving. After he moved out, different people told us they saw Charles around town. They said that he married Mom just to stay in this country. He never went away to school; he was still in Houston all along. He lived on another side of town and worked at a gas station.

Why did he leave? Why did he lie to us?

Like the drug raid at Dad's house, I did not get answers to my questions.

Once again, it was just Mom and me. Like before, she struggled to make ends meet. If we were on assistance, it did not seem as though it helped. Mom could barely afford the rent, let alone the other bills. We were not in subsidized housing. I did not receive free/reduced lunch. I do not know whether it was even available. All I know is that we did not have a whole lot of food in the cabinets or in the refrigerator.

Spaghetti became the bane of my existence. I grew to hate spaghetti because it seemed like we ate it every day. One night, I was looking for something to eat and nothing was really there. Mom was at work and I was alone. I wished I had the Kentucky Fried Chicken from Brema's job that we had regularly when Charles was with us. I even wished for the times when Charles made Fu Fu. I was so hungry I would have eaten the Fu Fu made with dough instead of rice and with the spicy sauce even if it was so hot that it made my eyes water and my nose run. I even wished there was spaghetti that night, but there was none. I was so hungry. I looked in the refrigerator. Nothing was really there except condiments. I found a box of Lipton mashed potatoes. The mashed potatoes had some kind of chicken-flavored powder packet to mix in while the potatoes cooked. I followed the directions on the box, cooked the mashed potatoes, added the seasoning, and sat down to eat. It was hot and tasted delicious. When you're hungry anything tastes good.

It's funny how over the years I have heard other people speak of their hungry days and the love they had for government-supplied food that was available. Some people swear they miss the days of canned salmon, government cheese, and canned soups that were made as rations for the armed services, but were often part of the items people could get in the poor and needy assistance lines.

Later that night after eating the chicken-flavored powder packet mixed in with the potatoes, Dad called. Sometime during the conversation, he asked me what I had for dinner that night. I embellished a little and said, "Mashed potatoes…uh and chicken…and vegetables…and it was good." I do not know why I told him that. I just did.

The next day, I took the potatoes to school for lunch. As good as I thought it tasted the night before, it was disgusting the next day for lunch. I never figured out why Mom and I did not have food on a regular basis. In Texas, Mom regularly brought home Wendy's salads from the salad bar. The salads were always mounted high in the bowl with the lid smashed down. The cheese was usually smashed onto the lid so that I had to scrape it off and put it back into the salad. The salad was always soggy. Mom made the salads at the end of her shift, so it had sat in the refrigerator overnight with the Ranch and French dressing on it sprinkled with sunflower seeds and raisins. After sitting in the refrigerator, and then in my lunch bag until it was time for lunch the next day at school, the salad did not always seem so fresh. I took salad to school for lunch day after day anyway. It was all I had.

After taking salad for lunch so many times, one girl in school asked me, "Are you a vegetarian?"

I said, "What? No, I am not a vegetarian."

I did not know what a vegetarian was until Michael Jackson claimed to be one in the early '80s. After she asked about me bringing salads for lunch all the time, I tried to vary the things I took for lunch, but there just were not that many options available in our house. Once Charles left, we did not have the Kentucky Fried Chicken from Brema's job as a regular source of meals. When Mom stopped working at Wendy's, the salads were few and far between as well. It was either feast or famine. I preferred to feast.

I usually took my lunch to school when I lived with Mom because she was not able to give me money to buy lunch. Back when I was in the second grade at Madge Youtz in Canton, my friends and I planned to take lunches to school. Mom did not have any bread or lunch meat. Creativity kicked in and I made a cornbread, egg, and bacon sandwich. Of course, the other kids made fun of me. They laughed and asked, "What kind of sandwich is that?" As adults, my friend Camela and I still laugh to this day about that lunch.

Some days we did not have anything at home for me to take for lunch. When I attended Olle Middle School, I made up stories that I forgot my lunch money or had lost it on the way to school. Sometimes, I flat out asked to borrow money in order to eat. I had no intentions of repaying the money and knew that I could not even if I wanted to. Most of my white friends who loaned me money never asked to be repaid. My eyes widened with shock when they reached into their pockets or wallets and I saw fives, tens, and sometimes they even had twenty-dollar bills. But one day, I asked the wrong person.

I remember it clear as day. Her name was Jena. She was a very tall, tomboyish, black girl. I asked Jena if I could borrow a quarter to get a fruit punch. She agreed, but told me that if I did not pay her back she would have to beat me up because she could not loan out money and not have people pay her back. I was scared. I knew that I did not have the money to pay her back and that I had no way of getting it either. I took my chances anyway. I took the quarter from her. Fortunately, I was able to borrow lunch money from one of my white friends. With the change from buying lunch, I gave Jena her quarter back before her deadline.

The fear of physical pain from Jena was nothing compared to the emotional pain that I experienced at home. Mom would always get upset whenever I talked about Dad. One day he sent me a card in the mail for my birthday. It had five dollars in it. I immediately asked Mom to take me to McDonald's to get a chicken nugget meal. Back then, McDonald's had a special that included chicken nuggets, fries, and a drink. The commercials featured Hakeem Olajuwon of the Houston Rockets. I loved to get that meal. It was "Unbeatable" as Hakeem used to say in the commercials in his strong Nigerian accent. I was so excited about being able to get McDonalds. I called Dad to thank him. It seemed like a totally appropriate thing to do to me, but Mom hated it. She did not like me thanking him for small acts of kindness because she felt that he should have been more of a financial provider for us in general. She said that the $50 he sent once a month was a drop in the bucket compared to the cost of living she had to maintain as a single parent with a budding teenager.

Things changed on both ends of my family concerning money. When at Dad's house after the drug raid, it seemed that Carol always hustled for me to have food for lunch. I may not have had lunch by the time I left for school in the morning, but usually by lunchtime, she was there with a small paper bag full of my favorites: a turkey sub-sandwich, Doritos, Ding Dongs, and a strawberry New York Seltzer to drink. When I came from class out to the schoolyard, Carol was there. She was happy and stood there with the biggest smile as if she was so proud of herself for being able to hustle up lunch for me to eat. Carol usually worked out a deal with the local liquor storeowner and ran up a "tab" that she would pay off when she got her check on the first or fifteenth of the month.

Sometimes her food stamps would come in the mail right before my lunchtime, and she would have time to go to the store, get food for my lunch, and bring it to the school in enough time for me to eat before lunch was over. I've even seen Carol find the mailman down the street and get her mail from him. We would fly down 5th Street with Carol waving her left arm out the window, and her right hand honking the horn until it was time to change gears as she drove Dad's red, Dotson 310. She would shift gears with ease, and continue honking the horn and steering with her right hand to get the mailman's attention and get him to stop.

On the opposite end was Mom and her financial struggles. With Charles gone, Mom searched for a place with cheaper rent. I had just started the seventh grade and I did not want to move again. Trying to hold on to some type of stability, I lived with my friend Frances and her mom during the first semester of my seventh-grade year. There was not much food at Frances' house either. I remember stealing Ramen noodles and Kool-Aid from our friend Nick's house so Frances and I could eat one night. Nick's mom was a single mom too, but we figured she could afford for me to take the noodles because Nick always dressed nice with name brand clothes and shoes.

Frances and I joked, "They won't miss them" and said, "It's ok because there's nothing to eat at home."

My theft did not stop with the Ramen noodles from Nick's house. Desperate times called for desperate measures. I walked in the *Kellogg 5K* walk for the *March of Dimes* more than once with Mom's friend from church who worked for *Kellogg*. I prayed for God to forgive me when I used the money I raised for the march, to buy food to eat. I made a promise to God as I stood in line at Burger King. I promised that I would return the money as soon as I got more. I was only thirteen at the time. It was not until I was twenty-two years old that I was able to keep my promise.

One morning when I dropped my son Jaylon off at daycare, I saw a jar labeled for the *March of Dimes*. I immediately thought, *Oh my God... this is my chance to return the money I spent back in Houston when I was hungry.* I thought of my promise from so long ago, and I put twenty dollars in the jar; the amount I stole in order to eat at Burger King after the march and for lunch during the following days at school.

Times were hard after Charles left. Mom was involved with other men, but she stayed married to Charles. I always believed he would come back to be with us someday soon. *He'll be back and we'll be a family again.* I kept hope alive in my head that things would go back to how they were, although Mom did not seem to be concerned about Charles' whereabouts or his return. Emotionally, I still held on to Charles; and when I became an adult, I was determined to find him one day.

After I married, and both my husband and I had started our careers in Canton, my husband helped me find some information about Charles on the internet, including his phone number and address. I called Charles and spoke to him. He told me that he divorced Mom, remarried, and had a child. He later divorced again, and was living with another woman. During the summer of 2012, Mom, my sons Jaylon and Jordan, and I visited Houston. While we were there, I spoke to Charles again. He said he wanted to see all of us, and Mom was willing to see him. Charles said he wanted to take us out to eat and we agreed to meet before returning to Ohio. I sent him a text to follow up, but never heard back from him. I called and left a message on his voicemail. I did not hear back from him. I called again and Mom left a message on his voicemail. No response. I did not hear from Charles anymore. I wanted to see him and ask him why he left us. I wanted closure on the whole situation.

No closure when Charles left, and no closure later either.

That old saying about seasons has played a role in my life: *Reason, Season, or Lifetime.* People come into your life for a reason, a season, or a lifetime. When you figure out which one it is, you will know what to do for each person in your life.

Mom being with other men always made me want to stay away from home. When I stayed away, the place I went to the most was Frances' house. I was happy to be invited to sleepovers at any of my white friends' homes too because I knew I would have something to eat.

I was a regular at Stephanie's house. Stephanie lived in a beautiful neighborhood close enough to Olle Middle School that we could walk to school from her house. It was cool to go over to Stephanie's and stay in the two-story home with a large swimming pool in the backyard. Lying on the beach chair in the backyard and talking on the cordless phone with my

Hollywood sunglasses on made me feel so special.

Stephanie's family had a computer in the office which was the first room of the house after coming in the front door. Stephanie's computer even talked! Stephanie's house was "it" for me. I spent time there to get school projects done with a better chance of getting an "A" because Stephanie's parents took us to the library, bought the supplies we needed, and provided general support until the project was complete. I knew Mom could not afford the stuff that I needed for school projects, and I did not want my grades to suffer because of it.

Stephanie was a cheerleader for Olle. When she had slumber parties, I was invited along with the other cheerleaders. I was one of few black girls that tried out for the cheerleading squad. Even though I did not make the squad either time I tried out, I was always invited to do things with the cheerleaders. I liked the slumber parties the most. We ordered Domino's pizza with sausage and mushrooms, listened to popular '80s music by Cindy Lauper, Duran Duran, Guns and Roses, and of course…Wham. We also watched movies like *Goonies* and *Back to the Future* until we fell asleep.

During middle school in Texas, I had several white friends. My best friend from fifth and sixth grade was white. Race did not seem to be an issue. At that time, MTV did not play R&B or rap music videos. I liked what I saw on MTV. No one could tell me that I did not look like Madonna. I watched popular '80s sitcoms like *Who's the Boss* to get ideas of what to wear to school the next day from the character Samantha. I was connected to mainstream white America, except for one thing…I was black.

History for much of black America is based on a vision of life that we see and then try to emulate. Black children often attempt to blend in, and oftentimes it works, but it can be a strange moment. There is no right or wrong unless you cannot truly be a part of the finished product; for example, when black and white kids attempt to do each other's hair.

Sleepovers at Stephanie's house included me tagging along with her to babysit two neighborhood children. As we were sitting and playing with the children, the little boy hung on Stephanie and gave her a hug and a kiss on the cheek. The little boy had blonde hair, blue eyes, and was missing his two front teeth. He was only about four years old. His little hands were clasped together, gently dangling in front of Stephanie as he held her from behind. She sat across from me on a different couch. I smiled as I watched their bond. He was behind her on the couch as if he was trying to climb on her back. His face was right next to Stephanie's face. Every so often, he would kiss her on the cheek.

At one point, Stephanie said, "Give Corey a hug and kiss."

When Stephanie told him to kiss me, he loosened his clasped hands and removed his arms from playfully hugging Stephanie. As he hid behind Stephanie, he looked over her shoulder toward me.

After a long pause he said, "No." Another long pause and then he said, "She's black."

He came from behind Stephanie to plop down next to her as if he was mad and no longer wanted to play. I did not know what to say or whether I should say anything at all. I sat there and acted as though I did not hear what he said. Stephanie and I never talked about that incident. I never returned to help her babysit there again.

Although the babysitting incident triggered a significant race-relation awareness in my life, I knew I still wanted the other experiences at Stephanie's house in my life. I wanted to live like Stephanie and her family. I wanted a home, stability, and the ability to support my children's education. I wanted food. I loved the thought of having a pool in the backyard for my children and their friends to enjoy. I wanted the highest quality of life that I could attain. I wanted it all.

Even though I did not babysit anymore with Stephanie, more babysitting times were on my horizon. When I stayed with Frances and her mom, my mom started working for a white female attorney. Mom was the nanny/ housekeeper and was responsible for taking care of the attorney's daughter, Phyllis. Phyllis was a cute little girl with red hair. She was around eightteen months old. Some days I would go to work with Mom and help her tend to Phyllis. Mom was paid about $200 per week to work in the attorney's beautiful two-story condo. The attorney's husband was in drug rehab during the time that I went to work at the house with Mom. I remember Mom saying that the attorney paid thousands of dollars a week to have him in rehab.

While Mom fed Phyllis downstairs, I watched MTV as I made up the attorney's bed and cleaned the bedrooms and bathrooms upstairs. There was a bathroom just for the husband that I also cleaned. As I cleaned, I thought of being an attorney one day and being able to afford a nice place to live, to be able to have a nanny and housekeeper, and even to afford to send my husband to expensive treatment… if he needed it. I just did not want to have to struggle. The bathroom was large and masculine. The husband must have been a hunter because the décor was done in a hunter theme, with fishing gear, deer, and other wild game on a burgundy, hunter green, and navy blue color schemed border and wallpaper. I imagined all the possible perks in the life of an attorney as I scrubbed the toilet in his bathroom.

One day as I sat on the couch in the living room after finishing the up-stairs cleaning, while Mom was cleaning in the kitchen, the attorney opened the front door. She did not make eye contact with me. She unlocked the door and continued to look down as she struggled to pull the key out of the lock. She walked directly to the kitchen with her briefcase hanging from her shoulder. She held a paper bag of groceries wrapped in both arms and she had other bags in her hands. The way she entered the house, it seemed to me that something was not right.

The day before, I also went to work with Mom and I overheard my Mom talk to the attorney about Pastor Ed and Sister Sandra at our church, Abundant Life Cathedral. Mom told the attorney that she believed that the people from the church were listening to things that she talked about in our apartment. She told the attorney that she thought people from the church put "bugs" in her car. The next day, the attorney walked directly to the kitchen. I knew something was different from the day before. The child we nannied for was not there that day, so we just cleaned the condo. We were told Phyllis' former nanny *missed* Phyllis and wanted to take her out for the day.

Mom came out of the kitchen and into the living room, "You ready to go?" she said to me abruptly.

I looked up, then looked back at the kitchen, and then back at Mom who was heading for the door. I got up and walked to the door without saying goodbye to the attorney. I slipped out the door past Mom's outstretched arm with her hand on the door handle. As she shut the door behind me, her voice had hurt and anger in it.

"I just got fired," she said.

I looked down at the cement walkway that led to the stairwell. As we walked to the car, I stayed silent. My thoughts were stuck on the conversation about Pastor Ed and Sister Sandra, and the "bugs" in our apartment and car. I wondered if that was why Mom was fired. The stuff Mom said was weird to me. I know it had to be weird to the attorney. I was used to weird being my normal. She was my Mom. She said things that were weird, and that was normal to me. However, Mom was escalating in ways to which I had no understanding.

Mom cried and yelled that Pastor Ed and even guest pastors were listening to the things she did in the apartment and in her car because they preached about them at church. One night Roxanne and her sister Marcella were over and Mom showed them small holes in the wall.

"See, this is probably where they put them," Mom said.

Marcella walked over closer to the hole and ran her index finger along the wall and back and forth over the hole.

"Yeah, they do make stuff small enough to fit in a hole like that."

I shook my head and thought, *please do not encourage her*. I did not know what to think about the things Mom believed took place. It all sounded weird to me.

I finished eighth and ninth grade in South Vallejo. During the summer, I visited Mom in Houston. She had a party for me, with my closest friends, Roxanne and Marcella, in a hotel suite. We had pizza, chips, pop, and each girl had enough supplies to design and decorate her own T-shirt and hat. Throughout the night, different guests told me how much Mom missed me and wanted me to live with her. *Mom really wants me to stay with her*. I felt an obligation to stay. I did not want Mom to be sad and lonely because I returned to South Vallejo to live with Dad. I did not want her to think that I loved Dad more than her. So even though I was accepted to attend Hogan High School in South Vallejo, and had made the dance team there, I decided to stay in Houston with Mom.

The upcoming school year, I started at Hastings High School. While I was a student there, Mom started working in the cafeteria. Finally, for the first time in a long time, Mom only worked one job, instead of two. It was around that time that Mom's behavior became more and more strange. Her thoughts seemed to be worse each day. She told my Grandma Vickie that there were recording devices in the walls of our apartment.

"The people from the church put bugs in my car, Ma," Mom said convincingly. "The preachers, all of 'em…they preach about stuff I do in my apartment, Ma!" Mom continued, nearly in tears.

Grandma Vickie asked to speak to me. Mom handed me the phone.

"What is going on? Is that church a cult?" Grandma asked, confused, and not knowing what was really going on.

I did not know what to say.

One night, Mom stop making sense altogether. She described herself as being like Jesus with supernatural powers that could heal people. "Corey, are you sick? I can heal you. I can heal all that are sick, Corey. I really can. Bring them to me. I can heal them."

Mom repeatedly talked about healing people. I called Roxanne. She came over, and we tried to console Mom. Roxanne tried to hug Mom and get her to stop talking. Mom continued to talk as if she did not hear a word anyone said to her. She continued to talk nonstop. After some time trying to talk to Mom, we took her to the hospital. Mom continued to ramble. When the doctor approached her, she started talking gibberish as if she was speaking a language the doctor was supposed to understand because he looked like he was from another country. That night Mom was admitted to a mental ward for the first time, and was diagnosed with manic depression/ schizophrenia.

Chapter Seven

Left Behind

I stayed with Roxanne while Mom was in the hospital. When Mom was released, I did not know she had been released. One day after school, she came looking for me in the parking lot of Hastings High School. I was so afraid of Mom at that time because she was very angry and aggressive. She chased me around cars. When she caught me, she tried to force me to go with her, but I was afraid and did not want to go. I broke loose and ran through the parking lot with her chasing me. Soon, a security officer came toward us. I ran to him.

Out of breath, I told him, "That's my Mom," I said panting heavily. "She must have been released from the mental hospital," I added, holding my chest. It felt like my heart was trying to break out. "She's scaring me."

As I kept holding on to the security officer's arms, Mom walked away as if nothing had happened. I do not know where she went. The security officer took me to the main office so I could call Roxanne.

Since Mom was out of the hospital, and she was my Mom, I had to go back to stay with her. I slept on the couch in the living room; she stayed up throughout the night. Even though I was uncomfortable staying with Mom, I had already told her that I would stay with her instead of returning to South Vallejo. She started looking for a two-bedroom apartment. She found one, but it was not ready for us to move in. Since the lease was over at our current apartment, we moved in with my friend Amy and her mom Ms. Willa from church. We all attended Abundant Life Cathedral.

After going to a New Edition concert together, Amy and I became best friends. It was a nice arrangement: two single moms with two daughters that were best friends. Something can be said for the fact that I always had a way of making new friends easily, and that was a lifeline trait for me growing up.

At night, Mom, Ms. Willa, Amy, and I usually watched *The Arsenio Hall Show* on television while Amy and I got ready for school the next day. One night, the show was on and Mom still had not come home.

Where is she? I thought during a commercial break. Just then the phone rang.

"Hello."

"Corey?" I heard Mom on the other end say as if asking to make sure it was me.

I said, "Yeah…Mom where are you?"

"On my way home," she responded.

"Well, when will you be here?" I asked as I watched the next guest come out to shake hands with Arsenio.

"I'm not on my way there. I'm on my way to Canton. I tried to…"

I could not even hear anymore. I could not hear, I could not see the room I was in, and my body went numb. I was being abandoned. Left behind. Not wanted. Although I was independent, I was a child in need of parenting. I was a child trying to be grownup, in a grownup world of confused parents when it came to being responsible about raising me.

I started crying. *How could Mom just up and leave me in Houston?* My Mom's issues, as far as she understood them, overrode her need to parent me. That thought made me feel as if I was drowning by the tears that poured out of my soul.

Ms. Willa took the phone from me and talked to Mom. Ms. Willa, the same lady that encouraged me to get seconds when Mom and Amy told me I should not because they thought I was overweight, consoled me as I cried knowing that Mom had left me in Houston. Ms. Willa told me that Mom wanted me to go and stay with my cousins Roxanne and Eric.

So there I was again…staying with someone else.

I appreciate Roxanne and Eric's willingness to take me in, but at that point in my life, I had been in too many different households. At the same time, I wanted to finish a complete school year at one school, so I stayed in Houston with Roxanne and Eric and their sons Perry and Brandon.

Roxanne, Eric, and their sons lived in a two-bedroom apartment that was just enough room for their family, yet they took me in with open arms.

I stayed in the same room with Brandon and Perry. Their bunk beds were like the ones on *Different Strokes*. They slept in their bunk beds, and I slept on a chair held together by Velcro that folded out on the floor into a mini bed. Perry made room in the long, horizontal hallway closet for my things. The closet seemed to stretch from Perry and Brandon's room to the bathroom about six feet down the hall. Perry slid the door to the right, pushed aside the clothes, and helped me hang my clothes in the new open space.

Although the closet provided less space than the big, walk-in closet Mom had in her apartment, it was space enough for some of my things. The clothes that did not fit in the closet were kept in a laundry basket. Perry and I were close in age, and our moms were always around each other when we were younger. Like our time spent together while our moms worked back when I first moved to Houston with Mom, being around Perry made adjusting to my new surroundings easier. It really made the transition better because I was able to talk to him. I never really focused on the fact that Mom left me. I chose to spend time being silly with Perry.

However, the time soon came when I had to leave Houston. The school wanted to know who my legal custodian/guardian was. Eric and Roxanne did not have legal custody of me. The school began to ask questions regarding my parents' whereabouts. The only way that I could stay in Houston was for Eric and Roxanne to gain legal custody of me. That sounded too permanent to me. More importantly, I did not want my relatives to have legal custody of me just for me to continue to go to school in Houston.

At the age of fifteen, I answered one of the most important questions of my life at that time—*where do I go from here?* At that point, I had two options: go back to South Vallejo with Dad, or go to Canton with Mom. I thought about South Vallejo: Da' Posse was divided, drugs were too abundant, too many people I knew were in jail or going to jail, and others that I went to school with were dead. Furthermore, Dad was never gainfully employed after his time in jail. He was close to losing his home to foreclosure, he had already lost two cars to repossession, and he was struggling to get by. Plain and simple, life did not seem too hopeful there.

I thought there was no way I was going to amount to anything by going back to South Vallejo. The environment was not conducive to success. At that point in my life, I knew I wanted more out of life. During my time in Houston with Eric and Roxanne, my grades were good. I had my first job. I wanted to continue to get good grades and work to support myself legally, not by selling drugs as I once tried to do in South Vallejo.

I decided to give Canton a try. Arrangements were made for me to move to Canton during the Christmas break. As far as I knew, my family in Ohio knew that I was coming. However, when I arrived at the airport, there was no one there to pick me up.

I called Mom and her response was, "Y'all play too many games. You need to stop playing games."

She did not believe that I was at the airport.

I called Roxanne and Eric and told them what happened. "I wish I never came here. I want to come back!" I said as I started crying. "Nobody is even here to pick me up," I said through my sobbing. "Didn't my grandma know that I was coming? Did anyone know that I was coming? What is going to happen to me here?"

I cried until my cousin Karen picked me up from the airport and took me to my Grandma Vickie's house where Mom lived.

Motivation

Chapter Eight

BFF

I was in the tenth grade when things fully started to unravel for Mom. It was also in the tenth grade when I met Kim who has been my best friend ever since. Kim and I were both new students at Hastings High School, and we were in the same English class. We both had braces, and we both had mothers who were dealing with depression. Kim was tall, lean, and had the most beautiful skin and defined facial features that I had ever seen. Her beauty masked all the hurt and emotional pain she held inside.

Although Kim has been my best friend since Hastings; I never fully understood her impact on my life enough to acknowledge her as my best friend until her wedding day when I gave the toast as the matron of honor. Kim has always been a person I could talk to about anything. We were both able to talk to each other about dealing with our mothers' illnesses. Kim, at an early age, became the mother while her mother was the child. Kim worked at Kentucky Fried Chicken full time while in high school to help cover household expenses for her mom, sister, and herself. Kim's mother not only dealt with mental illness, but she also had a brain tumor.

When I moved to Canton to reunite with Mom after she left me in Houston, Kim and I stayed in touch. One day I received a call from Kim. When the phone rang, I do not know why I felt the way I did, but I sensed that it was her and that something was wrong before I answered the phone.

"Hello," I said, unsure if I wanted to answer the phone.

"Corey…my mom died."

I could hear the tremble in her throat as she tried to continue talking without crying.

"I found her on the couch where she sleeps."

I do not remember anything else Kim or I said. We both cried.

During the summer break, I invited Kim to come to Canton to visit with me and Grandma Bluchelle. We needed to be there for each other. As adults, Kim shared with me that she felt that the trip to Canton that summer saved her life.

She said, "I don't know how I would have handled life without my mother if I didn't go to Ohio."

As adults, Kim and I have discussed our mental health. I asked her one day if she was concerned about becoming depressed. She said she thinks about it, but quickly thinks about what her mother went through and shakes herself out of it. Sometimes things seem too hard to bear, but I know I do not want to become depressed, and for the same reason, I shake myself out of it. In both of our mothers' cases, they were not able to shake the pitfalls of their mental health.

Chapter Nine

The Attack

I understood that it was not Mom's fault that she left me in Houston and moved back to Canton without me. I blamed myself. The morning she left, Mom tried to whisper in my ear as I got ready for school. As she continued to pull on my arm to lean me down toward her so that she could whisper in my ear, I continued to try to comb my hair.

"Mom, what is it? I'm trying to get ready for school," I said.

She just continued to try to whisper in my ear. I was already running late. I did not want to miss the bus. I should have just listened to her. That morning, she tried to tell me that she was leaving. I did not listen. That night, she left.

Mom's struggles through mental battles with reality, and my struggles being a teenager, became a ready-made for TV movie. Many times, I was afraid to go to sleep at night because Mom would be awake all through the night walking around and talking to herself. I did not know if she would do something to herself or to me. Sometimes she would just have blank stares as if she was deep in another universe. Other times, she would say that "they" were spying on her, "they" had microphones in her car, "they" put micro-cameras in the apartment walls, and "they" were ruining her life. I did not know what to believe, but I knew one thing…I wanted Mom to get help.

In Canton, I moved in with my Grandma Vickie, Mom, and my two uncles. They lived in public housing that we affectionately called "The Jets." My Grandma Vickie lived there for as long as I can remember. We lived there when Mom had me at seventeen. Now, I joined her in the three-bedroom, upstairs/downstairs townhouse in Southeast Canton. I remember it used to be so much fun playing with my uncles when we were little. Uncle Jason is a year older than me, and Uncle Travis is a year and a half younger than me. We had the same neighborhood friends, went trick or treating together, and played together as kids. Once I moved back to the Jets, Uncle Jason and I would go to high school together as teenagers. Mom seemed fine for a while, but she always said different things about my hair, or how she did not deserve me, and that I was too good for her. Soon, she started saying that I should not live.

One Easter weekend, I stayed at Grandma Bluchelle's house. After church, I went to visit Mom. I will never forget that day. It was the day my worst fears came true—Mom attacked me. We were all sitting in the living room talking. Mom sat in a wicker chair that was away from where everyone else was sitting. It was the same wicker chair that moved with Mom and me from apartment to apartment until she got tired of it. My Grandma Vickie asked me to get something for her out of the utility room. I got up to go to the utility room in the kitchen and I had to walk by Mom. I looked at her and smiled. She looked at me with a stern, cold stare and looked back down toward her lap. All the while, Mom was mumbling inaudibly.

After some time, my cousin Michael and I headed toward the front door to leave and go back to Grandma Bluchelle's house. Unnoticed, Mom went into the utility room. When she came out, her mumbling became louder. Before we knew it, Mom rushed toward me with a pair of scissors. She grabbed the top of my head. Her hand clasped tight around a fistful of my hair. Michael jumped over the couch to get to where Mom and I were, just in time to prevent Mom from ramming the scissors in the direction of my head and neck. With one hand struggling to stab the scissors in my direction, it seemed like she used a death grip to continue to yank and pull me by my hair with all her might. My Grandma Vickie, Uncle Jason, and Michael tried to restrain Mom, but to no avail.

Mom had unbelievable strength. She continued to pull and yank me right and left like a rag doll while holding tightly to a fistful of my hair. She used so much force that I began to lose balance as I reached to the top of my head to try to loosen her grip. My eyes watered from the pain. At the same time, the pain choked me. I could not scream. My family tried to persuade Mom to let me go and to give them the scissors.

"Come on, GG; it's ok," I heard Grandma Vickie say.

"Give me the scissors, GG. Don't hurt her," Uncle Jason said.

Michael, in his soft-spoken voice said, "Just let her go, GG."

Eventually, Mom's grip loosened and Michael rushed me out of the house. After getting me to the car, Michael went back in to help calm Mom down. I felt an unbearable throbbing all over my head. There was a massive amount of hair that continued to come out with each graze of my hand. I do not know for sure what Mom was trying to do. I did not know whether she was trying to cut my hair, or if she was trying to hurt me with the scissors.

After that incident, I knew that I was not going to live in The Jets anymore. *Where am I gonna go from here?* I thought as Michael drove me back to Grandma Bluchelle's house. I knew that I could no longer live with Mom. For that matter, I was afraid to live with her. The Department of Job and Family Services (JFS) got involved. We had to appear in court. JFS immediately recommended foster care for me. The court ordered my removal from the home because, "Mother is a danger to her child." The Shelter Care/Pre-Disposition Judgment Entry dated April, 23, 1990 states, "Mother attacked child with scissors—mother has severe mental problems—mother has threatened to kill child." That same document ordered my placement with Grandma Bluchelle. Grandma Bluchelle surely did not have to take me in. She was a retired widow who had not only reared her own five children and twin nephews, but who had also raised three grandchildren.

I became the fourth.

During the '80s crack epidemic, many children were placed with their grandmothers. In each generation, there is a new social or economic issue as the cause of separating families such as teen pregnancy, high unemployment, lack of healthcare, and the rising incarceration rates. In my case, mental illness was the cause.

Dad flew in from South Vallejo for the court hearing. The experience had my eyes, ears, and mind wide open. I became highly interested in the court system and focused in on every nuance. I wanted desperately to go into the courtroom. To my dismay, they did not call us into the courtroom at all. Everything was handled with the caseworker while we waited in the hallway. It was nothing like TV court with *Matlock* or *Perry Mason*. I was disappointed.

After becoming an attorney, I went back to the Stark County Domestic Relations Court to pull my juvenile file from the archives. The documents in my Dependency, Neglect, and Abuse (DNA) juvenile file contain a lot of familiar names. It was interesting to learn that as an attorney, I worked with some of the same people who were involved in my DNA case. Adrian Chenault was my caseworker and is still a caseworker today. Attorney Frank Motz was my guardian *ad litem* in my DNA case. He's now retired, but he was also once the head mediator for the Stark County Domestic Relations Court. I worked with him during my career as a judicial attorney in Summit County. He later coordinated the mediation for my divorce. Jim James was the referee that presided over my DNA case. During my divorce, he was the presiding judge in the Domestic Relations Court and was the assigned judge for my divorce case. Robert Horowitz's name is highlighted as the county prosecutor on the subpoenas issued in my DNA case. He was still the prosecutor when he hired me as an intern pending my bar results. The first job of my legal career was as a juvenile assistant prosecutor in his office.

Chapter Ten

Drugs

Both of my parents experienced demons so severe that it led them down a path to drugs. It was a very hurtful situation, trying to understand why my parents allowed their lives to spin so far out of control that they would use drugs to cope. Mom lived a horrendous way of life when she began using crack cocaine. I hate the way that I found out about her using.

I was a young mother by then. I went home to Bowling Green after a day of classes in law school at the University of Toledo College of Law. I was tired, and I sat on the couch after settling my son Jaylon down with an after-school snack. The phone rang. It was Mom. She sounded frantic. She called to tell me that some man had just cut her throat. I screamed and shouted questions in an attempt to understand what she was saying. I did not have a clue that it was drug-related. I was only in my first semester of criminal law, but I went on a quest to investigate the matter and get the Canton police involved.

Later that week, I spoke with the lead detective on the case. He told me that he was not going to pursue the case any further because it was drug-related.

Drug related? How in the world is this case drug related? I thought.

I later found out that Mom's house was a crack house. As long as addicts agreed to share their drugs with her, they could use drugs at her house. She also allowed a drug dealer to live in her house and sell drugs from there. One day, a man Mom knew knocked at her door. He did not have money to buy the drugs, but he knew the drug dealer was there. That meant drugs were there. He just had to get past Mom to get to them. He first asked Mom to use the bathroom. As she turned to direct him to the bathroom, he came up behind her and sliced her neck from left to right directly across her throat. She grabbed her neck and fell to the ground. Trying to fight off her attacker, Mom turned in his direction. He overpowered her and began violently swinging the knife in her direction. With the man standing over her, Mom fought back aimlessly swinging her arms to protect herself from the knife. The blade repeatedly slashed her hands. Her hands were slashed across her fingers and thumb, with deep gashes that injured vital nerve endings.

To this day, she is unable to make fists with her hands. At times, she holds her hands limp as if she has had a stroke. Mom was able to get away from the man and run to a neighbor's house for help. Aunt Shanie described the house as if it were straight from a crime scene on TV, except the blood was real, and Aunt Shanie had to clean the blood off the walls, floor…and off my Mom.

Mom was on crack. I was in denial. Mom said that a family member introduced her to crack.

"I would not do that to my worst enemy," she said.

I do not understand why my relative introduced Mom to drugs. At the same time, I knew Mom was an easy target to get money from. She was easily swayed to give away her disability check for drugs and housing. All her sass and beauty did not protect her from the effects of drug abuse. Her beauty slowly faded as her skin became darkened and unhealthy, her hair brittle, and her appearance shabby.

Her experience with symptoms of manic depression and schizophrenia incapacitated her, but the drug abuse debilitated her. There was one time that Mom was home for a weekend visit from the mental hospital, and she went with a relative to a social gathering at their friend's house. I later found out, it was not just a social gathering. It was a drug fest. Mom came home throwing up all over herself.

Aunt Niambi put Mom in the tub with all her clothes on and tried to clean her up. I was so disgusted and distraught that I did not even talk to Mom, and especially not to our relative. It was so stupid to even offer a woman on mental health medication alcohol, let alone any other drug. I resented our relative. I blamed her for being selfish enough to get Mom hooked so that Mom could supply our relative's addiction. Having someone to blame for

Mom's condition eased the pain of seeing Mom addicted to crack.

Mom returned to the mental hospital and completed the treatment plan. She was released with a fresh attitude, and a desire to do right. She got a job. Aunt Shanie helped her to find an affordable apartment. Mom always decorated her apartments with expensive looking style and class on a small budget. Her apartment was fully furnished with mail order items from very nice catalogs. She even had a full set of leather furniture. She had an African theme for her decor with different masks, paintings, and drawings that she made herself. She also had a beautifully hand-carved wood dining room set with a buffet cabinet, a washer and dryer set, and a bedroom suite. She had a full entertainment center with a large television and stereo/CD player. She had everything to make her apartment her home.

As time passed, Mom's behavior crept back to the dark side and became more and more suspect. One night, my son Jaylon and I stayed the night with her. I woke up in the middle of the night to go to the bathroom. Mom was up and dressed. I had learned to trust to be alone with her again, even to the point that I had my young child with me. I never wanted to give up on Mom.

I could have walked away. I could have done that, but at what cost?

I did not need her in the sense of bonding with my Mom; but she was the woman who brought me into this world, and I stayed trying to be her daughter.

"Mom, where are you going?" I asked as she attempted to slip out the door.

"Oh, just for a ride," she responded.

Mom's ride must have been a journey because she did not return until the next morning. I did not think too much of it then, but the evidence became all too clear as things began to come up "missing" from her apartment. First, it was the three-disk CD changer stereo that I had given her, then the TV, then her bed.

One night as I studied for a law school exam, Aunt Shanie called.

"Corey…hello, how ya' doing?"

"I'm fine."

"Well, I just called to tell you that I am on my way to get your mom's furniture."

"What do you mean 'on the way to get it'?"

"Your mom sold all her furni…"

"No, I didn't!!!" I heard Mom in the background, interrupting Aunt Shanie.

Mom sold her complete leather living room set, and my aunt knew the people who traded the furniture in exchange for crack and money. Mom received $500 and some crack for an entire leather living room set. The $500 bought more crack. The $500 was smoked up in one day. It was sad, but the story is not over.

Mom still had things of value in the house, and one by one, the items were sold. The brand new carpet that was once so plush and clean was now heavily soiled and worn from all the traffic of drug users. Another one of Mom's apartments was turned into a crack house.

Aunt Shanie went to pick up Mom's hand-carved wood dining room set and buffet before she could sell them. Unfortunately, she did not return fast enough to pick up the washer and dryer. They were the last things of value in Mom's apartment that found their way out of the door. I am sure they were exchanged for a lot less money than what they were worth, just so Mom could buy some crack. Everything worth anything was sold. Mom even sold the soap, her grocery items, and her toiletries. Anything of value equaled more crack, even if it was just to get the crumbs from the bottom of the dealer's pocket.

Never in my wildest dreams did I imagine that Mom's ultimate thing of value would be up for sale...her body.

At this point, Mom was deep in the addiction. She had sold all she had, and now the only thing of any value was her body—and that was not a final sale. It was sold as a continuous rental to whoever was willing to stop and give Mom money or a fix. With all I had witnessed, my heart screamed, *it's not my Mom; it's something that has overtaken her.* I stayed in denial of the fact it was my Mom. The woman who birthed me sold her body as a commodity. As if having my own out of body experience, I kept my heart from seeing what my mind knew was true. The oldest profession was for others, and I hated that any woman would, or had to, sell her body. The reality check was heartbreaking.

Chapter Eleven

Not My Mom

I was still a very young woman, but years of dealing day-to-day and month-to-month with Mom's drug addiction and mental complications had me in need of my own fix. I was seriously in need of relaxation and an escape from the stress and sorrow I had been experiencing because of Mom. Now in Canton, and after starting my career as a prosecutor, I tried to enjoy a relaxing Saturday afternoon at Jaylon's baseball game. Nothing was out of the ordinary that day, except that I did not take my cell phone to the game with me. I just wanted to relax.

I did not think of work or anything other than my son's game. Just as Jaylon walked up to bat, my husband, Craig's cell phone rang through the cheers of the crowd. My cheers for Jaylon were interrupted by Craig calling my name. I thought he was calling my name in order to tell me to quiet down so that Jaylon could concentrate. Craig thought I cheered and said things to the umpire way too much at the games. I could not help it. I was a cheerleader and I played softball in high school, so being involved in school activities was in my blood and I was not a quiet spectator. I cheered and led the team in chants.

Craig was trying to tell me that the call on his phone was for me. I took the phone, confused as to who would call me on Craig's phone. It was an old acquaintance of mine. She apologized for interrupting me at my son's game, but said that she needed to tell me about Mom.

I took a deep breath and might have rolled my eyes upward. As I listened to her, the carefree Saturday I had planned turned into a dark and dreary day of gloom. She told me how she had wanted to talk to me before about the things she saw Mom doing. She told me how Mom would come over to her house looking for food and other items to sell. She said she did not want to give Mom the things she asked for, but that sometimes Mom would just take what she wanted. Other times, she would just give Mom money because she knew that Mom would go to the streets if she did not give Mom the money. My friend said that she thought that if she gave Mom what she wanted, Mom would not go out turning tricks to get crack. She thought that as an attorney, I may be the only family member that was financially able to get Mom some treatment.

As she told me her concerns, I thought of all the times I had spent what little extra money I had to buy things for Mom, or to give her money with the same intention as the young lady who called. One day, Mom called begging me to bring her some food. She said she was hungry and did not have anything to eat. I immediately dropped what I was doing and took her some food. She, in turn, exchanged the food for crack. Then she wanted me to bring her more food. I refused. She blamed me for what she was doing to get drugs. After listening to her yell, scream, and try to guilt me into bringing her food, I started to cry. Through my tears, I thought, *I should just take her the food.* Dad was in Canton that summer. He offered to take her a plate of the dinner we had that night. Although Mom acts like she hates Dad, that night she liked him enough to take the food from him and actually eat it.

I listened as my friend on the phone continued. "I just wanted you to know because I held back for so long, not telling you about your mom," she said.

Not long after that, another friend told me that she dropped someone off after Bible study and Mom came up to her car as if the car belonged to a dealer that my mom could buy drugs from. Surprised by who was in the car, Mom supposedly had a *don't tell Corey* look on her face.

I did not want to hear about Mom being in the streets. I did not know what to do, or if there was anything that I could do. As far as treatment for Mom, I had already gone that route a few times before.

Chapter Twelve

Jail

When I was an assistant prosecutor, Craig worked for the municipal court as a computer programmer. While running a test program, he saw Mom's name and looked further into the information. He later saw Mom in the lobby waiting to go into court. He immediately called to tell me.

"Hey, I just ran this test report and it said your mom had to appear in court today. I went out to the lobby and she is here. She was charged with possession of drug paraphernalia."

"What?!" I responded in shock. No one had told me that my mom had been arrested.

Immediately, I requested to leave work and I ran over to the municipal court from my office to find out what was going on. By the time I got there, Mom had pled *No Contest*. She was found guilty and sentenced to an outpatient drug program. The jail time was suspended on the condition of her compliance with the drug program.

The arrest and court appearance were not enough to scare Mom straight. After she was released, she did not attend the drug program, or appear at the show-cause hearing to explain her failure to comply. As a result, a warrant was issued for her arrest.

Usually, the police do not seek out individuals who have warrants. Instead, if a person is pulled over for a traffic offense, or arrested for some other reason, a warrant search is performed. If the person has a warrant, then they can be arrested. However, if the police know where a person is who has an active warrant, they can go after them for an arrest. That was the case with Mom's active warrant. She was on drugs again and she was not taking her prescribed medicine for her mental illness.

Unsuccessfully, I attempted to get her into a facility with dual treatment to treat her mental illness as well as her drug addiction. I found a location in Cleveland, but the clinic addressed addiction to heroin, not to crack. It was explained to me that crack is not life-threatening when a person is going through withdrawal. With heroin withdrawal, it is life threatening and it is better for a person to have professional medical assistance when trying to beat the habit. Also, being admitted to that facility had to be voluntary, and Mom would not consent to treatment.

I thought long and hard about what I could do to get Mom help. I knew she was not going to voluntarily go to any treatment facility. The only option was to act on the existing warrant. I knew her address and I knew she was home. Arranging Mom's arrest was one of the hardest things I ever had to do.

What played in my mind was, *it's for her own good. I'm doing the right thing.*

Mom was arrested without incident and transported to the county jail for booking. She got treatment while serving her jail sentence for her original charge. After being released from jail, Mom was clean for about nine months. Although she went to Cocaine Anonymous, had a mentor in the program, and was doing well...Mom started using drugs again.

What is it going to take? Perhaps she needs to know that I love her. Perhaps I never shared with her how I appreciated that she worked two jobs to try to provide for me. Perhaps I did not show my gratitude enough. My daydreaming and nightmares continued on and on.

One day while driving Mom home, I told her that I loved her. I told her that I appreciated all that she did to try to take care of me. At that time, I was a mother of one son, with another on the way. I told Mom that I wanted her to be around to see her new grandchild. I wanted to be able to feel comfortable with Mom visiting with and caring for my children. I told her if she continued to use drugs, it was not going to happen.

After Jordan was born, Mom continued to use drugs and go to jail; that was the vicious cycle of her life. One day after taking Mom home, I called her later to talk to her. She did not answer. That night, I received a call from the same woman who called me during Jaylon's baseball game.

"Hey Corey. Your mom is out there right now in the streets."

I went out to see for myself. I parked nearby where Mom stood. I watched as she approached a couple going to get into their car. It was still light outside. I did not understand what she was doing.

I went up to her, "What are you doing, Mom?"

The people walked away from her, shaking their heads.

She said, "I was trying to get some money they owe me."

"Mom, come on. Get in the car."

I took her home.

I called to check on Mom later that evening. She did not answer the phone. I went back to the street where I saw her earlier that day. *Why is Mom out here?* I was surprised to see her walking toward any car that passed by her. I sat in my car, parked under a streetlight, and continued to watch her. She never once noticed my car or me, even after walking right by me in my car. After about a half hour of watching her, a car finally stopped next to her. I watched Mom walk toward the car. The passenger opened the door for Mom to get in. I started my car and sped off in her direction. I slammed on my brakes just as my car seemed like it was going to crash into the other car. I threw my car into park, jumped out, and started yelling at Mom.

"What are you doing?! What are you getting into that car for?" I yelled and yelled until it felt like my veins in my head were going to burst. I started seeing stars because I was screaming so hard. I was in as much trouble as she was in because I was in denial of the facts—the truth.

"I'm not doin' nothin'," she said innocently as she stepped away from the car. She was being childlike in her shame.

"Yes, you are. Stop lying!" I screamed.

My head began to hurt as if the tears that filled my eyes were too heavy to hold. The warnings I had received during the phone calls were true. Mom was arrested more than once for solicitation. I was in defiance of what I knew, but would not accept. I made excuses: *It must have been a mistake. She was just standing outside her apartment. The bust just so happened to be in an area known for prostitution. After all, she was still in her work uniform when she was arrested; she couldn't be selling herself in her work uniform.*

But I was finally seeing it for myself. There was no denying what Mom had been doing.

One morning Mom came over to my house at 6:30 a.m. When I answered the door, she said, "I was trying to catch you before you left for the day."

That seemed strange because it was the weekend. I wanted to sleep in, but I allowed Mom to come in.

"The people I was with left me at another house," she continued as she came inside the house. She continued to talk. I no longer listened. I went to get her a pillow and blanket so that she could lie on the couch. I returned to my room to go back to sleep, but I could not sleep. I did not feel safe with her in the house. I kept thinking that she might come and attack me…again. I did not know if Mom was high or coming down from one. It was hard for me to gauge because I did not know how badly Mom was addicted to drugs.

All I could think about was a friend from high school who was killed by her boyfriend. He hit her over and over again with a baseball bat because she would not give him money to buy drugs. I did not know if Mom was capable of the same thing. I envisioned Craig coming home and finding me and the kids dead. I could not accept the visions my mind created. I got up. I returned to the living room and woke Mom up.

"Come on. I'm taking you home," I said.

It was very hurtful to think about the emotional distress that I kept bottled up because I was so angry that Mom allowed herself to hit such an all-time low in her life. The most upsetting thing was that the drug use was not just hurting her, but it was also hurting her family. I did not feel comfortable having my children around her in fear that she would do something to them while she was high.

What makes people want to smoke crack? What makes a person want to continue smoking crack when it hurts the family so much? I'm being selfish. But, she acts as if she does not care. I often argued with myself.

On one hand, I did not think that it should bother me when it was not my life that was upside down. On the other hand, I could not ignore it or stay in a state of denial. It was my life. She was Mom. She was my children's grandma. I loved Mom. I could not help but be bothered by all of her actions.

When I was in the second grade, I remember lying on Mom's lap while we watched television. At the time, it was rare for us to be home together just relaxing. For that single moment, Mom was not stressed about work. Right then, I felt loved. Mom rubbed her hand along my head. She gently ran her fingers along each strand of hair in my ponytails. It was such a special moment, and I have longed to have that moment again ever since then. As an adult, there are times when I need a hug, want a hug, or just want to be told things will be okay. It hurts to this day that I do not have a real parent/child relationship with either of my parents. I do not feel emotionally attached to Mom or to Dad.

Throughout my life, I was not sure whether I loved my parents. I felt as if I was not with either of them long enough to have any significant attachment with them. I always questioned whether I truly loved my parents, or whether I simply felt I loved them because I was expected to. I have questioned whether I know what it means to love anyone. That might be because as a teen and young adult, I did not tell my parents that I loved them even when they said it to me. At times, I felt that I did not know how to love yet.

It pulls on my heart to put it in words. Because of the lack of an emotional connection with my parents, I have always craved that in my relations with others. Trusting enough to love, it makes it a learning process with each person that comes into my life. I know I'm a loving and giving person. Sometimes I have felt uncomfortable talking about love, but I know the love of God and His mercy and forgiveness. I know compassion, empathy, joy, and sorrow. Those must be all the components of love, so I do know love. Becoming a mother taught me how to give and love. I am now learning how to love those that I disagree with the most, and to commit to self-care in order to show love to myself.

In my life, as an adult, every time I started to say, "I love you" to either of my parents, I literally paused and thought whether I loved them before I allowed the words to come out. I said it, but somehow it was an empty statement. To me, they were words without meaning.

There are only a few times when I truly connected with people on a personal level. I preferred cordial acquaintances without any real attachment. Moving a lot could be the cause of much of that. Extended family living situations might have caused the other part. It was not until I had my first son that I felt true love. And, once my second son came along...I knew, without a doubt, that I loved my children. As for others in my life, I was not so sure. It seemed that my parents, the people who should have cared about me and loved me the most, abandoned me and turned away from me at times in my life when I needed them most. It helped me strive for a strong connection with my own children. Deep down inside of me, I never wanted them to ever question my love for them.

Other family members and friends have been there for me and shown great love and admiration for me, but it did not, and does not take the place of the love I wanted from my parents. Sometimes we mislead, or we are misled, when it comes down to the fairytale, or the white picket fence and 2.3 kids ideology, or the TV shows of the *Leave It To Beaver* type image of love that blinds us to what family love truly is.

It is interesting to me to witness how people loosely say, "I love you." It is such a serious feeling—a serious statement, and yet some throw it around so lightly and without much sense of the magnitude it holds. I always tell my children that I love them. I think about the hugs I longed for as a child, and I make sure that I give my sons hugs at any given time. I do not want my sons to ever question the love I have for them.

When Mom used drugs, I felt my love for her was concealed by my fears, and she did not feel my love due to how the drugs clouded her soul. I feared that if I showed love, I would become emotionally attached to her. I feared that the attachment would only be interrupted by her not being there again whether it was another stay in the mental hospital, jail, or the ultimate departure...death.

Chapter Thirteen

Mential Ward

Here we go again, I suppose that was my feeling again as Grandma Bluchelle called to tell me that Mom was committed to the state hospital for the third time. I had the same thought when I walked through the cold corridors to the ward where Mom was. I felt closed in, and also felt I could not wait to get back outside of those doors. It was as if I needed to escape. The scary movie of being trapped played in my mind. As I passed the residents, I always thought that Mom did not belong there. I saw people arguing with themselves, women with makeup haphazardly painted on their faces, others with their hair matted and uncombed, and I smelled the stench of body odor that could make tears come to anyone's eyes.

I disavowed the truth of my Mom having mental illness. I wondered why she had to be in the mental ward. To me, Mom did not have "the look" that I began to recognize and associate with people that have mental illness. To me, "the look" is a blank, empty, lost stare. It was not until years later that I saw Mom with "the look." Either I never saw it before, or maybe I did not want to see it.

Constant contemplations and dreadful spirits haunted me. *Why does it have to be this way? Why Mom? This is what has caused her not to be Mom? Did this create the situation of me being the mother and her being the daughter, like Kim and her mom?*

In my sophomore year in college, I was determined to see a movie that came on television called, *Out of Darkness* starring Diana Ross. Diana Ross portrayed a woman who, in the height of her medical education, began to experience symptoms of paranoid-schizophrenia. It's as if the

83

illness just comes upon a person at any given time, but there are signs. The movie sheds light on the complexities of mental illness. Seeing the previews, I immediately connected to the movie. I hoped the movie would help me understand Mom's illness.

I had so many questions.

Why did Mom think that people were doing things to her? Why did my mother think that everything that happened was with the intent to irritate and annoy her? Why did Mom think that I was working with other people to do things to her? Why did Mom think…?

I needed to know more. I wanted to know more. The movie brought out emotions I did not know that I had regarding Mom's illness.

I think a major part of what bugged me about all that I felt and saw, was the fact that I am an educated woman; and yet, I was still unable to decipher what was going on with my Mom. I was a bright child. I might have been older and wiser than many I knew; yet, I was in the dark about my Mom's illness due to denial.

During my junior year in college, Mom asked if she could live with me in Bowling Green. At the age of twenty and being in college, there was no way I wanted to live with Mom. *What college student does?*

However, I knew she was sick, and I could not see how I, as her only child, could say no to her. Once she moved to Bowling Green from Canton to live with me, Mom secluded herself in the bedroom. She wanted to be in the dark, and there was always something that "they" did. If there was anything misplaced or out of place, it was blamed on someone who came into the apartment, when no one had come through the door. It was so irritating trying to reason with her.

She believed that someone or something did things just to *fuck with me* as she would say all the time. At one point, my friend Candi and I arranged for Mom to move into Candi's apartment. Candi lived in an apartment complex across the street from me. In turn, Candi moved in with me. I could walk over and check on Mom daily on the way to or from class or work. This arrangement was a bit less stressful for me. However, I could not ignore the events that would take place. They became a constant stress in my life, even though Mom did not live with me.

Mom began to put blankets over the windows. She kept the television on, but covered it with a blanket. She wanted to hear the TV, but did not want to see the screen. During one visit that I had with her, Mom made her bed. When she finished making her bed, she started to look for the remote to turn the channel. She became very upset when she could not find it. She began to cuss and yell that "they" came into her room and took it.

"They are always playing games," she said.

I was frustrated trying to understand why she said those things. I looked for the remote and asked her when she last had it. I lifted the pillow and there it was.

"Oh," she responded.

"Mom, just because something is missing doesn't mean that someone took it."

She shrugged, "I'm sorry."

"How can someone come in here and take something and you not see them?"

She responded, "Have you ever thought of a secret passageway?"

Of course, I had not, but I did not want to tell her that because I knew that it would just feed into her paranoia.

I answered, "No."

With a confident grin, she muttered, "Well, I have."

I continued to check on Mom on my way to class or work. Mom's mental health continued to decline. She stopped taking care of herself and stopped answering the door. She even barricaded the door closed. I could not get inside. I called one of the social service agencies for help. When the social worker came and was not able to make any headway with Mom, she called 911. The police had to force the door open.

Once they forced the door opened, the medics went inside the dark apartment to find Mom under blankets, with the TV blasting, and a sheet over the TV screen. Her kitchen was filthy. There were clothes all over the place. It appeared she had not cleaned in weeks. Mom squinted and tried to raise her arms to shield her eyes from the daylight. She had not been out of her apartment. She chose the dark inside instead. She looked horrible as the two men, one on each side of her, guided her to the ambulance. It was the first time I saw Mom in a straitjacket.

She was hostile and shouted, "I don't want to go to the hospital. Corey, why are you always sending me to the hospital? Why can't ya'll just leave me the fuck alone?"

The EMTs put her in the ambulance and shut the door.

Like the character Paulie in *Out from Darkness*, Mom made many attempts to restart her life back to normal, including trying different medicines to treat her disease. However, it has been a never-ending cycle since I was in high school. I wanted Mom to do well. When she did well, she had an apartment, a job, a car, and took care of herself. But the normal routine of her mental illness cycle was that after doing well for a while, suddenly she would start to think that she did not need her medicine, and she would refuse to take it. Slowly, the paranoia would take over again. She would stop taking care of herself and her apartment. She would not comb her hair or get dressed. She would sit around in the dark and be up all night. She would sleep all day or start using drugs and abusing alcohol. Eventually, a caseworker would come and find that she was a threat to herself, and Mom would end up back in the state mental hospital.

There was very little that I could do because Mom has legal rights. Unless she was a threat to herself or others, she could not be forced into treatment, or into taking her medication. After being admitted to the mental hospital in Bowling Green, Mom did well and worked at Rally's and Wendy's. She had a social life with friends she made at work. She did well for about a year before there were issues between her and her landlord. She made a lot of accusations. I guess my denial allowed me to ignore the signs that her paranoia had started again. She came to live with me during my senior year at BGSU. Slowly, her paranoia increased to the point that I could not ignore it. Although Mom did not physically attack me again, she damaged my apartment.

I came home from class to find that she had poured flour all over my carpet. She told me it was a way to freshen the carpet. I was shocked. Not long after that, my mother cut up my couch with a knife. She cut the screened-in living room window and threw the trash outside. I lived on the second floor.

I was concerned about Mom's behavior. I had flashbacks. In my mind, it was like I was a scared teenager on the couch in Houston again. I hid all the knives and sharp objects. I was awake all night because I was scared that Mom would do something to me if I fell asleep and could not protect myself. I felt like a scared little child. In reality, I was not a child. I was an adult, pregnant with my first child. At the same time, I was afraid to go to sleep at night because I was not sure whether Mom would do something to hurt me and my unborn child.

Several years later, Mom was eventually committed to Heartland

Behavioral—formerly Massillon State Hospital, after several failed attempts to have her "pink-slipped." When a person is pink slipped, they are involuntarily admitted for mental health treatment. As it was explained to me, Mom had to do more than what was considered the norm for a person with schizophrenia. She had to do more than make threats. There has to be an imminent, serious threat with actual attempts to hurt somebody. Mom's behavior became more and more erratic. Finally, she was pink-slipped.

Most of the time, I feared Mom because of the things she chose to do. She would come to my house in the middle of the night screaming, yelling, and demanding that I let her in. I had all kinds of flashbacks and fears. I called the police for her to leave. However, during the day, she came to my job at City Hall and acted out so horribly that security escorted her out on a number of occasions.

"Hey, we had to arrest your mom again; but don't worry, we made sure she was ok," an officer told me as I returned to City Hall after lunch one day. Eventually, the Service Director banned her from City Hall. Although I was a member of the Mayor's Administration, Mom could not to come to City Hall without being arrested. I was scared.

I was scared when I pulled into the parking lot at work. I was scared walking from my car to the City Hall entrance. I was scared to pull into my driveway at home. I was always scared that Mom would attack me again. It was as if I was once again the scared tenth grader running away from Mom in the school parking lot after she was released from the mental ward. I felt defenseless even though I was a grown woman.

She went to the bank almost daily demanding that the manager give her money from her account. I had to leave work to go to the bank to get her to leave. Sometimes, Aunt Shanie went to take her home. Other times, Mom went to local businesses where people knew me and told them I was dead. Another time, I had to pick her up from a local restaurant, she had walked to. It was not close to her apartment. When she arrived at the restaurant, she was tired and worn out. She had large deep bruises all over her arms. She told the owner that Aunt Shanie was trying to kill her, and that Aunt Shanie was evil.

On another occasion, I left work to pick Mom up from a local community health clinic. A friend of mine from high school called me. She was the receptionist at the clinic. The clinic was even farther away than the restaurant, but somehow Mom got there. She did not have an appointment, but she went there anyway. As she usually did whenever she went somewhere, Mom announced that I was her daughter. My friend called me to let me know Mom was there. And just like every other time, I went and picked her up and took her home.

Another time, she refused to leave from in front of the downtown YWCA. It was a really hot day. Mom was overdressed for the weather. She walked up and down the street until she fainted. Someone went to help her. Mom told them that she did not want to go inside the YWCA.

Instead, she screamed, "Corey Minor Smith is my daughter! Call my daughter!"

I am glad that the person who helped her knew me. She called me on my cell phone and told me what happened. I got there, but not before the ambulance arrived. A part of my job with the City was recruiting for the Police and Fire Departments. I knew the medics on the ambulance because they helped me with recruitment efforts during my time as the Director of Compliance for the City of Canton. They allowed me on the truck to see Mom. She was in a daze. They told me she was dehydrated, and her blood pressure was extremely high. They offered for me to follow the ambulance to the emergency room. I was stressed to the max at that time. Right in the midst of all the stuff happening with Mom, I was overwhelmed with one of the most emotional times of my own life… my divorce.

Determination

Chapter Fourteen
Learning to Cope

Emotionally broken by Mom's sporadic and unexplainable behavior, I participated in the National Alliance on Mental Illness (NAMI) twelve-week program for people who have loved ones with mental illness. I needed to know how other people dealt with the unexpected acts of psychosis. During that program, I learned that mental illness does not discriminate. No matter the race, religion, gender, or age, anyone can become mentally ill at any given time. Mental illness not only affects the person with it: it affects the whole family, and it affects friendships.

My children wanted to see their grandmother. At the same time, it was difficult to explain to them the things that she said, the things that she did, or the way she dressed. It is just difficult in general having a family member with mental illness. It was as if we did not understand each other.

As Jaylon became older, it appeared that he had seen enough. He did not ask, like Jordan did, to see Grandma G.G. anymore.

The first night I attended NAMI, I was more than ready to share all that was on my mind. I unloaded all the emotional baggage that I carried about Mom. In return, I wanted to hear the stories of others about their loved ones with mental illness. I wondered how their stories compared to mine. I was the only one there who spoke from the perspective of a child with a mentally ill parent. Most of the people in my NAMI group were the parents, grandparents, or spouses of mentally ill loved ones. Even though the others were not in the exact same situation as me, we still had a connection. I wanted to know from them how to love Mom despite her illness.

91

During my NAMI class, people in my group had the same thought about their loved ones: it's as though they know how to "play the system." They know just what to say and not to say. They take their meds, talk politely to the doctors, and then they are released only to come out of the hospital to start the behavior again that caused them to go to the hospital in the first place. Each time Mom acted out, she was arrested and the police took her to the hospital. Each time, she was released.

One time, my cousin Rae convinced Mom to admit herself. She agreed to go to the mental ward at a local hospital. They kept her there for about five days and then released her. Dealing with Mom's illness caused increasing stress on a daily basis. As she got worse, it reminded me of when I was pregnant with my first son and Mom lived with me. I had flashbacks of Mom attacking me with scissors like she did when I was a teen. Unfortunately, my fear did not go away as I stood in the emergency room with Mom hoping to get her pink-slipped. I thought I would be able to get Mom admitted when she threatened to kill herself.

It started when I was driving to take her home. She was rambling and it was as if I waited for her to put the words together that I feared she would eventually say. After a whole bunch of talking, she finally said it. She said she did not want to live. I did a U-turn and took her to the emergency room at the local hospital. But her statement was not enough. She did not say enough, she did not do enough to warrant an involuntary admission. She was released after we sat in the ER for six hours.

A few days after being released from the ER, Mom broke windows out of someone's house. She got arrested, and was later released...*again*. Upon being released, she started her destructive behavior all over again. She broke windows in her apartment. She cussed out the neighbors. She cussed out the landlord whenever he came to show the neighboring duplex unit to prospective tenants. She was arrested because her yelling, screaming, and cursing became so disruptive that others were complaining...but she was released later that day.

No one wanted to move in next door to Mom. After writing all over her apartment walls with blood-like red liquid, not cleaning her apartment, and having six cats living with her without even one litter box in the place, she said that she could not live in the mess. She then broke into the duplex next door and moved in. When the police arrived, she said that someone else messed up her apartment. She was arrested again. After being released from jail, she was found a few days later in the middle of the street yelling and screaming at cars in oncoming traffic. Someone called the police. Mom was arrested and taken to the hospital. This time, she was pink-slipped. Mom had finally done enough to get pink-slipped.

After she spent a day at Heartland, I went to visit her. At that point, I reflected on Mom's long journey in that facility in some form or fashion. I lost track of how many times I had been there before to see her. In the beginning, it was just me, a teenager without a driver's license, so Grandma Bluchelle took me for visits. As a young mother, I went with Jaylon when he was a baby and still in a stroller. However, that summer, I was established in my career, a mother of two, and in the midst of my divorce from my husband of twelve years. Over the years, my mother and I had crossed the threshold of that facility more times than I can remember.

Once again, I followed the staff member who led me down a series of hallways to the wing that housed my mother. The staff member opened a hallway door, and I was hit with the stench of stale urine. When we finally went through the last of three locked doors, I followed the staff member to a small open area that appeared to be used as a place for the residents to eat. There were two other patients in the area who had loved ones visiting them.

The area was dark and drab with only one of eight light panels lit. It was depressing, silent, and dark. The surroundings were somewhat familiar, even though I was not taken into the wing with the patients as had been the case during previous visits. It was uncomfortable to be in such close proximity to other families who should have had a bit more privacy while sharing personal thoughts and feelings, and while discussing the intimate, particular details that had led to their loved one being hospitalized. There were about five tables with three chairs at each table.

To the right of me, I could see through the window as the nurse led Mom to the door. Mom appeared to be very drowsy. She had on an oversized, gray sweatsuit with a T-shirt trimmed in lace. The T-shirt was long enough to hang out from under the sweatshirt and make it look stylish. I was glad that she looked decent. She had on her asymmetrical bob-styled, blond wig, but she could barely walk on her own. The nurse was very kind and polite as he led her between the tables and chairs and over to the table where I was sitting.

"Mom, are you okay?"

She could hardly hold her head up. Her head slowly drifted back and reached her shoulder area before she jerked it back to an upright position again. Her eyes were closed, and she struggled to try to open them and look in my direction. Her head continued to slowly fall forward until she jerked it back to an upright position. She did this over and over again. It was very frustrating to see her that way.

I asked, "Mom, did you sign the release?"

I was referring to the release papers that would allow the facility to talk about her condition with me. Instead of answering my question, she mumbled some profanity about some woman who did something she did not like. I had no idea what she was talking about. I just needed her to sign the release so that the staff could talk to me without any consequences. I wanted to be able to find out about Mom's treatment plan. I wanted to know how long she would be in the hospital.

"Mom, did your caseworker come by?"

She slowly lifted her head and struggled again to open her eyes in the direction of my voice. She tried to look me in the face even though her eyes did not open wide enough for her to see me. She mumbled incoherently. The visit was frustrating and meaningless.

If she was asleep or in such a drowsy state, why did they bring her out for the visit?

She could barely talk, walk, or open her eyes. She even began to drool as she tried to move her head and form words. Even though she was there physically with me for barely ten minutes, I rang the bell for the nurse to lead her back to her room. Mom needed to sleep.

Eventually, Mom was released from Heartland once I was able to find housing for her with the help of community organizations. Mom had an intense treatment plan with a team of specialists that engaged with her daily. Mom and her nurse, who was also her caseworker, had a great relationship. Mom was doing well once again.

After about a year, Mom's nurse accepted a new position. She was no longer assigned to my Mom's case. Mom cooperated with the newly assigned caseworker and continued to receive services. By 2012, I decided to run for Judge of Canton Municipal Court. Mom was one of my biggest supporters. She passed out my literature wherever she went. Often, people would let me know that they met my mom on the bus…downtown…or at the grocery store.

"She really loves you," I repeatedly heard.

Slowly, my campaign signs became more apparent. Mom's behavior was not just of a campaign supporter; she was obsessed with finding locations for my signs. She used a hammer and nails to hang a banner on a vacant car lot building. Unfortunately, it was removed before I could get to the location to remove it.

"Mom, are you taking your medicine?" I asked one day toward the end of the campaign.

"I don't need that medicine…I'm fine."

Aunt Shanie and I kept a close watch on Mom and stayed in contact with the intervention team assigned to her case. Mom seemed to do well. She met regularly with her high school friends. They took turns making dinner for each other. Each weekend they went to a different friend's house for a "girl's night out dinner." However, Mom's behavior became more erratic. She started accusing her friends of lying to her. Soon, she did not want to participate in girl's night out.

Aunt Melody started to take Mom to the store and to complete errands, but soon after Aunt Melody started, she stopped because Mom accused her of stealing her money. Aunt Shanie moved in with Mom to be more available to help her. Not long after moving in, Aunt Shanie had to move out because Mom accused her of stealing from her and damaging her clothes among other false allegations.

Mom no longer answered the door for any of the intervention team members. Day after day, there was a different behavioral issue with Mom. She moved at least three times by 2013. One day, she unexpectedly called me in the middle of the day.

"Corey, what are you doing?"

"Working…where are you?" I asked.

"On my way to Houston," she responded.

"What do you mean you are on your way to Houston?"

"I'm leaving my life. I'm giving everything away and going to live in a shelter in Houston."

"What?" I said dumbfounded.

The thought of Mom being in Houston made me think that maybe she would reach out to Roxanne, so I called her. Roxanne said that she had not heard from Mom because Mom stopped talking to her. As with her other friends, Mom accused Roxanne of hating her, lying to her, and wanting to kill her. Roxanne was in Canton. She was not able to confirm if Mom was really in Houston.

Eventually, Mom called and said that she made it to Houston. I did not believe she was there.

How could she have gotten there that fast, I thought to myself.

"Where are you?"

"In the shelter."

"What shelter?"

Mom could not remember the name of the shelter. She put an employee on the phone to tell me the name of the place. I looked it up online. It was real! Mom left Canton and rode the bus to Houston just like when she left me in Houston and rode the bus to Canton. To make matters worse, Mom's landlord called to tell me that Mom left the apartment full of furniture, dishes, clothes, and other household items.

"You have until tomorrow to get the stuff out. I did not know she was leaving. I tried to work with her. I have someone in my family like that...I tried to work with her."

I understood the landlord's position. I thanked him for helping Mom and asked for time to coordinate with my family to clean out the house. Right after work, my friend Andrea and I met Aunt Shanie at the house. My eyes looked like Michael Jackson's in the *Thriller* movie when I saw all the stuff in the house. We had the rest of that day and the next to get all of it out. We did the best we could with the help of Uncle Jason and Travis. Most of Mom's things were donated to Goodwill. Other things were given to people we knew who were in need.

Mom was in Houston for about three weeks. She did not follow the rules, and her behavior led to her being kicked out of the shelter.

Mom returned to Canton and stayed with "a friend," as she put it. I had never heard of the person before. It was near Christmas time, and Jordan and I went to visit her and take her a gift at the friend's house. Mom had a room to herself with space enough for a twin-size mattress and TV on the floor.

Fortunately, the intervention team was still willing to provide services to Mom. I kept them informed of her whereabouts as I knew them to be. Mom wanted help finding a place to live. She reluctantly worked with the intervention team for a while to get help finding a place. Eventually, the caseworker located housing and the apartment complex manager was willing to work with Mom even though she had several evictions on her record. Once again, Mom had an apartment. I helped her move in. However, she became aggressive in her verbal communication and behavior. One day, she hit one of the caseworkers, and it quickly became apparent that it was time for Mom to have consequences for her behavior. The caseworker filed a police report and a charge was filed against Mom.

But that was not the only sign that Mom was starting to act out again. She began complaining about the apartment. She claimed that the glass from the microwave door *mysteriously* fell and broke. The property manager said that Mom requested a work order for leaking pipes. When the pipes were assessed the manager determined that the pipes were purposely damaged. Soon after that, the apartment manager evicted Mom because of her threats against neighbors, and for an even more easy case… non-payment of rent.

The caseworker located Mom at a local motel that rented rooms for long-term stays. Mom refused services, but the caseworker continued to try to engage her. Mom refused. Mom's behavior worsened. Eventually, she was committed to the hospital…*again*. I attended treatment plan meetings at the hospital with the doctors, floor aides, and the intervention team caseworker. Mom was also in attendance. She was very aggressive toward all of us. The meeting ended before we could complete a plan.

When I returned for another meeting, Mom's attitude had totally changed. She was in the hospital for over a month and she wanted out. She was cooperative and even agreed to consider a group home upon release.

She is just agreeing because she wants out. She's not going to stay in the group home, I thought.

I had grown in understanding. The cycle continued. By December 2, 2015, Mom was released to a group home after we toured the facility. I was appalled at the condition of the home and thought to myself, *People pay over $900 a month to live here and share a room with a stranger!*

After seeing the home, I knew Mom would not be there for long. The intervention team vowed to find other housing options.

Late at night on December 8, 2015, Mom called me very upset. She accused the group home staff of not feeding her, and complained that she did not want to be there. The next day, I called one of the caseworkers to explain what Mom told me.

Silently, I held the phone, shaking my head as I listened to the caseworker say, "A man helped your mom move out her belongings. Her whereabouts are unknown…if after twenty-four hours we have not heard anything, we will file a missing person's report…we want her safe."

Later that day, Mom called me yelling and cussing at me with accusations that I just wanted to put her in the hospital.

"Don't call me. Don't you come nowhere around me. Don't call me unless you find me a place to live."

She hung up. I had no idea where Mom was, or what I could do to help her.

After that incident, Mom refused any help from the intervention team. She lived with other people, and soon was in housing that she found herself. It seemed like every other week, she came to my job and was verbally aggressive as she cussed at employees and demanded to see me. Whenever she came, someone would call me on my cell phone to warn me not to return to the building from court or come downstairs if I was in my office.

Mom has come to my house in the middle of the night so often that I had re-occurring dreams where I am awakened out of my sleep from hearing someone banging on the front door and frantically ringing the doorbell. Paralyzed by fear, I have come to realize that the sounds are not real, only because I do not hear them followed by her screaming for me to open the door and other vulgarly aggressive demands.

From the repetitive cycle of Mom's condition, I am now on a quest to help others that have family or friends with mental illness. There is no clear solution. The person must want to receive help. When they do not want it, it can be very stressful for family and friends who want to be supportive.

I reached a point of total frustration when I called Aunt Shanie. I was grocery shopping and very emotional when I started crying, "Why am I a lawyer? There has to be something more that I can do…what can I do?"

Aunt Shanie talked me through my frustration with her words of wisdom. I was determined to increase awareness about mental health resources in the media, presentations, and advocacy.

Like *Out of Darkness*, I wanted to see *The Soloist*, and later in 2016, *The Secret She Kept.* Based on a true story, the most moving for me so far is *The Soloist.* I wanted to understand what led to the main character Nathaniel's diagnosis and how his family handled his illness. I wanted to know more about the lives of others who dealt with mental illness. The movie seems to suggest that it might be best to let people be who they are with the mental illness. In the case of Nathaniel Ayers, Jr., it was best to be his friend and work within his world with mental illness, rather than to make him fit into the world of being "normal." Nathaniel could not live in an apartment as is the norm for many people. Instead, he preferred to live on the streets. Nathaniel could not play his violin dressed in a tuxedo before an audience of well-to-do, high society people. Nathaniel chose to share his gifts in the street before others who were homeless.

At the end of the movie, the camera zooms out from Nathaniel among a formally dressed crowd. Nathaniel is clearly dressed in ragged clothes with a tattered tuxedo jacket adorned with bright colored patches. However, the more the camera zooms away from Nathaniel, his different appearance does not seem so noticeable. It is as if he begins to blend in with the rest of the audience. Even though the audience members are dressed in black tie tuxedos and formal gowns, as the camera continues to zoom out, you can no longer see Nathaniel's bright colored decorations on his tattered tuxedo jacket that he wears over disheveled clothing. When the camera zooms out to it farthest point, Nathaniel does not stand out from the rest of the audience at all.

I have gotten to that point with Mom. No matter how she dresses, wears her hair, or where she hangs out…she is my Mom, and I love her. If her behavior is questionable, I love my Mom. No one could make Nathaniel be who he was not. I cannot make Mom be who she is not. I will continue to think of the times when we can be together with joy and happiness. I will continue to think of how it is a pleasure to see that my children are the joy of her life. I will continue to think of the times when she is happy, when we can talk, and when we can enjoy time around each other in peace.

When she is well, the good times with her are truly invaluable. It was during the better times that Mom helped me with Jaylon when he was a baby. Without her help, I may not have been able to finish my Bachelor's degree in four years. One of my most joyous memories was during my law school graduation. As I listened to the keynote address, I looked back to find my family among the crowd. My eyes focused in on Mom, Dad, and Jaylon sitting together. Mom and Dad were there together…for me. I started to choke up. It was a vision I had never had before. Mom was not at any of my other graduations. She did not come to my wedding. But, on that day, my family was together.

Chapter Fifteen

Friends and Schools

I often reflect on all the schools I attended, and the impact that had on my education. Going back and forth between Mom and Dad during my elementary school years meant that I attended several schools. At one point, I was technically in the third grade, but doing fourth-grade work in South Vallejo. Then I moved back to Houston and I felt that I should have been placed in the fourth-grade. The administrators in Houston chose to place me in a third-grade class where I excelled despite the fact that I was once again in a new school. Something in me, despite all the moving around, made me excel when it came to my education. I loved learning.

Due to all of the moving around between different schools, I have seen and attended various types of structures for higher learning. Stafford Elementary was a large warehouse/factory style building with an open floor plan - no interior walls. Some classrooms, such as the band and music room, looked like real classrooms with real walls and doors, but most of the classrooms were in open areas. The classrooms had real walls and doors, but the rooms must have been the offices in the warehouse before it was converted for school use. It was quite unique and looked nothing like the schools in the late '50s *TV* shows, *Leave It to Beaver and Gidget,* which most of the schools were patterned after during my early school age years.

Without real walls, doors, and windows…the neighboring class—if they were too loud—could be very disruptive to what was going on in your own classroom. Fortunately, that was only a temporary site. After going on to the fourth grade and starting the fifth grade, Mom and I moved again. This time we moved to Alief, a suburb of Houston, where I attended another elementary school.

That school was Smith Elementary School and it was even more unique than Stafford. The entire building was a circle. Like Stafford, Smith was an open space without walls. Movable partitions defined the classrooms. However, worse than Stafford, the partitions did not go all the way up to the ceiling because the ceiling was extremely high. Sometimes, it was very loud inside our partition because all the classes throughout the building were in the same area.

From Smith Elementary, I entered junior high at Olle Middle School. While I was in the middle of sixth grade and after Charles left, Mom moved again. That was it for me. I did not want to move again. I wanted to finish a complete school year without moving. I enjoyed Olle Middle School and wanted to start participating in after-school activities, so I asked Mom if I could stay with my friend Frances and her mom.

Frances lived in our complex in the Westwood Apartments. She was a grade ahead of me and very popular in school and on our school bus. I met most of my friends on the bus through Frances. I was included and allowed to sit with the seventh graders in the morning before the first class bell rang because I was with Frances. She had a large network of friends, not only at Olle, but at Jane Long where she previously attended school.

Frances was known for her very large breasts. She was well endowed even at an early age. Often I would catch boys' eyes glued to her breasts. She was tall, which made her breasts eye level for most boys our age. It seemed almost daily I heard the boys daring each other to touch her breasts, trying to "accidentally" bump into her, or sitting around guessing what size her breasts were. In the seventh grade, it appeared that Frances wore at least a DD.

I, on the other hand, was teased for being "flat as a board." I started wearing baggy shirts so no one could see or even try to estimate my bra size. I admired Frances. Not because of her breast size, but because I viewed her as the big sister I never had. We eventually had most of the sixth and seventh graders that knew us at Olle believing that we were sisters. We told people that we had different dads. To us, it certainly explained the difference in our appearance. We looked nothing alike. Frances was taller than I was. She was full figured, with a dark complexion. She wore a Jheri curl cut short with a tail. I was short and thin, with no breasts, a light complexion, and longer hair. I did not even look like "Mummy"—Frances' mom.

We called her "Mummy," instead of mom or mommy, as a mimic of her strong West Indies' accent. Mummy reminds me of a mother love figure. She is short and cuddly with a strong West Indies' accent. Her very presence was gentle, loving, and kind. She did not have much, but she was willing to share what she had. Even when she yelled at us, her accent sounded so cute that it was hard to receive her yells as discipline. Instead, it made me want to just give her a hug and kiss on the cheek. Whenever I reached to hug her, she seemed to quickly forget why she was mad. She just hugged me back and would reach up to give me a kiss on my cheek while she giggled and held me tighter.

She worked as a nurse and rode the bus to and from work. I remember Mummy seemed to always wait for her income tax return to buy a new car. I do not know if the income tax never came, or if it just was never enough, but for as long as I stayed with them, and for as long as I have known Frances, Mummy never had a car of her own.

I do not know what Frances could have possibly said to Mummy for her to be willing to allow me to stay with them. She was a single mother struggling to make it with her and Frances, let alone having another mouth to feed by taking care of me. Mom and Dad did not give Mummy any money, food, or anything else to help with the cost of providing for me. I stayed with Frances and Mummy during the week. On the weekends, I rode my bike at least five miles to Mom's new apartment across town. I rode my bike far with my bagged up clothes in tote to wash during my weekend visit. I stayed with Frances and her mom the remainder of sixth grade and into the seventh grade.

Dad invited me to come to what seemed like a once in a lifetime opportunity to go to Hawaii the summer of sixth grade. I was excited to go. Hawaii was absolutely beautiful. We visited with a lot of Carol's family, including her former sister-in-law. She was married to Carol's brother, Mark. Uncle Mark's daughter, Ioni, showed me all around the town. We walked everywhere. She introduced me to her older friends and she introduced me to smoking cigarettes. She, and one of her friends, smoked with ease and even made smoke rings. She tried to teach me how to smoke. Carol smoked, but I was not impressed when I saw her doing it. When I was younger, I tried to smoke cigarettes. Before anyone else was awake, I would grab cigarette butts out of the ashtray, put them in my mouth one after another, and light the crumpled, ashy end. The smoke burned my eyes and the back of my throat. To take off the burning sensation, I drank left over cups of warm juice and pop that were left out overnight by Carol and Dad's company. That was all it took. I had no further interest in trying to smoke. But, seeing Ioni and her friend make smoke rings, I wanted to try it again. I tried and nearly choked to death. I started and gave up smoking in the same day.

When we returned to South Vallejo, I spent the remainder of the summer getting reacquainted with old friends from Patterson Elementary. I was back in South Vallejo before the end of my eighth-grade year and it was cool to have friends from elementary school who could introduce me to new friends and teachers.

After ninth grade, I was back in Houston and met friends at the Abundant Life Cathedral (ALC). Attending ALC was a great experience for me as it made me feel good to be associated with something I loved from years before, like Bible Baptist in Vallejo. With ALC, my spirituality developed on a teenage level rather than as a child in children's church at Bible Baptist in Vallejo. I enjoyed my Sunday school classes designed for teenagers. Attending ALC also helped me make friends with other teens I met at church who also attended school there. Cynthia and I were the closest among all those I befriended. Sometimes, I would go over to Cynthia's house after church, then go back to evening church with her and her family, and then return home with Mom after church.

I was impressed with Cynthia's home life. They were the first black family that I knew personally in Houston with an actual house. It was nicer than where I lived in South Vallejo.

* * * * *

Old Friend

My old friend, Angela, is someone whom I will never forget. Cancer took her away when we were teenagers.

I always complimented Angela on her hair that looked so soft. The strands of her Jheri curl seemed to fall just right with a smooth, silky texture. During one of our first conversations, I asked, "Who does your hair?" as I reached to touch it.

She gently moved her head away before my fingers could feel her silky curls and said, "My mom."

Her hair had such a natural sheen to it that it did not seem as though she had to use activator, if at all. I wanted her mom to do my hair too. Mom always did my hair in the kitchen of wherever we lived at the time. I wanted my hair to look like Angela's hair.

One Sunday, Pastor Ed announced that Angela's cancer had returned; it had been in remission when I first met her. Our church prayed and prayed for Angela's recovery. As a church, we trusted and believed in her healing. I remember seeing her in my mind when the announcement seemingly echoed through the church. She was a young teenager; quiet, soft-spoken, but an intelligent young lady who knew and shared the word of God in our youth group like she was a grown up. A few months after Pastor Ed's announcement, Angela lost her battle with cancer and passed away. At the funeral, I waited in line to take my turn at the casket and pay my last respects to my friend. In the casket, she had on her glasses, and her smooth, soft beautiful coco skin was fully exposed by the fact that she did not have any hair. Standing at the casket, I realized why she gently moved her head away to avoid my touch. The hair I had admired was really a wig.

Angela was Pastor Ed and Sister Sandra's oldest child, which added to a very emotional time for the church; especially for the teenagers that were close to her, including me. It was the first time I can remember showing any emotion. It was intensified because I lost a friend.

At the burial, Pastor Ed said, "Ashes to ashes, dust to dust" while sprinkling dirt along Angela's coffin. All of a sudden, I dropped to my knees and broke down crying. To this day, I become choked up thinking about that moment. I still do not know how I regained my composure, or who helped me get up from my bended knees.

Chapter Sixteen

Wannabe

During the second half of eighth grade, I was back in South Vallejo. Even before the drug raid, it seemed as though I was around drugs a lot. The opportunity to sell drugs could have been a possibility if the "right" wrong people had entered into my life. I was only exposed to the kind of drug dealers who never fully made it to the top. I saw the consequences of selling drugs on a daily basis; someone was around one day, and then you did not see or hear from them. They all either ended up with jail grabbing them, or worse—in a coffin. The young guys that I knew that sold drugs had the popular items of the time: mopeds, triple fat gooses, Troop tennis shoes, Guess jeans, a pocket full of money, and Jheri curls. My friends and I were called Da' Posse, and we thought we wanted to deal drugs so we could have all the cool stuff we saw other people with.

We were thirteen and fourteen-year-old girls when we met grown men, who we did not know, in a motel room in South Vallejo. One of my friends acted as if something was on the back of one of the men's pants. She continued to brush his butt with her hand as she said, "You have something on your pants."

In reality, she was feeling on his butt...groping him. Although we were dead serious about selling drugs for them, they refused to put us on their payroll.

"It's too risky to have y'all out there on the street," one said as he walked from one side of the room to the other counting the big stack of money in his hands.

According to the other man, "Y'all be easy targets. I need my shit sold, not for y'all to get robbed."

With that one sentence, our drug-selling career ended before it started.

Although I did not sell drugs, I did hold drugs for someone; his name was Stan. Drug dealers in South Vallejo often had someone hold their supply for safekeeping until they needed more to sell. Holding was easier than selling, and I could get paid for doing it. I was so excited when Stan agreed to let me hold some money and dope for him. He even gave me a "double-up." After a drug dealer sells the drugs he has on hand, he may give double the amount to a person that gave him money to buy the drugs that he sold. Once the drugs are sold at a profit, the dealer gives the person double the amount loaned. It's like providing a loan and receiving your money back with 100% interest. In my case, I did not give Stan any money, but he paid me double what he had me hold for him. I was excited to have money of my own, especially since I did not have to do much to earn it.

My friend Felicia and I rode the bus to Kmart for a spending spree. I nearly spent all of my money buying stuff for me, and gifts for family members. Unfortunately, the day after I gave the money and dope back to Stan and received the double up, he got busted! He was back in the slammer at the age of sixteen, and my job holding his product was over.

Chapter Seventeen
Underage Drinking

E ven though I was often around drug dealers and their product, I did not have a desire to use drugs; instead, I started drinking. In South Vallejo, my friends and I could pay a crackhead a dollar, and he would go to the liquor store and get anything we wanted to drink. One of my friends had an older sister who rented motel rooms for us, and we would go there to drink without getting caught. My friend's older sister was always at motels in South Vallejo. I later learned that she was a prostitute.

One day her pimp said, "I'll have you working for me too," with a smirk on his face as he looked down counting his money.

I looked at him and said, "No, you won't!" I stood there with my arms folded across my chest as if to dare him to say anything else like that to me again. He never did.

I quickly found out that beer was not my forte. Drinking a "forty" was the popular thing to do; however, beer was just too nasty tasting to me.

"Come on, Corey…just drink it down to the top of the label…drink it to the label. You can do it, drink it to the label," my friends would say.

"PUGHAHH…YUK!!! That is nasty," I said. "I don't like beer!"

"Ahhhh…you weak…you weak," they would tease.

Well, I was not weak for long. I left the beer alone and started drinking much stronger drinks like Night Train, Cisco, and Thunderbird. Those were still nasty tasting, but they worked for me at the time to pass the cool test. I think back now and wonder how I ever let that nasty stuff pass by my lips.

I hosted drinking parties in Dad's basement when no one was home. Once, Carol came home early. She found us in the basement with rap music

109

blasting. We were all sitting around with a cloud of smoke filling the entire basement like a foggy day in L.A. L.L. Cool J blasted from the boom box speakers and silenced Carol's entrance into our hangout spot. Some of us were sitting on the couch drinking and talking. The guys were smoking weed and taking turns shooting pool. It was a scene all too familiar to Carol. She and Dad always had people in the basement doing the same thing. The only difference was they listened to Bootsy Collins, Earth Wind and Fire, or the Commodores while they did it. I was becoming a product of my environment, doing as I had seen her and Dad do all the time. Still, Carol chased all of my company off. In that instance, she was sending a message of, *do as I say, not as I do.*

The guys that were in the basement with us were drug dealers. Apparently they had sold to her before. At least that is how it seemed when they yelled at her in retaliation.

"Bet you ain't gonna be mad when you come around for more," one of them said as he laughed and ran up the driveway.

The drug raid at Dad's house had not happened yet. I was in denial about Dad and Carol using drugs, although, I had reason to believe it. After all, I found drug paraphernalia around the house all the time, and I was able to describe how to freebase by the time I was nine years old.

One New Year's Eve, my friend's sister rented us a motel room as had become a common practice. That night, I drank an entire bottle of Night Train. It seemed as though I did not stop to take a breath. I thought that drinking the bottle all at once would not have any effect on me. I sat on top of the dresser in the motel and guzzled it down. One leg dangled off the front of the dresser, the other leg was propped at a ninety-degree angle. I braced my position with my left hand outstretched behind me atop the dresser, and my right hand held the bottle to my mouth. Leaning my head back, I guzzled all of the liquor down.

About an hour later, we walked around South Vallejo and hung out. Soon, I could barely walk. Felicia teased me and started pushing me. I tried to push her away, but my arms just flailed and hung at my sides. She barely pushed me on my shoulder, and I fell to the ground. I could not get back up, and I got angry and scared because I could not get up on my own. I started to cry. By the time we got back to the motel room, I felt sick and tried to make myself throw up. Hugging the toilet, I stuck my whole hand in my mouth trying to gag. That was my last ride on the Night Train.

Chapter Eighteen
Joyriding

It seems that the teenage rebellion years are all stereotypically the same. At least, that has been my experience since it seemed that I did all the disruptive things others did as a teenager: underage drinking, partying, attempted drug sales, and riding in or driving cars without a license or permission. Being involved with drugs and drinking was not the only thing that was leading me to a life of juvenile delinquency. I also took Carol's car; not once, not twice, but all the time. I kept the spare keys in my dresser drawer. When Dad and Carol were away, I picked up my friends in the old cream-colored, two-door Nova, and drove all over South Vallejo and the Crest. I did not have a driver's license, but Carol taught me how to drive when I was eleven. She used to take me to the parking lot at the nearby city park in Dad's red, five-speed Datsun 310.

Carol thought it was good for me to know how to drive in case Misty ever needed medical attention and there was no one else around. Misty was a severe asthmatic and had life threatening asthma attacks. By the time I was thirteen, I was rolling around town with my friends. One day, I took the Nova when Carol was at home sleeping. I knew just when she was in the deepest sleep because her snoring was so loud it echoed throughout the house. I waited until the snoring was at its loudest, then I left in the car. I got away with taking it, and that was the beginning of many more times to come. Over and over again, I took the car whenever I thought it was a good time to leave. If Dad and Carol were not home, and were not expected to be back for at least two hours, I would take the car.

Late at night, after everyone that lived with us was sleep, I took the car.

This time, I took it and drove to the Crest to see Ron, an older guy that I had a crush on. As my friends would say, I was "sprung" over him. When I returned, Carol was up waiting for me and she was not alone. A police officer was at our house. She had called the "Po Po" on me. I did not care, and it was apparent in the way I talked to Carol and the officer. Carol told the officer that he could take me with him.

"I ain't putting up with this shit…her daddy ain't even here."

I shrugged my shoulders and said, "I don't care if you take me to juvy."

Without any response from anyone, I added, "She is the one who taught me how to drive."

The officer continued to write in his small notepad. Without a word, he went to his patrol car and returned with a metal box the size of the shirt gift boxes that Mom put clothes in at Christmas time before wrapping gifts in pretty, colorful Christmas paper. But, this was not Christmas, and there was nothing pretty about the way the officer opened the box and snatched out the paper. The officer snatched out a three-page carbon copy form and clipped it to the top of the metal box. He continued to ask questions like my name, my age, and confirmation of the house address…and then he continued writing. When it appeared he reached the end of the document, he signed his name at the bottom, tore out the middle sheet, and handed it to Carol.

He said, "I'm not going to take her in this time." Then turning to me, he warned, "Young lady, you'd better change your attitude or you're going to end up in a lot of trouble. I would hate for this nice lady to call us again and I have to come back, arrest you, and take you to juvy."

My bravado was playing out. The kids called it *punkin' out*. I was not as tough as I wanted to be when it came to standing-up to authority with a badge. I began to envision the cop car and the back seat with the bars over the windows. The handcuffs attached to his huge thick black leather gun belt threatened my frailness. His look—it scared me straight for the event at hand. My heart beat at full speed. My breathing rapidly increased with deep breaths. I focused on not allowing the fear to show on my face, and I thought I was being successful at it. I shrugged my shoulders again as if to say, *so what if she does*, but the words did not come out of my mouth. I could not let them know they were "pumpin' fear in my heart" as Da' Posse referred to intimidating situations.

That truly could have been a turning point in life. It was a prime example of reverse psychology. I believe had I cried, acted scared, and begged not to go with the officer, he would have taken me to juvy to teach me a lesson. But, I was without any emotion. I was cold, hard, and on the verge of being an adjudicated juvenile delinquent. If I were taken to juvy, it would have made me worse. Some believe that sending kids to jail just helps them become better criminals. Had I been taken into custody, who knows what would have become of me. In my case, I did not go to juvy, but life in South Vallejo was leading me down the path to become a criminal.

Chapter Nineteen

Murder

As a member of Da' Posse, we made sure that we walked down the street in a group of at least three at all times. Like any other day, we walked down 5th Street one sunny Saturday afternoon. Unlike any other day, we talked about joining the female affiliate of a nationally known gang.

Becka's older cousin dated a guy that could get us initiated into the gang. Felicia and I discussed what we would be willing to do to become real gang members.

"Yeah, I think I will kill someone before I die," Felicia said.

"It's not that hard, I think I will kill someone too," I said confidently.

This conversation appeared so simple at the time. That's what TV and the movies can do; they trap a young person's mind to become desensitized to reality. Kids brag and often talk as if they do not care which in some ways is true if you have no concept of the hurt and pain one can cause, or if you have never felt the hurt and pain of the end-result that is experienced by each and every person connected to brutal events.

How could we, at the age of fourteen, have such a casual conversation about murder?

It was the lifestyle around us. Sex, drugs, and violence—all the things that grasp society's attention, were in South Vallejo daily especially in my neighborhood. Each person to your left or right can most likely feel and say the same thing about somewhere they lived.

Whether it is urban or suburban life, kids want to be king of the hill. Whether it is based on real or false images, they brag thoughtlessly. Today, it's scary for me to think of the ease in which we talked back then about

115

killing someone. But, the Bible tells how powerful the tongue is. We did not realize how our mere words would take form.

A few months later, two fourteen year olds were outside of a two-story building in the Bay Area fog. Our faces streamed tears; our hearts pumped adrenalin. We were hypertensive to all things out of fear. I could hear the air Felicia inhaled, and as a bird flew above us, I could hear the wings seem to whistle in the wind. I could also hear cars cutting through the fog, although they were far away. Eerily, we were alone; no people were seen, just a couple of cars in the parking lot including the car we arrived in.

We were at an abortion clinic. The dark brick structure had a glass sign on it that read, *Women's Clinic*. We stood at the big double doors, scared to pull them open. I remember rubbing my forehead, feeling old. I had to be old, I was at a place that did not exist for kids. I was at a place to support a friend in a life-altering decision, and I did not want to be there. I pleaded with Felicia not to get an abortion. At the same time, I asked God for mercy, and for Him to help me help her in another way. We were only fourteen, but I figured I could help her raise a baby.

I believed that getting an abortion was not the right thing to do. The day Felicia was scheduled to have the abortion, I said to her, "We can learn how to take care of a baby."

I had no idea of how to take care of a child, and had never done so. Up to that time, I had never really been around babies, but I figured we could go to the library and check out books to educate ourselves.

That morning before we left for the abortion clinic, Felicia's Aunt Dee was at the house. Dee was Felicia's mom's younger sister. Dee and her boyfriend lived with Felicia and her grandma when I first met Felicia, but they had moved out since then. Felicia was three or four when her mom died. Since that time, Dee was the one that always did things for Felicia, and it seemed to me that Dee would do anything for Felicia. Living in her own apartment, Dee visited Felicia's grandma nearly every day all throughout the day. However, on that day, Felicia did not want her aunt Dee to be there.

"Why won't she just leave?" cried Felicia as we waited that morning for her aunt to leave so we could go to the clinic. Aunt Dee did not know that Felicia was pregnant. Felicia ran to her grandma crying and repeatedly saying, "Why don't she just leave?"

Felicia's Grandma knew about the looming abortion.

Felicia did not tell Dee about the abortion because she knew her aunt would chastise her about the unplanned teenage pregnancy. Naturally, Felicia was ashamed that she was pregnant at fourteen. Felicia was scared, and I was scared for her.

"It's ok, Fe," her grandma said as she tried to console Felicia by holding her head in her lap and caressing her hair. "Why don't you just tell your auntie? You know she loves you."

Felicia did not want to hear it. She jumped up off of her grandma's lap and ran to the bathroom. I could hear her sobs as I waited in the hallway until she came out.

Dee eventually left, and it was time for us to leave to get to the clinic for Felicia's appointment. We were late because Dee did not leave soon enough, and because of Felicia's fear of the procedure. Even after Dee left, we did not go to the clinic that day because the car would not start. We had to reschedule. So the next day, we were headed to the clinic, however Aunt Dee picked us up to take us. I was shocked, but I did not ask any questions. I figured that after the first appointment was cancelled, Felicia must have told Dee about the pregnancy and her decision to have an abortion. We traveled to a clinic about an hour away. Aunt Dee did all of the driving as we sat in silence.

As we sat in the waiting room, I could see the anxiety in Felicia's face. Aunt Dee might have been upset, but I believe she took on the role of being cool and composed as her young niece was about to go through a very serious procedure.

I had not even started my period, let alone started being sexually active yet. There were boys who tried to have sex talk with me, and boys who were always trying to do the stereotypical things such as dry humping and bump and grinding with our clothes on, and also others who said they wanted to touch me down there…but I would laugh it all off. However, at fourteen, I was not having any of it; but Felicia, on the other hand, was having sex and was getting ready to abort her first child.

The nurse appeared in the door with a smile. No…it was not really a smile. It was an, *I'm sorry, it's going to be* all right kind of empathic upping of the corners of her mouth. She called Felicia's name, and I watched as Felicia slowly rose from her seat like a ghost from the ground, and then her body went toward the nurse as if she were on a conveyer belt. It seemed to be the longest journey from her seat to the doorway that I had ever witnessed. Felicia had a habit of holding her hands together with her arms fully extended out in front of her when she was nervous or scared. As she walked toward the nurse, her habit and nervousness were on full display.

When Felicia was almost to the door, she gave what appeared to be a final look back in my direction. Our eyes locked for a moment, and we both froze in time. It seemed as though she wanted reassurance from me. Maybe she wanted me to plead with her again not to go through with the procedure. I could not bring myself to look at Felicia with any expression at all. Our eyes had connected, but I went into a daze. Something broke the connection, and I looked down and acted as if I went back to reading the magazine in my lap.

This was a serious thing, and I felt Felicia was making the wrong decision. Maybe I should have tried once more to stop her, but at that point, I was there to support her with whatever decision she made. When I looked back up to smile at Felicia, she had already turned and headed through the doorway. I only saw the hood of her sweatshirt and the words, "Da' Posse" that were on it as the door closed behind her.

Da' Posse was us; our young friends, relatives, cousins, and all of the people we hung out with. And Felicia was removing the first member to be *born* into the group.

I tried to keep my mind occupied as I scanned through magazines from the tables in the waiting room. Eventually, I became tired and fell asleep. It felt like I was asleep for a long time before Felicia came back through the door with the assistance of Aunt Dee. She was a little weak, but she felt fine. She did it. At the age of fourteen, and despite my pleadings for her not to do it, and overcoming her fear of Aunt Dee…Felicia had an abortion.

Being young and naive, we asked to see the fetus. The nurse assistant told us, "We do not keep the remains. The remains are immediately taken to a lab."

Felicia and I never discussed what happened that day at the abortion clinic, or the choice she had made not to carry her child to term. It was never mentioned to any of the other Da' Posse members. Although I tried to talk her out of it, it was a personal decision between Felicia and God. Who was I to judge her for her decision, when there were decisions I made every day that were displeasing to God? I simply prayed for her, and for her emotional stability if the decision ever came back to haunt her. I thought it would be terrible to go through life thinking, *What if I had that child? Would it have been a girl or a boy?* Or to think later in life about the possibility that her child would be old enough to have a grown child.

* * * * *

Fighting

La Neisha was in my English class. She tried to be my friend when I was new to Franklin Jr. High. She did school girl stuff and passed notes in an attempt to be my friend. She did not do anything to me, except try to be my friend. The Da' Posse members had issues with La Neisha; they just did not seem to like her at all. Who knows why? That is how it is sometimes. When girls do not like you, they just do not like you. There is not always a reason behind it. It could be because of hair, skin tone, body type, mixed race issues, all white, all black, all Hispanic, or some cool clothes that somebody had and the other hated to acknowledge.

There had been heated verbal exchanges among different Da' Posse members and La Neisha. Yet, there I was, along with my friends from Da' Posse, on the way to La Niesha's apartment complex. We hung around the complex and waited to see her. After a few hours of being there, we sat on the stairwell across from her apartment. When she and her mother pulled up in the parking lot of the apartment complex and saw us, I saw the nervousness in her mother's eyes.

It seemed as though she tried to figure out whether she was going to park the car in the parking lot or drive somewhere else. We were waiting for her daughter and somehow her mother knew it. Some of us sat on the stairs, others hung on the banisters near the stairs that led to La Niesha's apartment. We were dressed in hoodies, jeans, and tennis shoes. We were hanging out in front of La Neisha's apartment with the intent to fight her for whatever reason that sounded good. Her mother did not park in the parking lot; instead, she drove up on the sidewalk and the lawn between the apartment buildings. She parked the car directly in front of their apartment. Her mother parked the car in a way that blocked our access to La Neisha. The car protected La Neisha as she jumped out and ran right down the enclosed stairwell into her apartment. Her mom stayed parked right there until we left. We did not get La Neisha that day, but it was not over.

When I look back on young drama and all the reasons Da' Posse wanted to fight La Neisha, it often mimics adult dramas. Children learn from adults. Simple-minded dislikes leading to confusion, arguments, broken friendships, and many types of discords, often filter down to how our children behave in handling life with others.

I felt at ease with my friends. I did not think we were violent at all. We just helped each other out. If one was in trouble, we all were in trouble. If one got in a fight, we all got in a fight. This *one for all and all for one* mentality led to other fights. So...it happened again when Jasmine, who gave me her old clothes from *Spiegel* catalogs, had a problem with Monet. Monet was going to the prom with a boy that Jasmine had a crush on. Jasmine did not appreciate the fact that Monet accepted his invitation to go to the prom when Monet knew that Jasmine liked the guy. Monet was not a member of Da' Posse.

Monet stood her ground, and the heated conversation escalated between her and Jasmine. All of a sudden, Jasmine stopped talking and just started swinging. That was *our* cue to start swinging too. Monet did not back down. She swung at whoever swung at her. Fortunately, Jasmine's sister saw the fight from her bedroom window across the street and ran over to break it up. If Jasmine's sister had not broken up the fight, there would have been no stopping it. As I look back on it now, that was inappropriate to the umpteenth degree; but as a teenager in South Vallejo, my friends became my top priority. I was down for my friends. Everything else just did not seem as important.

"There she go! Let's get her..."

SMACK...PUNCH...KICK.

The fight with Jasmine went down and Jasmine's sister was the only authority figure involved. That was not the case with La Neisha. Although we did not get La Neisha that day at her apartment, we went to school and jumped her during lunch. Some of Da' Posse members felt that she started rumors about us, some did not like her because they may have liked the same guy La Neisha liked, and others just did not like her just because they did not want to. It did not matter what the reasons were. We all ended up fighting her, and all of us ended up in the principal's office afterward.

I was not initially called into the office after the fight with La Neisha. While I was in my advanced English class preparing to discuss *A Tale of Two Cities*, I heard that all of my friends were in the principal's office.

I asked to go to the bathroom, but instead I went to the principal's office to find out what was going on. When I entered the office, I overheard Mr.

Brown talking.

"Another discipline problem from Da' Posse," said Mr. Brown as he looked at each of them with disappointment. "Isn't that what's on your sweatshirts? Is that what you call yourselves?" he asked.

It was believed that we were a gang because we were the same group of girls that were always together. When we started dressing alike, the assumption heightened. We wore plaid lumberjack shirts of different colors randomly selected for any day of the week. We also wore sweat jackets with "Da' Posse" ironed on the hoods in white letters. The fights confirmed the assumption of our gang affiliation, and it was time for school officials to take a stand.

When I walked closer to his office door, I saw each of my Da' Posse friends sitting, one by one, in Mr. Brown's office.

I walked into the principal's office asking, "Did you want me too, Mr. Brown?"

Mr. Brown peered over the top of his glasses and glared at me, before saying, "Were you involved in the fight during lunch?"

Thinking that I did not do much, if anything at all, I scanned the semicircle my friends formed in his office as they sat in front of Mr. Brown's desk. When I saw Bianca, I was scared to say anything but yes.

Bianca was the smallest, yet she talked the most mess, and usually started the fights whether it was her issue or not. Bianca was wire thin with short hair. She usually wore her hair pulled back into a ponytail with just enough for a half-inch of hair extended past the rubber band that held the little tail of a ponytail. To top it off, she would have a pink sponge roller in the front of her head to curl her bangs. I hardly ever saw her bangs without a pink roller attached. She might have done that like some girls—who had been targets of bullies for being "too pretty to other girls"—who wore their hair in an incomplete fashion to attempt to shield their good looks so that the bullies would take the target off of them. Also, partially put together hair, made you seem tough.

It is no wonder that no one could believe that I was involved in jumping La Neisha. I was the one whose dad would not let her do anything. I was the one that "didn't do anything," according to my friends. I did not cuss, could not drink a forty to the label or smoke weed. I was not sexually active and had not even started my period. So in this instance, I felt like I had to prove myself. I was tired of other Da' Posse members thinking I was not down. I was down; and even if I was not down, they probably would have beaten me up if I did not at least say that I did something to La Neisha during the fight.

But what had happened was, all I did was initiate a kick in La Neisha's direction. I do not even know if it ever landed. There were so many people bunched up together, I do not know who did what. In any event, all of us were suspended for the fight.

"Ahhh, but Mr. Brown…it's the end of the year and people are supposed to sign yearbooks tomorrow."

Each of us moaned and groaned as Mr. Brown said, "Suspended. All of you are suspended!"

"Whose fault is it?" he said. "You all have to take ownership and accept the consequences of your actions."

I should not have been involved at all. I should not have invited myself to the disciplinary meeting in Mr. Brown's office. We were suspended from school at the end of our eighth-grade year. Tina, one of the older members of the group, was smart. She did not even get involved in the situation at all. It was her graduating year.

"I can't let nothing get in my way of graduating," she later said on our way home after school. She did not care if any of Da' Posse said anything about it, and no one did. No one tried to fight her. She went on to Vallejo High School the following school year.

I learned my lesson. I did not want to ever get suspended, drink, smoke weed, or take the car again. All of the things I thought I wanted to be a part of, no longer seemed as appealing as they once were. I thank God that I woke up. Luckily for me, my eyes opened. The negative behavior I was involved in was no longer desirable to me. I realized that I no longer needed to be viewed a certain way in order to have value.

Preparation

Chapter Twenty

Time to Focus

"This isn't even a 3.0, Corey!" Mom looked at me in dismay when she saw my report card from Franklin Jr. High. Throughout seventh and eighth grade at Franklin, I did not even know what a 3.0 was. I remember wanting no less than five As and two Bs when I attended Olle Middle School, because that would get me into the coveted Honor's Breakfast in addition to being on the Honor Roll. But before Mom brought my GPA to my attention, I did not associate the grades on my report card with the number…the GPA. Drinking, hanging out, drugs, a drug raid, fights, stealing the car, bad grades, and my friend's abortion…things just did not seem so cool anymore.

Where was the guidance? Where was someone to say that this stuff was not right?

I thought about my life. I wanted to do better.

By seventh and eighth grade, a lot of what I envisioned for my life was based on TV or other peoples' lives—like Lina's life. Lina attended Franklin Jr. High. By the end of eighth grade, I wanted to be just like her. I wanted to look like her. I wanted to dress like her. With Kelly and Jasmine's hand-me-downs, I came closer to having a neater appearance like Lina had. Lina always dressed nice. She looked nice, and her hair was always perfectly done. She was voted best dressed by our ninth grade class. At Franklin, Lina stood out to me because of her neat, clean, nice appearance.

Lina hung out with Da' Posse sometimes. She always looked much nicer in appearance than the rest of us. She wore color-coordinated outfits like clean white, form-fitting slacks with a white turtleneck, a designer mustard gold colored shirt, and a designer coordinated purse. Her hair was well groomed and looked smooth and shiny as though there was always just enough sheen. I liked when she wore it pulled back into a bun with soft, feathered bangs.

We were only going to the park, but Lina always looked like she was prepared to meet and impress the finest people in the world. Da' Posse wore jeans, T-shirts, and gym shoes from the local flea market or Filipino owned stores, and our infamous lumberjack flannel shirts or hoodies with Da' Posse on the hoods.

We loved to go to the Filipino owned stores because they had all the kinds of cheap clothes that we liked. We had T-shirts with neighborhood sayings like "5-0 Double Up" with a caricature of a black male wearing a donkey rope gold chain, Troop tennis shoes, a furry Kangol hat, a Run DMC T-shirt, and baggy jeans all while leaning on a Mustang 5.0.

I had to go home to get my keys before going to hang out at the park. Lina said she would come with me. I was hesitant. I really did not want her to see my house, but at the same time, I was excited that she wanted to come with me.

Dad, Carol, Misty, and I lived on 5th Street in South Vallejo. It was a two bedroom, single family home with a laundry room that was used as a nursery for my cousin, Jason, when he was a baby. The exterior was stucco, painted pink. Dad refinanced and made some renovations to the house after the time when he, Mom, Uncle Louis, Aunt Pat, and I lived there. The pink exterior was changed to light blue with navy blue trim along the windowsills and doorframe. To the right of the house was a quarter-acre vacant lot that extended to the sidewalks that made the corner end of the street. There was a large, wooden, six-foot fence that enclosed the right side of the house, and the backyard was adorned with a plum tree and a pear tree. When Dad lived there with my Aunt Pat and Cousin Jason, my Uncle Louis built a wooden back porch and stairs that led from the upper part of the house to the backyard and basement door. A portion of the basement was paved with cement. It was a favorite past time of everyone in the family to play pool in the basement.

However, there were people and things at the house I did not want Lina to see. I thought about Leonard who slept in his old olive green car outside of our house. During the day, he was usually on our couch in the living room watching TV. There he sat proper and upright with his legs crossed. If his drink was not in his hand, he had one arm gently crossed over the other on top of his crossed legs. His legs were long. The foot of the crossed leg seemed as though it would touch the ground next to his other foot. He appeared to claim his dignity in his upright posture. All the while, he drank gin and any kind of orange juice he could find, while smoking cigarettes all day long. It did not matter if it was 100% real orange juice, orange drink, orange pop, Tang, Sunny Delight or orange Kool-Aid…Leonard added it to his gin. I hated to come home thirsty after walking home from school, and being ready to make a cup of Tang, only to find that Leonard used the last of it for his gin and juice.

I did not want Lina to know who he was, or for her to see him and ask who he was. I did not even want to try to explain who he was. In all actuality, I did not know who he was. All I knew was that he sat in our house all day long and slept outside our house in his car all night. Dad said Leonard only came in our house to watch *Perry Mason*. He even had the nerve to get mad at Dad for turning the channel from *Perry Mason* to watch a football game. One day, Leonard got a paper route. It did not last long, but he bought us donuts in the morning after his paper route and watched TV all day long until it was time to go back out to his car for the night.

I also did not want Lina to see Derrick who randomly came by our house with salvaged computers that he gave to Misty and me as gifts. Derrick thought the computers would be helpful for us in school. The only problem was that the computers never worked. Dad said Derrick was a genius even though he did not have a job, was homeless, and sporadically came by our house to eat and sleep for as long as he needed during his time between different friends' homes. Dad also said that Derrick worked on computers and fixed them all the time. The computers he brought for me and Misty never worked. He *worked* on them, but never seemed to be able to fix them. Misty and I did not have a working computer for as long as I lived with Dad.

If Lina saw the children that we discovered were living in our basement, I really did not want to explain them either. Carol had a friend who ran, with her three children, from an abusive marriage. The boys were the most handsome and well-behaved boys I had ever seen. The little girl was beautiful with cocoa smooth skin and long beautiful silky hair that her mom kept neat in ponytails. The mother and children spent a lot of time with us. Carol was a friend to most, especially if someone had a hardship.

That is why we had Leonard sleeping in his car in front of our house and sitting on our couch during the day watching TV. That is why we had Derrick coming and going anytime he wanted to and that is why we had the mother and her children staying in our basement.

The children's father was a military man. He was strict, and he made the kids do drills he learned in the military. However, he took it too far most of the time. If he demanded that the boys stand at attention, they had to stand at attention. If he went off, fell asleep, or in some other way seemed like he no longer was paying attention to them, but came back to find the boys wobbling with weakened legs or if they had dozed off from exhaustion, the father would beat them and make them stand at attention longer. I never would have thought that the kids were physically abused because they were so happy when they ate and played with us.

As far as we knew, the mother and children stayed in our basement for about two weeks while the mother got on her feet after leaving her abusive husband. About three months later, Carol discovered that the children were still in the basement. They were abused by their father *and* mother. Their mother beat them and told them not to make a sound. She came to check on them, but she did not take them with her. She left them in our basement where they could not eat or play with us. In fact, they could not make a sound or in any way let us know they were there. But even without them doing anything to draw attention to themselves in the basement, Carol discovered that the children were there.

It brought tears to Carol's eyes to see how skinny and sick the kids looked. The children did not know how long they had stayed in our basement alone; they just knew they had to be quiet. Carol bathed and fed them. They were too weak to play with us. Soon Child Protective Services (CPS) came for them. Their mother came later. She yelled and tried to fight Carol for calling CPS. She was later arrested for child abuse. It is no wonder why I am now an advocate for children in my adult life.

Uncle Sammy and his girlfriend Jane were two more people I did not want to be at the house when I arrived with Lina. Uncle Sammy was nice, but he was always drunk. His girlfriend Jane was nice too, but she usually looked so skinny and worn out that I felt sorry for her every time I saw her. The story is that Jane used to be a very attractive woman before her former husband beat her and nearly killed her. Jane had a thick scar over her left eye which remained nearly closed shut. She looked at everyone with such timidity that it seemed as if she would cry if anyone said anything to her. She always wore a hair scarf, skinny-legged pants that revealed the true size of her thin legs, an oversized T-shirt, and flip-flops.

Jane was always seen walking behind Uncle Sammy around town. They did not own a car and seemed to walk everywhere. She walked behind him as though she were afraid to walk too close for fear of stepping on the back of his shoe and getting hit for it. She seemed afraid of walking too far behind him for fear that he would hit her for not keeping up and making them late for appointments they did not have. She usually did not talk a lot. She said hello with a quick wave, and an even quicker head turn either to the ground or away from whomever she spoke to. Eye contact was not a part of her demeanor.

Jane had four beautiful children who attended Patterson Elementary with me. I knew her oldest daughter Connie from Franklin Jr. High. She seemed slightly embarrassed to talk about her mom. Whenever I talked to Connie, I could see Jane in her facial features. I saw how Jane must have looked before her face was gashed open with a beer bottle. I saw Jane before the keloid scar that was on her face from just above her eyebrow, crossing over her left eye to the top of her left cheek. Connie knew her mom was still being beaten even if it was no longer by her dad. Now, she was being beaten by Uncle Sammy.

Uncle Sammy walked with a cool swagger and a forty-ounce bottle of Olde English 800 Malt Liquor in a brown paper bag to warm the chill on his hand. He walked with a slow double bounce with each step he took. His back was slightly hunched with his head bent downward, but he walked with an air of confidence as if to say, *Even though I'm drunk. I'm still cool.* His regular dress for the day was a fitted plain T-shirt, jeans, and flip-flops. He had dark tanned skin, thick, dark wavy hair, and a thick Cheech and Chong mustache. He looked like a darker version of Cheech Marin. When he was drunk, he acted like the Cheech character in the Cheech and Chong movies. He and Jane showed up at our house sporadically at any given time.

Whether it was the middle of the afternoon, or late at night…semi-permanent or recurring characters walked through the doors of our house and acted as if they resided under our roof. Uncle Sammy and Jane were usually on the couch drinking beer by the time I came home from school, next to Leonard on the other couch drinking his gin and juice. Uncle

Sammy fussed and cussed about anything and everything.

I wanted Lina to be able to come to my house and bypass all the people she might see that were not a part of my immediate family. I wanted her to be able to walk through the door, ignore the stains in the carpet and heavily worn furniture, or people smoking weed from a bong. I wanted her to be able to bypass it all and go straight to my room. The room I shared with Misty had been transformed from a drab room with dingy white walls and run down brown carpet, to a pink girly room with dark pink fluffy carpet and pink daybeds. Our bedroom was the cleanest looking room in the house because it had the newest stuff. I hoped those things would keep Lina's attention away from my clothes that were neatly stacked on a makeshift shelf of large cement blocks with a wooden board on top. I wanted her to appreciate the newness of my dark pink carpet and pink daybed. I wanted her to imagine being in an immaculately clean room, with matching coordinated posters of: New Edition, Pebbles—the singer, not the Flintstone character, Al B. Sure, Bobby Brown, M.C. Hammer, and Mickey Mouse, while we talked about Bobby Brown going solo since he was her favorite member of New Edition.

When we arrived at my house, I saw Leonard's car outside. That meant he was inside watching TV all dignified with his legs crossed and a cup of gin and juice in his hand. I told Lina to wait outside.

"I will just be a second," I said as I slipped in the screen door that I opened only wide enough for me to be able to get in.

Lina waited outside while I ran in, got my key, and a couple of dollars out of my piggybank, and yelled out, "I'm going to the park with Jasmine and them" to Carol as I ran out the door.

That was close, I thought to myself.

I wanted a better life. I saw the consequences of selling drugs. I felt the consequences of drinking too much, and the effect it had on people's decision-making abilities. I started to pull away from Da' Posse. I applied to transfer to Hogan High School instead of my neighborhood school, Vallejo Senior High School. The other Da' Posse members were going to Vallejo High. Girls from the rival neighborhood, the Crest, were going to Vallejo High. I figured we would be in more fights than there would be school assemblies.

My transfer request was approved. I was to attend Hogan High School at the start of tenth grade. I also tried out for the dance team and made it, but I was back in Houston before the school year started. I was enrolled in Hastings High School to start my tenth grade year instead. Hastings was a different world than what I was used to. Everybody dressed nice. There were a lot of girls like Lina at Hastings. School there was like a big fashion show. I did not have a lot of nice looking clothes, but I wanted to look "nice." I watched the popular '80s sitcom *Who's the Boss,* starring Tony Danza, to see what Samantha had on during each episode. Samantha's outfits usually helped me think of something to wear. I found clothes that fit me in Mom's walk-in closet, and I wore them to school.

There were two sections of Hastings: Hastings North and Hastings South. I was assigned to Hastings South which was connected by a half-mile long sidewalk path to Elsik High School. My cousin Perry went to Elsik High School. Although we eventually lived in the same household, we attended two different schools.

There were thousands of students at Hastings; Franklin did not compare in number. However, because I wanted to be just like Lina, I was determined to be voted "Best Dressed" like Lina had been at Franklin, even though it would not be time to vote until my senior year. I also felt that I needed to go to three proms because that is what Lina did as a student at Franklin. I do not know what I was trying to accomplish, but being like Lina seemed good enough to me at the time. My time at Hastings was short-lived. Five months after Mom left me in Houston, I moved to Canton, Ohio.

Chapter Twenty-one
Stability

O nce I moved to Canton, I attended another high school, Timken
Senior High. Dad's sister, Aunt Niambi, helped me to expand
my goal setting from beyond being based on what Lina did at Franklin
Jr. High to establishing my own goals; but our relationship was rocky
in the beginning. Aunt Niambi, Michael, and Juba lived with Grandma
Bluchelle. When I first came to live with Grandma Bluchelle after Mom
attacked me, it seemed as though Aunt Niambi did not want me to live
with them. She fussed about anything and everything that I did. Once, I
accidently stepped on her toe, and she acted as if I had purposely stomped
on it repeatedly.

She complained to Grandma Bluchelle, "She stepped on my toe. She
stepped on my toe and did not say excuse me," as if she was going to cry.

I looked back at her and said, "I'm sorry Aunt Niambi, I did not know
that I stepped on your toe."

She ignored me. I later overheard her tell Grandma Bluchelle that
because I was there, Michael and Juba wanted to move out. Although
they were both grown, she felt that I drove them away. Michael was not
a kid. He was a grown man who made the choice to go and live with his
girlfriend. Juba soon followed and moved in with his girlfriend.

Once both of the guys were gone, Aunt Niambi and I strangely became
close. Wherever she went, Aunt Niambi took me with her. I even went to
visit her in Cleveland where she taught school, and I hung out with her
when she was in Canton on the weekends. I felt as though I became the
daughter she never had. Aunt Niambi encouraged me to be excellent in

all that I did. I soaked up everything she taught me. With her words of encouragement, she helped me to be confident in who I was.

She taught me a new word every day to increase my vocabulary; like *reiterate*. "Re-it-ter-ate," she said with such precision and strong diction as if to pronounce each syllable exactly as it should sound.

Throughout my time at Timken, I still emulated Lina. I attended three proms and was voted "Best Dressed" my senior year. I wanted to do even more. I wanted to do whatever I had to do in order to be successful and live the life I wanted for myself. Once I moved in with Grandma Bluchelle, all the moving and changing schools in the middle of the school year that I had previously done was finally over. I finally enrolled and stayed in one school for the rest of my high school education. With Aunt Niambi teaching me the value of education, I focused on earning the highest grades I could, and I participated in all the extracurricular activities that I always wanted to participate in.

Although Aunt Niambi helped to build my self-confidence, it met a big blow when I did not make the National Honor Society (NHS). I felt wounded. I became silent. I did not speak up for myself because I was scared of any other consequences that might come my way after I did not make the NHS. Even with all the things that I participated in, I still managed to keep my grades up, but that was not enough for me to get inducted into the NHS at Timken. After fourteen schools, I was finally excelling. I was in honors classes and extra-curricular activities, but I was not inducted into the NHS, and that hurt me to my core.

This disappointment might be the best lesson I learned, and the one that I want all to know and understand. *Never leave yourself open to chance.* Assume nothing when it comes to recognition. One's achievements are measured by human biases in the end, no matter the scoring or classing system.

The morning the inductees' names were announced, I had an orthodontist appointment. I missed the morning announcements. Someone delivered a yellow rose to each inductee during homeroom. When I arrived at school, I was excited. I just knew that I had been chosen for induction. There was no way I could not have been...or so I thought. My achievements were finally going to be recognized and rewarded outside of earning Student of the Month my junior year in November of 1990. I had worked hard and I knew I was going to be named as a new member of the NHS; and I could not wait for it to be made official.

When Grandma Bluchelle dropped me off at school after my orthodontist appointment, homeroom had just ended. I ran to my homeroom class. When I arrived, the homeroom teacher was not there. I asked the students who were in the class if the new members were named.

"Yes," one said. Mr. Kisha is the chair. He can probably tell you who made it."

In haste, I ran down two long hallways and up two flights of stairs to Mr. Kisha's chemistry class. Mr. Kisha was such a gentle, soft-spoken teacher. He was tall and lean, with a head full of white hair, and he wore black rimmed eyeglasses. Nearly every day in class, he wore a long sleeve, white button down shirt, thin black tie, black trousers, and black loafers. He was known for telling stories about Walla Walla, Washington or referring to "a little red caboose."

When I arrived at Mr. Kisha's room, I was out of breath and could not speak clearly. Mr. Kisha appeared in the doorway.

"Mr. Kisha, the National Honor Society members were named this morning. I wasn't here. I came to get my rose," I said, still trying to catch my breath.

"Rose?" he asked puzzled. I don't have a rose for you, Corey."

"What?" I asked. "Wasn't my name called this morning? I made the National Honor Society, right?"

Mr. Kisha's put down the chemistry lab beaker and walked over to his desk. After skimming through the pages, he looked up slowly, shaking his head left to right as he said, "Corey, I'm sorry. Your name is not listed."

"What? Why not?" I asked in total shock. "I maintained a 4.2 GPA my entire senior year, I'm in almost every activity here, and I'm the Senior Class Secretary. Why didn't I make it?"

"Corey, I'm sorry," Mr. Kisha said again.

I turned around with my head down. My heart felt like it dropped from its place in my chest, and was somewhere on the floor being stepped on by any student that just happened to walk by me at the time. Throughout the day I saw different people with a yellow rose; a yellow rose that I felt should have been in my hand. I felt that all my accomplishments at Timken were in vain. I did not want to walk with my graduating class. I vowed to buy my own yellow cord to wear during the graduation ceremony. There I was a Senior Class Officer graduating without a cord.

Heartbroken, I attended graduation feeling unaccomplished because I did not wear a yellow cord representing the National Honor Society. I was on the stage with the other class officers and school board members, including Ms. Jeffries who I would later work with when I was the Director of Compliance for the City of Canton, but no yellow cord adorned my white graduation robe.

Aunt Shanie called the school to find out why I was not inducted. She told me that a school official said my character and integrity were called into question. The school official did not give Aunt Shanie any specifics. I was puzzled. I did not know what that meant or what I had done to warrant that perception of my character. I reflected throughout my junior and senior years at Timken thinking what I could have done wrong or when I had gotten into trouble.

Was it because of the disagreement I had with my homeroom teacher who incorrectly marked me absent or late more than one time?

I thought about the time I actively spoke out against my homeroom teacher for repeatedly making the mistake. I boldly announced warnings to other students who may have been incorrectly marked absent too often as well.

"Be sure she doesn't mark you absent," I would say as I looked in the teacher's direction and then rolled my eyes while she continued the homeroom attendance roll call.

Was it my cheerleading and gymnastics coach who recommended that I not be inducted because I dated the guy she warned us all not to date?

She said he was "a playa" and "no good."

"I don't want any of you dating him," she warned as she looked over her clipboard at the group of newly named cheerleaders for the Varsity and Junior Varsity teams at Timken. It seemed as though the whole group turned and looked at me. They all knew that I was already dating him at the time.

Perhaps it was because I verbally challenged my coach during gymnastics when she made me do fifty "cant's" for being late to practice. "Cant's" were rigorous exercises where we lay flat on our backs, arms outstretched above our heads, and our legs straight out with our toes pointed as we folded our bodies in half with the goal to touch our fingers to our toes. We did them as a team for our gymnastics warmup, but anyone was subject to do more as a consequence for being late, saying "I can't," or not dressing properly.

I remember on one occasion, my coach made a comment about me coming down late from the locker room. As she told me to do "cant's" others came down from the locker room late.

As each one came in, I said, "What about them, coach?" More of my teammates came down…"What about them? Aren't you gonna make them do cant's?"

The more I said it, the more irritated the coach became.

"This is my gym…you don't have to tell me how to run my team. You can leave if you don't like it," she finished.

Angered and embarrassed, I said, "I will," as I started to gather my stuff to leave.

Just as I walked toward the exit, my coach shouted, "And don't come back!"

I looked back. My team was on the floor in a circle as we were instructed to do at every practice. As I scanned their faces, they all looked like they had an expression of shock on their faces in anticipation of what I would say in response. My eyes looked from down at them on the floor to my coach standing behind the circle, clipboard in hand, and a smart-alecky smirk on her face as if she dared me to say anything else.

I stared at her. She had the upper hand, and she knew it. It was as if everything was in freeze frame. Unexpectedly, I blurted out, "I won't!"

I turned around and walked out of the gym. I was so mad, but I did not know what the consequences of my actions would be. Time soon told the consequence. I learned that I would not receive my Varsity letter that I earned during the gymnastics season. I practiced, I competed, I traveled with the team, but I would not receive my Varsity letter. I submitted a written appeal to the Athletic Director. He denied my appeal and affirmed my coach's decision.

I did not receive my awards for any of my competitions. My best friend on the team told me that it was silent at the awards banquet when I appeared on the video doing full spins on the balance beam.

"I feel like Michael Jackson," I said with each spin. Eventually, my coach pushed fast forward through the parts of the video that showed me. The awards ceremony concluded without any mention of my record, achievements, or even my participation. It was as if my contribution to the team did not matter, and graduating seventeenth in my class did not matter to me when I was not inducted into the National Honor Society.

Not being inducted hurt a lot. Graduation was supposed to be one of the most joyous days in someone's life, but it was heartbreaking for me. I was determined to make up for not being inducted in NHS in high school. I wanted to go to college and do well. However, I did not know how I was going to go to college. My parents did not save money for me to attend. I did not have a rich relative that was ready, willing, and able, to pay for my tuition.

I thought to myself, *how am I—a ward of the State—going to go to college?*

"Undesirable circumstances," Ms. Norma Washington said as she helped me complete scholarship applications. Ms. Washington was a teacher at Timken who helped students apply for college and complete scholarship applications.

It was just me and a few other students who sat in a study hall classroom and worked on scholarship applications when Ms. Washington told me, "You have many undesirable circumstances in your life that you managed to overcome in order to reach this point in your life. You ought to focus on that in any application essay you complete…the scholarship committees like to invest in students that overcome difficult things and still pursue their goals."

The question of how I was going to go to college was answered. I never really thought about anything in my life as obstacles, or as undesirable circumstances for that matter. I never thought twice about the things that happened in my life.

I did not want to spend time in counseling…dwelling on what Mom did to me. But to make people around me feel better about my Mom attacking me, and how was I coping with it, I went to counseling, but I stopped going soon after starting. I did not want to connect with my feelings; and quite frankly, after moving in with Grandma Bluchelle, I had stability…finally. That is all that seemed to matter.

Reflecting back, I realize that I had been through a lot. Some would have given up or used the undesirable circumstances as excuses. I thought about excuses that I could have made up. Instead, I created what I now claim as my life's motto…

Don't allow undesirable circumstances to be excuses for you to fail, but allow them to be reasons for you to excel.

With that, I was encouraged to pursue the excellence my Aunt Niambi always talked to me about.

It hurt not to receive my Varsity letter that I earned. It hurt even more not be inducted into the National Honor Society. However, I was determined to be "successful." I made it to college and achieved a 4.0 during my first semester at Bowling Green State University. It was a major accomplishment for me, but it turned into another wound to my self-confidence when upperclassmen told me I did not have hard classes.

"You did not even have a full class load," Andre said as he pointed at the credit hours section of my very first college report card. "Look at this… University Success…that's not a real class," he continued while looking at my report card.

He pointed at each grade and challenged the value of each class he considered to be an "easy A." My confidence seemed to be near death with each class he demeaned. His comments tormented me, but they also drove me to do better. I made the Dean's List the following semester. No more comments from Andre. I had a full class load. I had the required number of credit hours. I had the grades. I made the Dean's List then and multiple times thereafter. I had the academic success I so desired.

Chapter Twenty-two

Relation-Trips

With my first long-term relationship, I just knew that my boyfriend—at the time—would become my husband. As is the case with many young ladies, I had this picture-perfect life all mapped out in my mind when it came to that first guy; the first one I gave my heart to. My first Mr. Right was the guy my cheerleading coach had warned the whole team not to date. I was drawn to everything about him; and apparently, the coach could see things in him that I could not see.

He came from a good family, and his parents had been married for over twenty years. I admired that. It fell right in line with that life-long desire that I was always searching for of a stable and perfect family life. I figured that we would be like his parents one day. Mr. and Mrs., forever and a day, until death do us part. But his father lived in another city to complete his final years with a major company before his retirement.

That doesn't seem right…but at least they were married, I thought.

The longer I dated my first Mr. Right, the more I saw that he really did not have much respect for women. I recall him saying that it was his mother's fault if his dad cheated on her. He felt that because his mother used to go out to clubs and drink with his dad, she should not be upset that his dad chose to continue to do those things after she "got religion" and stopped doing them, opting on going to church instead. His theory was that if his dad was with another woman, it was his mother's fault because she wanted to be more involved with her church than to go to bars with her husband.

His *mentality* should have been a red flag to me, but I chose to blow it off. Unknowingly, often—although we have heard that it is not a good thing to have one in our lives—we, as women, are still drawn to bad boys. There can be things about him that we know are destructive to our future, but we are still attracted to them. We somehow think things will be different when it comes to how he treats us. Or worse yet, we think we can change him. Deep down, a lot of women want a man with a bit of an edge; we want the happily ever after, but we also still want to be wanted by bad boys.

He was also somewhat controlling; which caused a problem because I never thought of myself as the submissive type, and always stated what was on my mind. He would often comment on what I chose to eat. He was concerned that I would "get fat" because he saw it happen to his mom and sister. The timing of his comments always rubbed me the wrong way because I had already been through the stress of my mother pressuring me to be thin. In hindsight, maybe both of them were just trying to help me by looking out for my health, but I saw both of their actions as being controlling.

I said to him, "Just because it happened to your mom and sister, doesn't mean it is going to happen to me. I will eat what I want, when I want, and how much I want."

He just gave me a look and let it go for that moment, but he continued to make little comments every time I put something in my mouth, and I continued to make it known that I would do as I choose to do. Just like most girls want a bad boy, most boys want a girl with a bit of spunk to her. And I could give just as much as I got.

While still in high school, I continued to date him after he went off to college. I wanted to have a long-lasting relationship; I really thought we could make it work. I *needed* it to work. I never got a chance to witness that "you and me against the world" relationship in my own parents, but since his parents had been together for so long, I thought he and I could be like them. In my mind, it was going to be that way. We were going to make it for the long haul.

I was falling for him more and more because of the relationship I had created in my mind; one that was half based on reality, and half based on fiction and fantasy. But all that glitters is not gold. I felt good when my friends admired our relationship. I knew it had a few problems on the inside, but to others viewing it from the outside, everything seemed to be good as gold. I remember Camela and I drove around after leaving McDonald's one day. I called my boyfriend to see if he was home and to let him know that I was coming by.

"I wish I had a boyfriend that I could go visit," she said as I got out of the car. It made me think that I had something special.

I soon came to realize that my relationship was not *all that*. I began to hear stories about him being with other women. Of course, I did not want to believe it. I wanted to chalk it up to gossip by people who were jealous of what he and I had together. I wanted to rationalize that he would never cheat on me and that he was just being targeted to be the source of something for people to talk about. I wonder if denial of this sort is adopted more by women of a certain age—where we close our eyes to the truth about the nature of this kind of behavior from some men.

I decided to confront him. He denied it…just like I thought he would, and I believed him. Well, at least I believed him the first time, but then there was a second, a third, and a fourth. The stories became too numerous not to give them more consideration. The stories involved the same women. His excuse, to me, for being with these women was always basketball. He even showed me his alibi flier for a basketball tournament he claimed to be playing in. Once again, I chose to believe his story over that of at least three of my closest friends. Eventually, the stories, the sources, and of course the number of women involved multiplied.

"How much is it going to take?" Camela asked.

It got to the point where she and my other friends refused to tell me anything anymore. I could not blame them, even though I wanted to. Camela continued, "Why should we tell you anything? You don't believe us anyway…all you do is barely question him and end up believing whatever he says."

She was right; his lies were more believable to me than what I did not want to hear…the truth. I did not believe them because I did not *want* to. I believed him because I *needed* to. It was as if I made some sort of connection in my mind that if he was cheating on me, somehow I must have deserved it. He even got another young lady pregnant while he was away at college. It hurt me when I found out, but instead of breaking things off with him, I started questioning myself.

If he was messing around on me, what did that say about me? What does she have on me?

I reflected back on the justification he told me at the beginning of our relationship concerning his father – *she brought it on herself* mentality.

Did I bring it on myself? Did I drive him to the arms of another woman? Was I a victim? Did I make myself a victim? Or was I just another tool in his toolbox?

The sad part is, I had no answers for myself; nor did I push as hard as I should have to find the answers.

He came home from college on weekends, broke up with me, and before he returned to school we were boyfriend and girlfriend again. It took some time for me to open my eyes to the fact, but it became apparent to me that there was a pattern. Camela was right. I chose to believe him because I did not want to know or believe that he was cheating on me. I excused the child because he was supposedly conceived during one of our many breakups. Believing that my boyfriend was being unfaithful to me would force me to change my belief that we would be together forever with the picture-perfect life of happy husband and wife; so I remained in a state of denial.

I stayed with him even after I went to college. His behavior did not change, and neither did my acceptance of his lies. Our destructive pattern continued. When I was a sophomore in college, I drove to his college to go to his basketball game. He did not know that I was coming. I figured that I would surprise him. When I got there, I thought he would be just as happy to see me as I was to see him.

I was wrong.

"Why did you come here?" he asked in disgust. "You should have called," he said as he walked away, wiping the sweat from his head after snatching his towel off the back of his team seat on the basketball floor. He was furious. "I have plans and I'm not changing them."

My happiness turned to sadness as I followed behind him to the locker room area. He went into the shower area, and I waited in the hallway. After he came out of the locker room from his shower, he walked past me to greet other people. He did not even introduce me to any of them. I stood there like a little puppy waiting and longing to be picked up and shown to visitors.

Frozen in place, I stood there trying to hold back my tears until he was ready to go. When he was done talking, we walked to his dorm room. He did not speak a word to me on the way. Once we arrived in his room, I sat on the bed. He got dressed in silence until he reminded me again I should not have come without calling him. With those words, he left the room. I later learned that he had other plans with another girl.

I sat alone in his room. Visions of what he was doing to another girl bombarded my mind.

Did he kiss her with the same passion that he kissed me? Did he touch her the same way he touched me? Did he love her with the same depth that he professed to love me?

It dawned on me that what I thought was special, was probably just normal at best. I should have paid attention to the red flags in the beginning. I was devastated.

Sitting in his room alone made me curious. I had nowhere else to go and did not know anyone on his campus. Before I knew it, I was walking around his room looking at his things. I wanted to see for myself what he was doing in college. I began rummaging through his personal belongings. They say when you go looking for stuff, you are sure to find it.

I found more than I bargained for.

All of the allegations and suspicions that were surrounding him for so long were all confirmed that day. I found love letters, pictures with "just for you" written on the back, cards, trinkets, etc. All of them were from other women. Yes…*women*; as in more than one. I cried. My mind was spinning. I had thoughts of setting the room on fire. I wanted to rip everything in sight to shreds; especially the pictures of other girls on his wall. I thought I was the center of his universe, and yet his wall was proof that other stars filled his sky; and some shined much brighter than I did.

I wanted to throw everything I found all over the room; littering the place with the evidence of my broken heart. Somehow, I managed to restrain myself. I had already been humiliated and abandoned, there was no need to add a charge of arson or criminal damaging to the day's events.

Hurt and heartbroken, I carefully put everything back where I had found it and quietly left the room. It was a long drive back to my campus, but it gave me plenty of time to think and reflect. I felt embarrassed by his treatment of me in front of his friends, as well as by the wall of women in his room.

How stupid could I be to have believed his lies for so long especially when everyone around me was trying to point out the truth?

I came to the conclusion that I should finally leave him alone. Although

I was hurt and tried to distance myself from having any contact with him, it was not that simple. I told Janae about what I had found in his room. During my sophomore year in college, Janae was my roommate and she dated my boyfriend's roommate. Janae told her boyfriend what I shared with her and he told my boyfriend. My boyfriend now knew that I had gone through all of his things. He knew that I knew the truth about most of his lies and that he really was cheating on me. My boyfriend contacted me and said he wanted to visit me. Against my better judgement, I agreed. We had history, so I figured I owed him a chance to explain himself. Or at least, that is what I told myself for even entertaining the thought of listening to anything that would come out of his mouth.

He came to my job to take me to lunch. The whole scene played out like an episode on some cheesy sitcom where one character is infatuated with another character who will not give him the time of day. Once the character quits paying attention to the object of his infatuation, the terms of endearment, gifts, and *goo goo* eyes are missed. It seemed as if the lack of my attention was something my boyfriend missed receiving. This time he did not make up excuses and lies. This time, he apologized.

He said every apologetic thing possible…"I don't deserve you. I took advantage of you," Blah, blah, blah, blah…, and I fell for it. Hook, line, and sinker; just like every other time before. The pattern of our relationship did not miss a beat.

Why do I let him do that to me over and over again?

That question popped in my head, but deep down inside, I do not think I was ready to tackle the answer.

We were back together again for a while until one day he finally met "the one" that he felt he was in love with.

"She's everything you ain't," he said. "You're too good," he said. "You don't drink, smoke, cuss, or hang-out. She's like a homey that I feel comfortable around. I can hang with her without feeling bad about the things I like to do."

There was a pause in his final breakup speech. I said nothing; just stared at him in silence.

As if he felt that he could not hurt me anymore, he added, "When you love someone, you eat, sleep, and shit that person. I don't feel that way about you."

And with that last statement, he was finally finished. Matter of fact, he crushed my world with just a few words. I was heartbroken again. I could not believe that after four years, the man I loved told me that he did not love me. He loved someone else. The only good thing about it all was that he was man enough to tell me to my face, but that did not soften the blow, and it was not enough for me to leave him alone. I wanted him back. I had to make him love me.

There I was…an excelling student. I was doing well in college. I carried myself as an achiever. When it came to the ABC's of life, I thought I was on point. I was *Driven*. However, I was a total failure in facing the reality of what love was and was not, and how to handle what was right in front of me.

I was lost in my thoughts of feeling dumb over all the stupid things that I did for his attention, for his love, and for him to simply believe me. The mental torment I put myself through was agonizing. I spent hours upon hours hanging out at his parents' house with his mom or sister, just hoping to see him when he came home even if it meant seeing him with his new girlfriend. There were nights I peered into his bedroom window, hoping to dispel the rumors that he was with other girls only to confirm the truth. Then there was the time he accused me of being somewhere with another guy. I begged and pleaded with him to listen to me…to believe me. Even though he was cheating on me, I could not bear the thought of him thinking that I had been anything but faithful to him. I ended up holding onto his leg, crying as I continued to beg and plead for him to stay and listen to me. I was desperate. I would have done anything for his attention and for his love. It was as if he was more important to me than life itself.

Thinking about it all, I cried an uncontrolled cry. Snot ran out of my nose. Fear grew inside me from how I was reacting to wanting someone, as opposed to maintaining my self-dignity. When I went to the bathroom to get myself together. The bathroom was dark. I turned on the light. The light and mirror showed a disgusting image. What others throughout my life had said was pretty was not what I felt. It was not Corey Minor. The image in front of me was of a sick, weak, and tired girl. Her eyes were red, swollen, and running with tears. Her hair was all over her head. I looked pathetic!

My God, this is not me. I have to get myself together. I can't be like this. This is not me. I have to do better than this. I want better than this for myself, I thought as I looked in the mirror. I could not allow my self-confidence to be further wounded by chasing after any man that clearly did not feel the same about me.

I stared at the girl in the mirror. *I'm acting like this over a boy? Me? Why have I allowed a relationship to define how I view myself?*

I did not want to be that girl anymore. I saw a ghost in me.

For the moment, all I could think of was all of the immature and dumb stuff I did for his attention; I felt ashamed for wallowing in self-pity over wanting him at all costs just to call him mine.

* * * * *

Wake the hell up, Corey.

I was determined to focus on my studies, build my self-confidence, and get my life together. That semester I improved my grades, and I made the Dean's List the following semester. I committed my time to the Gospel Choir and the dance team instead of trying to continue a relationship with my ex-boyfriend.

Chapter Twenty-three

Free Loading Burdens

Up to that time in my life, I had not seen many relationships that were good examples of how a man should treat a woman. To some extent, we all learn by what we see and hear; all I had seen and heard about up to that time when it came to relationships was despair and destruction. I had no idea what a healthy relationship was. I grew to hate the relationships Mom had with men. Mom told me how Dad mistreated her. She told me how he literally kicked her out of the bed once. She said that someone had come to the door early one morning. She and Dad were both in bed, and Dad did not want to get up to answer the door. She did not want to get up either. However, Dad kicked her out of the bed and told her to answer the door. Mom said I was a baby at the time, and it was the first time we lived together as a family. Dad confirmed the incident when I asked him about it later. I asked him why he mistreated Mom.

"Young, dumb, and smoking weed," was his excuse.

After Dad, the new man in Mom's life was Steve. I was about three years old when she was in a relationship with him. One morning, as the door to Mom's room opened, Steve came out. That is my first memory of him. After that, it seemed he was at our house all the time. He was the first man I remember being around other than Dad. Steve was tall and lean with a very light complexion. He wore a press and curl hairstyle. He had sandy colored hair and brown eyes. With his press and curl hairstyle, he could have passed for a member of the '70s R&B group, Switch. He was a *light-skinned, pretty boy* with what was popular to say at one time…"good hair." Like other men to come, Steve did nothing to help us. Mom and I lived in what was called Highland Park—now known as Skyline Terrace, a subsidized housing project in Canton. For a while, Steve pretty much lived with us.

When we lived in Houston, I was about ten when Dwight came into the picture. He appeared to be more than six feet in height, and had a dark complexion. He had a solid build and broad shoulders. Dwight wore a Jheri curl with a long shag style, or what is also referred to as a "mullet." Some women seemed to like guys with long shags back then. Dwight dressed nice. He never stayed the night from what I can recall. He came and went as he pleased. Sometimes there were weeks in between the time he came to our house again; sometimes it was only days.

When I was in middle school, Mom became involved with Tony. Tony did not work. He had a Jheri curl shag too and was of a dark complexion just like Dwight. However, he was nowhere near six-feet tall and he had a strong country accent. He was from Louisiana. I did not get to know Tony well because he lived with Mom when I lived with Mummy and Frances, so I was not around him much. I could not stand it when Mom talked like him with phrases he used in his New Orleans' accent. She would often say, "Come see" when she wanted me to come to wherever she was. I hated it because it made me think she was thinking of him when she said it. I began to think that she enjoyed him living with her much more than she enjoyed me being there. I began to believe that she did not care if I was there or not, because he was there and that seemed to be all she needed.

"Corey, come see."

"Don't say that to me. I hate it when you sound like that," I said.

"Sound like what?"

"Tony."

"Why? What's wrong with him? What did he do to you?" she asked as if she did not know why I was upset. She knew that I did not like it when she said, "Come see" and she knew why because I had told her before. Maybe she thought my reason was a bit selfish, and maybe it was, but she could not act like she did not know why I felt the way I did...I told her every chance I got.

Tony did not do anything to me. He did absolutely nothing...that was the problem. Mom struggled. He did not work. He did not help her with the bills. He did not help her buy groceries. He did nothing to make our lives better.

Isn't a man supposed to provide? She was always criticizing Dad for not providing, yet Tony could do no wrong.

In my mind, he was nothing more than a freeloader.

"Just don't say that to me," I said to her again.

My weekends home were few and far between. I chose to stay with Mummy and Frances rather than with Mom and Tony in a tiny one-bedroom apartment. Watching them together was sickening to me. When I stayed with Mom during that time, I slept on the couch and did not want to hear them in the room together. It was too close for comfort to me.

Too close for comfort quarters was the same issue I had when an unknown guy stayed at our house one night when we lived in Stafford. I remember the night with the unknown man as if it were yesterday. It was my bedtime. I had to get ready for school in the morning. I went to take a bath, and purposefully stayed in the tub for a long time. I wanted to see how long it would take for Mom to notice I had not come out of the bathroom, but she did not notice.

The unknown man was the one to notice, not Mom...

"Is your daughter ok?" I heard him say.

"What do you mean?" Mom replied.

"She's been in the bathroom for a while."

Mom came to the door and knocked. I did not answer. I wanted her to be concerned and question why I did not answer. I pretended to be asleep. She continued to knock.

"Corey, are you ok...what are you doing in there?"

Knock, knock.

"Ugh?" I said in a sleepy voice, "Yes, Mom."

"Are you ok?" she repeated.

"Yes. I guess I fell asleep," I lied.

I finished my bath and got ready for bed. I made my usual pallet on the living room floor of our one bedroom apartment. That night I heard a song that I had always liked. It was Patti LaBelle's, *Love, Need, Want.* That night, for the first time, I hated the song. As the song played, I heard Mom moaning.

"Mmm...Mmm..."

I wrinkled my face into a questioning expression.

What is going on? I thought to myself.

More moans. I could not take it. I did not want to hear it. I slept on the floor on couch pillows that I had created into a pallet near the stereo. *The Quiet Storm* featuring the latest slow songs were on at my bedtime. That usually put me to sleep. That night I could not sleep at all. The moans from Mom's bedroom disturbed me. The music did not drown out the sound of the moans. Instead, it seemed to create the atmosphere they needed to continue having sex even though they could not hear the stereo in the living room. They could not hear the music, but their moans interrupted my sleep.

It made me hate the sound of the moans. It made me hate the song even more. It reminded me of Mom giving her *all* to a man—all of them—and they gave nothing in return. I hated them all. I hated that song.

I moved my pallet further away so that I could be as far away as possible from Mom's bedroom door. Even with the door closed, I could hear the moans. With the throw pillows held tightly over my head, I heard the start of a commercial before I slowly fell asleep. That is my one and only memory of the unknown stranger.

Shortly after Tony, there was Brian. The mistreatment Mom received from Dad was nothing compared to what she endured in her relationship with Brian. During the time that I lived with Frances and Mummy, Mom lived with a man who physically abused her. I had no idea of the physical abuse until one of Mom's friends told me about it. She told me how Mom wore sunglasses when it was not sunny outside. Mom did this because she had red marks on her face and black eyes, in addition to bruises on her arms. I was infuriated when I heard about it. With all the anger I felt toward that man, I did not say anything to Mom. I never felt the intensity of dislike for another person as I did toward Brian. My dislike of him was beyond hatred.

Brian had been in the military, and he sported a fade haircut. I did not like the way he talked to Mom or the way he treated her. During one of my stays with Mom, he constantly called her on the phone. He always seemed to be checking up on her whereabouts, but in a bad, obsessive way. I remember once, she said something on the phone to upset him. He hung up on her and then called right back. I hated it. I answered the next call.

"Why do you keep calling here and then hang up on my Mom?"

"Well, she made me mad and instead of cussing at her, I just hang up," he responded.

"Well, that is stupid. Quit calling here."

152

The dial tone is what he heard next after I hung up on him. As far as I was concerned, he got no respect from me. I did not care if he was an adult. I remember that he once told me that children should be seen and not heard. That rubbed me the wrong way. I responded by telling him that I was one child that would be seen *and* heard.

On another night after he started living with Mom, I was in the bathroom doing my teenage primping in the mirror. I heard what sounded like a clap of hands followed by Mom saying, "Oooo, Corey!"

I came out the bathroom in a flash. I saw the red mark on Mom's cheek. That man had the audacity to slap Mom on her face while I was there in the house. Even though I had *heard* that he put his hands on her, I could not believe it when I *saw* it for myself. At fourteen, I was straight out of South Vallejo, but South Vallejo was forever in me.

Anger consumed me. I rushed to the kitchen drawer to find the biggest knife I could find. With a knife in hand, I walked toward him and told him he had five minutes to get out or he was going to clean up his own blood. I could see in his eyes that he was sizing up whether a confrontation with me was worth the hassle.

I hated all the different men Mom chose to have as a part of her life. None of them, except Charles even though he left, did anything to help us. None of the men did anything for us: Dad (most of the time) - nothing; Steve - nothing; Dwight - nothing, unknown man - nothing; Tony - nothing; and Brian - nothing. Mom's relationships with men had a similarity to them that I saw in my first long-term relationship...they had a pattern, one that was destructive. Also, most of the men in her life mistreated her. In my mind, they were all freeloading burdens.

Like the other men, Brian did not support Mom. Like the other men, he did not provide for her. Like the other men, he was not good for her self-esteem. However, unlike the other men, he beat her. He was an arrogant user and abuser. He was a military vet who was supposed to serve and protect. Yet, with all of his military training to defend this country in the event of combat, he chose to use his skills on a defenseless woman—my Mom.

She told me that he roundhouse kicked her in the eye once. He beat Mom on more than one occasion. She had to wear sunglasses to hide the black eyes, and long-sleeved shirts to hide the bruises. He verbally abused her and made her feel like nothing.

I hated to learn about the abuse she endured while she was with Brian. *Why was she with him?* I thought. I was ready to stab him.

On that night, I had the knife. I had the power. That time, he was the victim, and I was the aggressor. I had the strength and courage to cut and stab any part of him. I wanted to let him know just how much I did not like him. I was in protector mode. He was not going to abuse Mom anymore. I wanted him to feel more pain in one night than Mom had each time he beat her. Even though I am not one to condone violence now, on that night, I would have killed him; just like Felicia and I said we believed we would do one day.

With both his arms raised in the air as he backed away from me, Brian reached the door, unlocked it, and left. Once the door closed, I ran to lock it and ran to Mom. I dropped the knife and hugged her as I asked her why he hit her. At that point, I told her all that I had been told from her friend about his abuse. I also let her know that I could not continue to stay there if she was going to let him be there. I definitely was not going to be there if she was going to allow him to beat her.

That night I had the right mind to throw all his stuff out onto the porch. I wanted to see his face when he came back and saw his stereo and clothes outside in the rain. But that was something Mom had to decide…not me.

I hated that he beat her.

Why do women stay in those types of relationships? I thought. *Is there any dignity?* I wanted to question Mom, but only thought it. *Is there any care for the lack of self-esteem and self-respect that is being shown in front of her child?*

I wanted to yell at her and shake some sense into her. It is difficult to answer these types of questions when you are not the one in those shoes.

Mom answered the questions. Her decision was made. I ended up back in South Vallejo to finish the seventh grade. She chose him over me. I hated that Mom still wanted to be with him. I awoke one day angered to think that he beat Mom and that I could do nothing about it. Instead of me, she continued to let him live with her. He got away with it…no domestic violence charges, no assault charges…nothing.

* * * * *

Unfortunately, it is not just older women who are involved in, and stay in, abusive relationships. It's not just women who have had a hard life; it can happen to women in all walks of life. We have a burden in learning how we will allow others to treat us, but it is a burden we must overcome.

I was repeating the cycle when I was involved with my first boyfriend, although I had witnessed that burden with Mom. I had to do some self-analyzing of why I allowed myself to stay in a destructive relationship. Delving into my own actions of being an enabler to the problems in the relationship helped me determine that I needed to do better with my life. That was the driving factor in me moving on.

After all the bad and/or indifferent things I witnessed as a child on my way to adulthood, I had two choices in life…two paths I could follow. I could wallow in the valley of sorrows and live a life of struggles for me and my children, or I could climb the mountain of a better life after each time I fell down and crawled around lost because of my parent's bad examples, but not using those examples as excuses to fail.

A child of parents who have dependency issues—drugs, alcohol, mental issues, poverty, low education, and possible connection to a crime-ridden life—can end up never being able to see the hope of having a good day, let alone a good life. That child could be the textbook statistic of reasons why the failures of the parents are often repeated. Children mimic what they see.

But there are also, as we all know, some who rise above the sins of their parents or unthinkable living conditions. I believe in, and have seen some, such as Viola Davis and Tiffany Haddish, who are among the millions of people who blazed a trail away from unhealthy beginnings and imperfect examples, to become successful.

I am one of those who had unhealthy beginnings and imperfect examples. However, I am a child who intended to strive.

I am Driven!

Like any child who will be tempted by the devil and have moments of *Why did I do that?* and maybe that child will make bad decisions, but will turn it around because of the examples of life that came before them did not push them the wrong way, but another way: a better way.

I'd like to think of myself as a climber with skinned knees, choosing to strive for the better. I have chosen to use my parents' faults and failures as a positive motivation for change, instead of giving in to living a rerun of my parent's lives. It is strange, but I can say I love my parents because I lived to have choices because they showed me how I should not live. I could have fallen into being a victim. At times, I did slip and slide in the wrong direction. I could be used and abused as a way of surrendering to the negative lessons poured over my soul. I could have boiled the poisons of sadness and not risen out of the pot.

We all wonder why some make it and some fail in life, when both have had the ugliest example of life played out in front of them. Mom, despite her worst times, was/is a survivor; and often, a slick conniving woman who used her mental issues as a tool. But one thing is for sure: she taught me to never give up. She did that by her living through all the gas she poured on her life, either by her own doing, or by what she let others do to her.

My Dad, simply put, was not a good man for much of the life I know. Although at times I fell into self-pity, and picked men who were not good for me because I did not have an example of a good man around me, those choices made me realize that I wanted better for myself. My mother and father actually taught me very well what is *not* good moral behavior in a relationship by how they lived their troubled lives.

* * * * *

My friend Janae was in an abusive relationship of her own. She told me stories of how her boyfriend beat her. According to her, he once beat her so badly that she stayed at her friend's house, out of town, so that her parents would not see the bruises. I was a witness to her boyfriend's possessive and jealous character.

During the first semester of her freshman year at Bowling Green University, Janae's boyfriend made her call him every time she left or returned to our dorm room from class. She drove an hour away to go to his college, pick up his dirty, stinky clothes so that she could bring them back to our residence hall. Then she would wash and fold his clothes, and then drive another hour to take the clothes back to him. He accused her of entering our co-ed residence hall from an entrance near the male wing so that she had to walk through that wing to see guys before getting to our room. Every day, I heard her explaining herself, crying, and justifying her actions. Then one day he came to BGSU, pulled a gun on me, took my car, then went to our dorm room, and beat her.

One night there was a party on campus. I was with a bunch of friends, and after the party was over, I began to drop people off who needed a ride home. As I was about to drop off the last passengers in my car, I looked in my rearview mirror.

"Ohhh my God! Ohhh my God…get out of the car! Get out right now!" I yelled at everyone in my car.

Even though his school was an hour away from mine, Janae's ex, Ramsey, was right behind me…standing right outside of my car.

What made him come up here? I thought to myself. I tried to quickly drive off, but somehow Ramsey got in my car after my friends got out.

"Get out of my car, Ramsey." I said.

"No," he replied.

"Get out of my car, now." I repeated.

"No…where is Janae? You are going to take me to Janae."

"I don't know where she is."

He stared at me for a moment and then continued to insist that I knew where she was.

"You are going to tell me where she is," he said as he reached into his jacket.

Out of the corner of my eye, I saw the gun. It was a 9mm, semi-automatic. Ramsey began to pull back the chamber. Most people would have been scared in that situation. I guess that I had seen enough at that point in my life that I just did not seem to respond at all. At the same time I thought, *this man is not crazy enough to actually do anything to me with that gun.* I finally got to where I parked my car at my friend's house off campus to avoid needing a parking permit to park on campus. I ran to her door.

In my haste to get out of the car, I forgot my keys. When I looked back over my shoulder, Ramsey had already gotten into my driver's seat and was getting ready to pull off in my car. I ran back to my car, stuck my arm in the window to get the keys, and he rolled the window up on my arm as he began to drive off. I could not believe that he was trying to drive off with part of me stuck in the door. I got my arm out of the car window and ran back to my friend's house.

BAM! BAM! BAM! BAM!

"April open the door!"

BAM! BAM! BAM! BAM!

"April!" I screamed louder.

In the midst of it all, I realized that Ramsey was probably headed to the dorm room I shared with Janae and that I needed to call the residence hall and let the night guard know not to let him in. I had to warn Janae that Ramsey was in Bowling Green. I had to let her know that she needed to hide in case he went to our room.

When April finally answered the door, I frantically told her what happened, and asked that she and her boyfriend take me to my residence hall before Ramsey got there.

I called ahead to my residence hall to notify the night guard. I tried to call Janae, but the line was busy. Everything happened so fast. As April and her boyfriend drove me to my residence hall, I stayed ducked down in the back seat of the car so that Ramsey could not see me. When we got to the residence hall, I ran in and scanned the sign-in list. Janae's date had not signed out yet. That meant he was probably still there. I almost wet my pants because I knew for sure that Ramsey would go off if he got there and found out that Janae was with another man. I had to get to our room and warn them.

I ran up all four flights of stairs and began banging on the door for Janae to let me in. She would not.

She said, "Why don't you use your key?"

I told Janae what happened after the party, and that Ramsey had taken my car and that he had my keys…"Now open the door quick!" I said, standing in the hallway.

I had to stand outside the door for about five minutes trying to convince Janae that Ramsey was not with me, and for her to open the door. When she finally opened the door, I quickly scanned the room. I did not see Janae's date. Thank goodness he was not there anymore.

I told Janae the whole story, and we agreed that we would work together to keep her safe. Unfortunately, the hall monitor was not in on that conversation. Ramsey and his manipulative ways had convinced the hall monitor that he needed to come to our room to give me my car keys.

Our hearts dropped when we heard a knock at the door. I went to the door and asked, "Who is it?"

The hall monitor informed me that a young man wanted to give me my keys. Then Ramsey interjected, "Corey, I just want to talk to you and give you your keys back."

I told him to wait a minute. I then told Janae to hide under my bed and not to come out for anything. I cracked the door and squeezed my way out.

I ignored Ramsey's apologies and took my keys.

He continued to apologize.

As I cracked the room door open to squeeze back in, Janae was right there. Ramsey saw her, pushed the door open, and all I saw was a fist swing toward her face. He barged into the room, grabbed her, and repeatedly punched her. Then he dragged her out of our room and down the hall. Somehow Janae managed to get away from him, and she ran into one of our neighbors' rooms. That did not stop Ramsey. He barged into the neighbor's room to get her again. He then pulled her back into the hall and continued hitting her.

I tried to catch up with them in the hall. Ramsey pushed me into the brick wall. I fell to the ground. I got up and ran to our room to call the police. Ramsay continued to drag Janae down the hall and then he threw her down the first flight of stairs. It seemed like our whole floor came out of their rooms to see what was going on. Girls were screaming; some asked what was going on, and others started crying as they heard Janae cry and beg Ramsey to stop hitting her as he pulled her down the remaining flights of stairs.

Eventually, the police arrived and Ramsey fled the scene. Police reports were taken, and the residence hall director requested that Janae and I stay the night in his apartment with him and his wife. The next day, our residence hall was locked and only those with keys could gain access. There were descriptions of Ramsey's truck posted all over the hall, with instructions for the police to be contacted immediately if anyone saw him.

That was it; I finally convinced Janae that there had to be a better man out there for her. She put an end to the relationship with Ramsey and stopped dating her abuser.

I wanted better for Janae. I wanted her to be with a guy that was nice to her. Thinking about what my mom endured, I knew what she had to have been going through. I wanted her to gain some kind of the strength. I wanted her to gain some self-respect.

One day we saw my future husband Craig and his friends at a football game. At that time, I was not interested in Craig, I introduced him to Janae. Craig was a good guy and I thought they would hit it off well. Soon after I introduced them, Craig and Janae started seeing each other regularly. However, one day, out of the blue, Janae left campus and did not let me or anyone else know where she was going. She did not even tell Craig.

It did not take long to find out where she went. She had gone to her ex-boyfriend's school.

She stopped calling Craig and he asked me if I knew what was going on. I had no clue. After he continued to ask, I told him it appeared that Janae had gotten back with her ex-boyfriend. A few weeks later in another conversation, Craig told me that he heard that I made favorable comments when talking about him to others. I always had favorable things to say about Craig. That was why I introduced him to Janae to help her get over her abusive boyfriend. I thought he was a good guy, and that was what she needed.

Craig then told me that if he had known that I thought so highly of him, he would have preferred to date me instead of Janae. I appreciated his kind words. Even though I was staying away from my ex-boyfriend and had gained strength over my life, I was also trying to be honest with myself that in the relationship area, I was still a work in progress.

However, that was not the end of the attraction between me and Craig. With the attraction cat out of the bag from our conversation, Craig and I both realized there was some interest in one another, so we began to talk more. We were not strangers. We met our freshman year at BGSU. During our freshman year, Craig and his line brothers came to our dorm room all the time. We all hung out together because Craig and Camela were pledging line brothers and sisters. At that time, I was so into my ex-boyfriend that I did not think about ever dating anyone; that is until I finally took off my blinders to life around me after ending my relationship with my ex-boyfriend.

Chapter Twenty-four

Humiliation

Once we started dating, I thought Craig was the greatest thing in my world. But I also once thought of him as being a wolf in sheep's clothing because it seemed that he was too good to be true. When we first started dating, things went well between us. We were inseparable. He would walk over to my residence hall to walk me to my classes. We ate together, studied together, and hung out with the same friends. Then, my ex-boyfriend started calling me again, and he seemed to call more frequently whenever Craig was around. Craig told me that he thought things were not over between me and my ex-boyfriend, and because of his suspicions, Craig broke up with me.

I still wanted to be with Craig and was determined to show him that there was nothing going on between me and my ex-boyfriend. I stopped talking to my ex-boyfriend completely, and even changed my phone number so that he could not reach me. I thought that was enough to show Craig that I wanted to be with him and only him.

Although we had broken up, we still did things together as if we were a couple. He regularly came over to my apartment, and I visited his. We went home on the weekends and still hung out with friends together. All of our actions were the same as if we were still a couple. However, I started to feel insecure and wondered if the time we spent together really meant we were a couple again. He had my car while I went to class, stayed at home doing homework, or was at work. He actually had my car more than I did, and I began to question whether he was just using me for my car.

I got to know his mom rather well over a period of time. I had open conversations with her as almost a second mom. She would tell me, "Craig's not using you; he likes you."

Craig's mom is affectionately called Bunny by her family and close friends. It was not until eight years into our marriage that I no longer called my in-laws Mr. and Mrs. Smith, but rather Papa and Bunny. For the majority of her working years, Bunny worked for group homes that housed people with mental illness. She and I developed a relationship through conversations and advice I would seek from her about Mom's illness.

Bunny was familiar with the stress that family members of the mentally ill tend to face. She seemed to understand my concerns and fears about Mom. Bunny also seemed to understand the tremendous responsibility I carried in caring for Mom while being in college. It felt good to hear words of encouragement from someone who knew about mental illness.

Although Bunny continued to tell me that Craig was not using me, and that he liked me and cared about me, I did not get that same assurance from him. During my time as a gospel choir member, the choir was scheduled to perform a concert in Canton at Camela's dad's church, and two of my friends from the choir and I went to Grandma Bluchelle's house until it was time for the concert to start. My friends made it a point to share their concerns about Craig with Grandma Bluchelle. They talked to my Grandma about my relationship with Craig as if I was not there.

They continued to stress the fact that, "Craig always has her car…she just goes to class or stays at home while he does whatever he wants."

At the time, I was being naïve about not checking and confirming his behavior right away, when in the back of my head I knew things were not right, but I did not want to confirm it. Craig was responsible for his behavior, but I had to share the responsibility in the fact that I was helping him treat me as he did. I was enabling his behavior by not wanting to find out the truth that was right in front of me.

It was not until years later, after I filed for divorce, that Craig's high school girlfriend told me that he used to visit her at her college in another city…and he used my car to do it.

* * * * *

I reflect on feeling uncomfortable and insecure about my involvement with Craig back then, but I could not bring myself to see what was in front of my face. At the time, I wanted to treat Craig with complete trust; maybe in a way to show myself that I was not being played for a fool again. However, just like in my first long-term relationship, my bond with Craig was an emotional tug of war.

Why was I repeating the cycle?

I tried to convince myself to leave him alone. I attempted to do that when I applied for a BGSU Exchange Program. I completed all the necessary paperwork, was accepted into the program, and my picture was displayed on the exchange program's office bulletin board that advertised the program and its participants. I was scheduled to leave the upcoming semester to attend the University of California at Berkeley.

Later that semester, I decided to travel to Atlanta for spring break with friends. Camela's younger brother, sister, and mom—Ms. Connie lived in Atlanta. Dad's sister—Aunt Doris, and her daughter Rhonda, lived there too. It was going to be a great trip because each of us would be able to visit our families.

Ms. Connie worked at a daycare. She arranged for us to work there during spring break. I remember being in the classroom with the preschoolers. I thought I did pretty well working with them. I was patient and very interactive with the preschoolers. I helped them complete their assignments and prepare for naptime.

During reading circle, I noticed that my breast felt extremely tender. I had not noticed my breast ever being tender before; even during my period. I tried to ignore it and continued reading, but when the children hung on to me trying to get closer to see the pictures in the book, I could not ignore the painful tenderness. It seemed to intensify with each child that gathered next to me.

One night after work, I sat alone in the living room recliner next to a tall lamp in Ms. Connie's apartment. As I sat in the recliner and counted the days on the calendar I used to keep track of my class assignments, I tried to figure out the last time I had my period. I remembered helping close friends move to their new apartment after they had their first child. That was the last time I remember being on my period, and that had been a couple of months back.

A missed period and tender breasts were alarming red flags for me. I knew I needed to see if they meant what I thought they meant. I decided I would make an appointment when I got back. I did not want to talk about it with anyone. I scheduled an appointment at the local Planned Parenthood where I got my birth control pills. I went to the appointment and gave a urine sample.

After waiting in the examining room, the nurse returned to the room and told me, "It's positive," as she smiled and showed me the results. "You are pregnant," she continued with a big smile.

I always had issues with taking the pills on time, the same time, and every day. My birth control pills…I guess I skipped them or was late one too many times. I did not want the nurse to know I was nervous and scared, but tears started to stream down my face. I did not say a word. With a faint smile on my face, tears slowly rolled over my cheeks.

It was so hard for me to stop thinking of myself as an unwed, teenage mom. Grandma Vickie was unwed and fourteen when she had my Mom. Mom was unwed and seventeen when she had me. And I was going to be a twenty-one-year-old unwed mom. Although I was not a teenager, it was difficult for me to think of myself as anything but an unwed, teen mom.

I did not know whom to tell my news to. I did not know whom to talk to about how I felt. I did not know if I was going to keep the baby. I did not know how Craig would respond.

Would he deny that the baby was his? I thought.

We were not officially a couple. We had not spoken to each other since before spring break.

School was back in session. Coincidentally, Craig called me for help with an English paper. I figured it was time to tell him. I had to tell him that I was pregnant, but I did not know how to do it. I agreed to meet him at one of the computer labs on campus to work on his paper. He showed me his assignment, and what he had completed up to that point. As he spoke, my mind was elsewhere, but I tried to focus. I gave him suggestions on how to revise his work.

"Thanks," he said as he turned to his computer and began to type. I stared at him as his fingers danced across his keyboard. We sat right next to each other in the computer lab, but I could not tell him. My mouth would not work.

I typed a message that appeared on my monitor: *tnangerp m'i.*

I tapped him on the shoulder and directed him to look at the screen. He read those two backwards words. His eyes appeared to enlarge as he figured out what the message said. He jumped up and ran out of the computer lab. After he ran out, I sat there alone. It did not seem like he was coming back. I finished my work while I waited for Craig to return.

He did not.

I packed up my notebook, English book, papers, and headed to my car.

When I arrived at the apartment I shared with Candi, she was there with another one of our friends from campus. They were talking in our bedroom. I went in the bedroom and stood while Candi lay across her bed and our friend sat at my desk. They finished what they were talking about and Candi turned to me.

"How was your day?" she asked.

"Fine," I replied.

"Did you get your English paper done?"

"Yes, I finally finished it. I'm glad. I was tired of revising it."

Candi continued, "I don't know the last time you talked to Craig, but he wanted me to tell you that his high school girlfriend is pregnant."

I looked at her with a questioning stare. "Why did he want you to tell me that?" I asked.

"It's his," she said.

My legs felt like noodles. I became cold. In my mind I thought I was lying on the floor with Candi and our friend patting my cheeks in an attempt to wake me up. In reality, I stood in front of Candi emotionless as I heard her next words.

"I don't know why he wanted me to tell you that when he could have told you himself."

Candi did not know that I was pregnant. At that point, I had not told anyone but Craig. While standing right in front of Candi and our friend, I tried hard to keep my composure. I did not want to show any emotion whatsoever. I did not want Candi to wonder why I cared about Craig's ex being pregnant by him. I did not want Candi to wonder what in the world was wrong with me if I broke down crying at that very moment.

I felt so hurt, so humiliated, so disgusted, and so embarrassed. Two women were pregnant at the same time, by the same man. I was not ready to face the reality that I was one of them. I was not ready for anyone to know I was pregnant. I did not know if I was going to keep the baby. I had two cousins in similar situations during high school.

I thought, *Oh my God! This is running in the family. I'm continuing a cycle.*

I hated myself for being in the situation that I was in. I hated myself for not thinking more highly of myself; for not valuing myself more than I had. I hated myself for not expecting more from a relationship. I hated myself for settling for less. I could not believe it was happening to me.

* * * * *

I expressed how I felt to Craig. He said, "You act as if you are too good for something like this to happen to you."

I could not say anything in response. It was the ultimate wound to my self-confidence. My self-confidence was dead. It seems as though from that point on, I tried to prove to him that I was not "too good."

I thought, *who is gonna want me now?* The situation was not a part of my life plan. It was definitely not the type of family I wanted to have. I wanted to go to college, get married, have a nice home, 2.3 kids, and a dog. *This was not a part of my plan!*

* * * * *

My pregnancy seemed to be the worst nine months of my life. I felt embarrassed because I was not married. I did not blame Craig for my unexpected pregnancy, but I always blamed him for getting two women pregnant at the same time. The situation was just disgusting to me. I asked him how it happened.

"I didn't even know you were still involved with her...why were you involved with both of us?!" I yelled.

No matter how much I asked, he would not tell me the details of his relationship with his high school girlfriend. He would only give me bits and pieces of how her pregnancy came about. He said it happened during Christmas break, he was drunk at the time, and it was only that one time.

I began to have visions of Craig with his ex. My mind went in circles seeing them having sex together.

When were they together? Why did no one ever tell me? How long has this been going on?

Foolishly, I listened to Craig tell me that he did not want his high school girlfriend to know about my pregnancy, but that he would tell her eventually. Every so often, I would ask him if he had told her yet.

"I'll tell her; don't worry about it," he said each time I asked.

After the initial shock of the pregnancy, Craig stayed at my apartment.

We continued to go home on weekends together, he met and visited with my family members that he had not met before, and our families met to discuss marriage and how we were going to raise a child together. From all of his actions, Craig led me to believe that he wanted to be with me. When the news spread about my pregnancy, many could not believe that I was pregnant.

Grandma Bluchelle often said, "Now-a-days, there are too many things available for young women to use if they do not want to become pregnant." As a mother of five, she said that back in her day they had the "can't help its" because contraception was not available. "Now, there is too much available for you not to get pregnant, if you don't want to," she repeated.

But Grandma Bluchelle had a heartbreaking secret. The two men that Dad and his brother and sisters knew as their cousins, were actually their brothers. Grandma more than likely knew it all along.

We laughed and joked about Grandpa being a rolling stone—like his daddy who was said to be "a playa 'til he died." Grandma Bluchelle's sister, Aunt Geneva, encouraged my Grandma to stand up for herself and her marriage.

"You need tah' put that religion on the shelf, and come back and get it later! I told her. You betta go kick that woman's butt and his too," Aunt Geneva said laughing as she told us the story.

Aunt Geneva did not want my Grandma to worry about being "a good Christian" and to feel that she just had to accept the fact that my Grandpa was cheating and had conceived two sons outside of their marriage. The other woman was my Grandma's cousin's wife. She did not carry my Grandpa's child once, but twice. Grandma knew her own secret. She excused it and said, "We had the 'can't help its'."

Grandma Bluchelle did not deserve the emotional turmoil of knowing that another woman was pregnant with her husband's children. She did not deserve to be disrespected. She did not deserve to be humiliated. I found myself saying those exact words about my own situation. Maybe that's why Grandma did not say much…my situation may have been a reminder of what she may have gone through. Maybe she did not know what to do.

"I was married to him. I had kids for him," she said when I asked her about it during my pregnancy with Jaylon.

* * * * *

I did not know what I was going to do with a baby. One thing I knew for sure was that I was not going to drop out of school. However, it seemed as though others wanted to live my life for me. They wanted to make my decisions for me. There were two family members in particular who thought that I would ruin my life if I kept my child.

Even though one of those family members had four children of his own with different mothers, he encouraged me to have an abortion. He offered to schedule, pay for, and take me to the "appointment." Perhaps one of the mothers he had gotten pregnant in college did not finish school. Perhaps he thought I would not finish school if I had my child. At any rate, as if his harassing me to have an abortion was not enough, another family member called and cussed me out over the phone, hung up on me, called me back to cuss me out some more, and then hung up again. She later called me again and suggested that I get an abortion.

Remembering or thinking about the time I went to the clinic with Felicia, my mind was all over the place.

I'm scared. I can't have an abortion!

With that statement screaming in my head, I decided I wanted to keep my baby even though family members made it clear that they thought I should have an abortion. I wanted to be successful. Success to me meant not struggling like Mom did. I was overwhelmed with confused thoughts. It seemed as though there was no way I would ever be successful if I kept the baby.

Repeating a theme in my life: *I'd like to think of myself as a climber with skinned knees, choosing to strive for the better.*

Knowing this, I still became an emotional wreck. I questioned whether my family members were right and I was wrong. I questioned whether I should have the baby. I often thought that I should get an abortion because I was so humiliated that another young lady was pregnant by the same guy at the same time that I was; coupled with the fact that I was not married.

Although some thought that I was going to drop out of college and not accomplish anything if I did not have an abortion, I knew that I would keep my baby, stay in school, accomplish my goals, and be successful. I was determined to make that my goal. *I was Driven!*

My pregnancy was emotionally difficult. I really thank the Lord for helping me through it. I used to feel as though I did not want my child to know Craig's other child. I was so hurt by the dual pregnancy that it caused me to be selfish.

There are so many children who do not know that the child they play with every day is their cousin, sister, or brother. Many do not even know their own fathers. I could not do that to my child. Immediately, the thought of keeping the children apart left my mind.

Chapter Twenty-five
JD to JD
Juvenile Delinquent to Juris Doctorate

I received scholarships, loans, and grants to attend college. I graduated with a Bachelor's of Arts in English. I was eight months' pregnant when I ran for the Bowling Green State University Homecoming Queen. I was a freshman when I set the goal to run for the homecoming title. Even though I was pregnant my senior year, I was determined to still pursue it. I did not expect to make it far in the running, but I made the top ten. The following month, I had my first son, Jaylon. Tammy, Camela's sister, once told me about the time she saw me running up the Gish Theatre stairs on campus to turn in a paper. She said she was inspired because she knew that I had just had Jaylon at the time, and yet I was running as if I had not just given birth. I remember that incident. My paper was due and the instructor was not going to accept any excuses for it not being turned in on time. I had just had a baby, but I was determined to turn the paper in on time. Tammy is now married with four beautiful daughters. She credits that encounter for keeping her motivated when she felt overwhelmed with family, a spouse, work, and school.

Before Jaylon was born, I wanted to participate in a study abroad program in Spain. I did not raise enough money to go to Spain, but I continued to strive for the goal to study abroad. At just six months old, Jaylon stayed my Aunt Doris and Uncle Etheridge part of the time, and with Craig and his parents part of the time, while I completed the last two classes of my undergraduate career in Guadalajara, Jalisco in Mexico. The following semester—after graduating with my Bachelor's—the morning after I returned from Mexico, I started a Master's program.

In two years, I earned a Master's of Education in Guidance and Counseling. I wanted to apply to law school in addition to PhD programs; however, I was afraid to take the Law School Admission Test (LSAT). I found a program that prepared students for a better chance of earning a higher score. It cost $1,000. I could not afford it. I applied for the scholarship. I was awarded $500 toward reducing the cost, but I had household expenses that needed to be paid; especially with a small child. I needed the $500 for those household expenses that could have been used to pay the other half for the program.

I remember being encouraged by my cousin Karen. She told me that I did not need to take the course. She told me that I was smart and could study for the test on my own. After talking to her, I realized that others had more confidence in me than I had in myself. I strongly considered Karen's encouraging words.

Even though I was awarded the scholarship, I studied and completed timed tests from a book Craig's friend gave me after he used it to study for the LSAT. I took the test and applied to various law schools. I was accepted to William and Mary College of Law among other law schools. I did not know the prestige of William and Mary at the time I applied. I applied there because I could earn a joint degree including a Juris Doctorate and a Master's in African American Studies.

Grandma Vickie told me about its rich prominence after she watched a program on the History Channel that featured the college. At the time I was accepted, it was one of the top fifty law schools in the country.

Although Craig was the center of the most humiliating time of my life in my mind, we eventually matured, resolved our issues, and married on June 6, 1998. The marriage was featured in *Jet Magazine*. It is a black and white picture of a couple who were both twenty-three, with an excitement in their eyes that seemed to show their happiness with each other and the potential for their future together. The photo caption detailed our education and career goals, with a blurb about our honeymoon plans. Twelve years later, the irony of that picture forced me out of denial and slapped me with reality.

After taking the bar exam, I said I just wanted to sit at home and have babies. I was joking, but I did want to take some time off. I went to Canton to be with Grandma Bluchelle as she fought ovarian cancer. Jaylon and Craig stayed in Bowling Green. It was also time for Jaylon to start school.

I started looking for work in Canton while Grandma Bluchelle slept. I met a local radio and TV personality named Ron Ponder. Throughout his career, he was heavily involved in local politics. He ultimately gave me many opportunities to work on television and radio with his production company. He told me about the County Prosecutor's Office and thought it would be a good experience for me. As Ron suggested, I called and scheduled a meeting with Robert Horowitz, the Stark County Prosecutor. Mr. Horowitz said he respected Ron and took Ron's recommendation seriously of meeting with me for the possibility of working with his office. I appreciated the opportunity to make some money, but I had three degrees and student loans that needed to be paid. I was disappointed that I would only make about $11 per hour.

Grandma Bluchelle was not getting better. I continued to take her to doctor appointments, natural remedy counseling, church, and anywhere else she wanted or needed to go. August quickly came. It was time to enroll Jaylon in school. I did not want to leave my Grandma. Eventually, Craig and Jaylon moved to Massillon and we lived with his parents. I started working at the Prosecutor's Office. I continued to go over and help my grandma as much as life would let me. Grandma Bluchelle died on September 17, 2001.

I received my bar results on November 2, 2001. Time seemed to move in rapid pace. My family encouraged me to buy my Grandma's house. It seemed like it was within days that we moved into Grandma Bluchelle's house on Hamilton Avenue. Reality hit hard with all of the expenses that go along with owning a home.

Not long after that, I became pregnant with my second son Jordan. During my pregnancy, I was tired, exhausted, and sometimes did not return to work after lunch. Adding to my exhaustion, Mom was not only in and out of mental institutions, but now in and out of jail and on and off drugs too. I left work two weeks before I was due to try to build up some energy and prepare to take care of another life. I was tired. I used my vacation and sick time to cover the time off work, but the paid time was running out. A budget crisis hit Stark County and lay-offs were imminent.

I was given the option of a voluntary lay-off since I was on maternity leave. I wanted to stay home with my new child, relax, and spend time being a mother… something I did not fully do with Jaylon. I made the decision that I was not going to return. I applied for unemployment in anticipation of being laid-off. Later, Craig talked to me about returning to work. He told me he was not able to handle our household expenses on his own if I did not return to work. I did not want to return, I resisted making the decision, but the conversation led to me returning to work.

I had not, at that point, told my supervisor whether I would return to work. My supervisor called me to find out whether I was going to return to work. Although, the maternity leave felt like a vacation compared to my strenuous life, and although I felt the kind of exhaustion that sleep could not remedy and I was not ready…I told my supervisor that I was going to return to work.

During my maternity leave, I applied for and started to receive benefits from Women, Infants, and Children (WIC). I did not make it to my initial Job and Family Services appointment because I was so tired. My cousin, Yvette took me to the second appointment. By that time, I was only eligible for WIC, and we had no cash or food benefits. Without the cash, medical, and/or food benefits, the unemployment compensation would hardly be enough to cover our household needs. I was back in the welfare line like when I received benefits during my time at Bowling Green after having Jaylon.

I had three highly respected degrees. No one is above needing help.

While I was student and new mom at Bowling Green, I received medical insurance, food stamps, and benefits from WIC. I also participated in a breastfeeding group. During a group session, the women—pregnant or already with a child—sat in a circle. I was still pregnant at the time. The facilitator wanted us to go around the room and give our name, what we were currently doing, and what we planned to do in the next five years. Each young lady stated their information. Some said they did not know what they were going to do. Others said they were in college and planned to finish. And, yet others said they were going to drop out and return to college after their children were older.

When it was my turn to talk, it was as if my whole life was planned out. I told everyone exactly what I was going to do.

"I am going to study abroad, graduate, start a Master's program, and then pursue a PhD in African American studies."

Everyone looked at me in amazement. The facilitator smiled at me and said, "Wow, Corey. Those are some great goals. Congratulations!"

Little did I know that a few years later I would receive welfare again, this time as an attorney.

Although I could not get cash benefits, I was at the welfare office grateful to receive whatever I was eligible for. I was disappointed in my financial situation. I was also physically worn out, exhausted, burned out, and just plain tired. I was not ready to go back to work. I completed school straight through without any breaks after taking advanced classes in high school. I participated in the honors program in college, completed a Bachelor's, completed a Master's, and even completed law school—all without a break. Each summer was spent taking classes and working to help pay for school. In addition to all of that, I had Jaylon during my senior year in college and potty-trained him during my first year of law school. While I studied for finals, prepared for graduation, and studied for the bar exam, I had to deal with Mom going in and out of mental institutions.

Now with Jordan in tow, I attended a mandatory staff meeting led by Mr. Horowitz regarding the County's budget and the need to lay off staff. No one at the time knew who would be laid off. Mr. Horowitz discussed the importance of voting and became angry as he described his frustration with people that did not go vote even when their jobs were at stake. Lay-offs were imminent, but the voter turnout was low. I immediately felt bad because I did not vote in that election.

I was scheduled to be induced on Election Day at 8:00 a.m. I planned to get up, get dressed, and go to vote before going to the hospital for the induction. However, I woke up at 5:30 a.m. I sat up in my bed awakened by a sharp sensation in my abdomen. I felt it again and again and again. After a short time, the sensation intensified and started coming regularly. After about three minutes of continuous intense sensations, I woke Craig up.

"I think I'm having contractions," I said while cradling my stomach with both hands.

We started to time them. They were coming every five minutes. Craig ran to the phone and started dialing.

"Ah hello…umm, I think my wife is having contractions. She is scheduled to come in for inducement at 8:00 a.m., her name is Corey Minor Smith."

I could not hear what the doctor said, but Craig responded with, "Ok,

I'll bring her right in." Then Craig hung up the phone and started calling our family members.

"Corey's getting ready to have the baby! We are on the way to the hospital."

I called Yvette. "Can you please meet us at the hospital?"

"Why? What's wrong?" she said before I could explain the situation.

"I woke up with contractions. I'm getting ready to have the baby. I was scheduled to be induced at 8:00 a.m., but I have to go now. Can you please meet us at the hospital and take Jaylon to school?"

There was no time to go vote, I was getting ready to have my second son. Even so, I felt bad hearing Mr. Horowitz's frustration with county employees that did not vote. He did not know who his frustration was aimed at in particular, but if they did not vote, they were the reason he was upset. The tax levy failed. I returned to work strictly for a paycheck. The caseload resumed. I was back in court. I wished I had not returned to work.

Chapter Twenty-six
Accussations

A fter about two months of being back to work, I was faced with accusations that I thought would ruin my legal career and my reputation. As a prosecutor, I was responsible for recommending orders for the court to issue while a juvenile awaited trial. In one case, I recommended that a juvenile be released to his mother's custody from the juvenile attention center. The court followed my recommendation, and the juvenile was released. I later learned that it would be that juvenile's final days with his mother. She was killed in a car accident the following week.

Sometime afterwards, my supervisor wanted to meet with me. I did not know what the meeting was about. My supervisor wanted to talk about cases that were assigned to me. My supervisor apparently thought that I intentionally disregarded her instructions on more than one occasion, and she disagreed with the way I handled cases.

She said, "I flagged this case. I did not want him released because he may be involved in gang-related activity!"

She referred to the case where I recommended that the juvenile be released to his mother who later died. I did not know she had "flagged" the case.

How is a case flagged? I thought as I watched her hold the case file in the air with one hand, and aggressively pointing at the file with the other.

Distracted by my trying to remember when she previously advised me about the case, I could no longer hear her words.

"I flagged the case and told you that I wanted to follow the case personally," my supervisor said as she held the case file in the air.

177

I don't remember her telling me that. The file was not marked, I thought. "And there are other things," she said, interrupting my thoughts.

A week or two later, my supervisor wanted to talk to me again. This time, she questioned my recommendation on a case because it was later learned that I knew the mother of the defendant.

"You knew the mom. You knew she was the mother of the defendant. She was in the courtroom…it says it right here," my supervisor said as she held up the judgment entry from the file. The top left corner listed those present at the pretrial.

"I did not know she was the mother. She never came into the courtroom," I responded.

"It says it right here," my supervisor said as she pointed to the left top corner of the journal entry with anger.

"Yes, but they did not come into the courtroom." I started to cry. I felt overwhelmed with feelings of no way out…no way for me to prove that I was telling the truth.

It was the practice of the court on occasion to just have the Defense Attorney, Prosecutor, and Intake Officer in the courtroom. It was the Intake Officer's responsibility to call the case and provide the names of those present for the court proceedings, even if they did not come inside the courtroom. It was just like the time Dad, Grandma, and I sat in the hallway during my custody case after Mom attacked me. I wanted so badly to go inside the courtroom then; however, we sat in the hallway. All the while we were considered "present."

In this case, like in many others, the journal entry listed the parent, the defendant, the Pretrial Release Officer (PTRO), the State of Ohio (Prosecutor), and the Defense Attorney. In this case, like in many other cases, all were listed, but only I—representing the State of Ohio, the Public Defender, and the PTRO were at the bench with the Magistrate. The pretrial was handled at the bench. I did not see the mother until I was on my way back to the office. I had not seen her since high school. Her son was not brought into the courtroom. I had not seen him before, nor had I known his name.

As the Prosecutor, I had the discretion to resolve cases according to my best judgment. I attempted to be fair. In the case where I knew the juvenile's mom and the one where I recommended the juvenile's release to his mom that was later killed, I followed the guidelines provided to me as the standards of the office. I, like the other Prosecutors in the office, took into consideration the information provided by the PTRO because that person had direct contact with the Defendant. The PTRO knew the most about the juvenile defendants and the services available for them in any given case. More importantly, the PTRO knew if juveniles participated in the available services as the court ordered. However, from my supervisor's point of view, my consideration of the PTRO's information seemed to create a larger question of my ability to prosecute cases.

My supervisor inferred that I followed the statements of the PTRO rather than her instructions. Hearing her statement about there being "other things" concerning my decisions, caused me to sit upright in my chair with a facial expression that said what I could only think to myself.

If there were other things, why had no one talked to me about these "other things" before?

I sensed that I was accused of something I did not do in addition to things that I did not know anything about. It seemed to me that I was now the Defendant and a case was being built against me. I felt that any and everything would be used to build a circumstantial case against me. A case would be built to present circumstantial evidence that I unjustly reduced cases, was insubordinate to my supervisor, or otherwise was just not a good employee.

I felt broken. Looking down at my shaking hands and bent over in my chair, I tried not to cry. As my heart increased with sadness, she told me to leave her office so she could think. It seemed that my supervisor wanted nothing else to do with me. She seemed to have nothing else to say to me. She may have been just as confused about why I reduced the case, as I was about being accused of reducing it—as if I had some ulterior motive or something. I would not risk my career to reduce a case to get somebody off. I would not take for granted all that I have been through to unjustly reduce a case. I sat at my desk and stared at the computer monitor. I was an emotional wreck. I was confused by my supervisor's accusations.

What did I do wrong? Why am I even here? She doesn't even believe me. There's nothing I can say for her to believe me. She thinks that I'm lying, I thought to myself. With those thoughts, I started typing a resignation letter because I felt like I was being accused of something I did not do.

I broke down in tears, holding my composure long enough to type a resignation letter, print it, and walk down the hall to take it to the Chief of Staff. I was overwhelmed with emotions that only I created. I walked down the hall to the Chief of Staff's office fighting to hold back my tears.

* * * * *

As a child, throughout my teenage years and even in college teen, in the past I did questionable things. I wanted to make up for anything and everything I did that made me "bad."

At this point in my life, I purposely wanted to do right, follow the rules, and do the best that I could. I did not want to ever lose out on the reward available for any one of my accomplishments because someone did not agree with something that I said or did.

I reached the Chief of Staff's office. "May I come in?" I asked, peaking my head through his doorway.

"Sure, Corey, how are you?"

I did not respond. I handed the letter to him and tried not to cry. He looked at it, read it, and asked me to explain.

"What's going on?"

I explained, as best I could, without crying. I generated in my mind a precise, concise, and definitive explanation of the word "mistake." Tiger Woods claimed he made a "mistake" and/or used poor judgment when he admitted to having affairs. Grammy Award Nominee, Bruno Mars, claimed he made a "mistake" when he was caught possessing cocaine in a hotel bathroom. MMA fighter, Thiago Silva, owned up to his "mistake" after being caught using a "urine adulterant" in an attempt to conceal his use of banned substances in the weeks leading up to a fight.

At that time, I tried to explain that I sincerely made a mistake. It was not intentional. It was not with any ulterior motive or for any benefit to me. I did not intentionally do something and was only sorry for it because I got caught. It was a mistake. I interviewed witnesses and consulted with the PTRO, but I did not follow up with my supervisor and had not known it was a practice to do so. I was advised it was my discretion to make recommendations to the court.

I was overwhelmed with stress and a sense of having no way to show that I was not lying. All I knew was that I would not risk my career and all that I had worked for to reduce cases and get people off because I knew them or because they were black. With all that floating through my head, I do not know the actual words that I used to tell the Chief of Staff about the situation. All I knew was that after my supervisor wanted me to leave her office, I felt that she lost all trust and confidence in me.

She once told me that she thought I would make a great trial attorney. With the accusations, I thought that she believed I could not handle my caseload and that I could not appropriately negotiate and resolve cases. I felt helpless with no support. I was the newest attorney. I was the only black attorney. I was the black attorney suspected of reducing a case that involved black defendants based on the recommendation of a black PTRO. No one specifically alleged those things, but it was how I felt based on the questions that were asked of me.

I felt that my character and integrity were in question. I felt humiliated. At that moment, I felt that I represented black people poorly. It was as if everything was against me and there was no way out. My supervisor made me feel like she was in a position where she had to "babysit me." It was as if she felt she had to watch over every case I prosecuted in order to make sure that I did not know the people involved, and that I did not reduce a case during a plea negotiation because I knew the defendants involved.

I put so much pressure on myself. As far as I knew, there had not been a black attorney on staff since Ira Turpin who later became the first elected black judge in Stark County back in the 1990s. There has not been a black judge since. I felt I would be the reason no other black attorney would be hired at the Stark County Prosecutor's Office. I thought that I would be the example of what could happen for any future cases with black people involved. I felt that I would not be trusted to handle any more cases with black people because I may know them.

I was saved from lay-offs because I lived in the county and was a county voter. The person who was ultimately laid-off was not a county resident. However, that person had over five years with the office versus me approaching a year and a half. She deserved to stay. She loved her job and had a passion for the job. I, on the other hand, was not ready to return to work. All of my life's challenges seemed to mount on top of my defeated emotional state and lack of self-confidence.

The Chief of Staff suggested that I go home for the day and take the weekend to think about things. When I returned to work on Monday, I was asked to meet with the Chief of Staff and my supervisor. By the end of the meeting they supported my resignation.

"Corey, you know that your supervisor has worked in this office for a long time, right?"

I nodded to respond in agreement.

"She then went on to work with a large private firm for an extended period. We are lucky to have her back in this office heading up the Juvenile Division."

I looked in her direction and acknowledged her accomplishments with a nod.

"It appears that you took the words of a pretrial release officer over your supervisor. In another case, you went to another attorney in a totally different division to ask for guidance. Tell us what happened."

In addition to the two cases that my supervisor brought up when she was talking to me alone, I was being presented with an accusation that I went to another attorney in the office instead of my supervisor for advice on a totally different case. *I was dumbfounded.* My supervisor told all the prosecutors in the Juvenile Division to go to that attorney with any issues while she was out on medical leave. That is what I did. I went to that attorney for advice on a case during the time my supervisor was out on medical leave. However, the Chief of Staff and my supervisor were then telling me that the incident did not happen during the medical leave, and that I went to the other attorney for guidance instead of my supervisor just because I wanted to.

Feeling confused about the new accusation and overall extremely nervous, I explained the situation the best that I could. They did not have a response. They told me to take my version of the events to the new Prosecutor. Mr. Horowitz had moved on and was now the Probate Court Judge. The new Prosecutor at the time met with me separately. He disclosed that my supervisor was outdone by the incidents in question. She had returned to the office on Monday just as upset as she was on Friday when she left after talking to me.

It seemed as though all hope was lost. I felt that the best thing to do was leave the office as I said, "I don't want her to feel like she has to babysit me as if I can't prosecute cases. I would like her to be comfortable with me in the office. It does not seem that is the case at this point."

"Well, there are other things that may come out if you stay," he said.

What other things? I wondered. But, it did not matter anymore. I was defeated.

Ultimately, I did not withdraw my resignation. I just wanted to leave quietly, no questions asked. No allegations made. I wanted to leave and preserve whatever dignity and respect I had for myself. Above all, I wanted my plaque representing my tenure in the office. Receiving the plaque, in my mind, meant that I did not leave the office totally disgraced. It represented an invaluable time in my career. I wanted my plaque like I wanted my Varsity letter in gymnastics, and like I wanted my yellow rose and cord signifying my induction into the National Honor Society.

The staff threw me a going away party. I was surprised to see a gift from my supervisor. I thought that she did not like me and did not trust me. She never said those things to me, but the accusations and allegations were so strong, I felt that way about our work relationship. I just felt horrible. I felt the only way to alleviate my overwhelming feelings of anxiety was to talk directly, one-on-one with my supervisor and the Chief of Staff before I left.

"I would like to just talk to you directly, positions and titles aside. I just want to talk person to person," I began during my talk with the Chief of Staff. "I would never risk all that I have accomplished for cases where I know the mother or because I did not want to follow the direction of my supervisor. I've worked too hard to get where I am to lie about cases."

He did not have much to say in response. He acknowledged my accomplishments and I left his office.

When I shared the same remarks with my supervisor, her response seemed to be like a pep talk that should have been given right before I went into the courtroom for the first time. It seemed that the "pep talk" would have been more appropriate during our conversation before working in the Juvenile Division.

"Corey, I think you will make a great trial attorney. You seem to be comfortable in the courtroom and enjoy being in court."

She had said those same words before I came to the division, and based on her words and apparent confidence in me as a trial attorney, I focused on my desire to be in the courtroom with the Juvenile Division rather than spending the majority of my time researching and writing with the Civil Division. I liked the action of the courtroom. I wanted to pursue the career of a trial attorney. The words she shared before I came to the division were the same words she shared as I was leaving. They were encouraging both times. I began to wonder whether I was leaving or if she was encouraging me to stay.

At the same time, I had the opportunity to be the Executive Director of a non-profit organization on a part-time basis. It would give me time to be at home with my children as well as earn a living that could meet our household needs. After being encouraged by board members to apply, I interviewed and was one of two people scheduled for a second interview, but I did not get the job.

With the money paid out to me from my time at the Prosecutor's office, I was able to cover the household expenses until I set up my home law office. By working from home, I could be with Jordan. When I had to go to court, Yvette watched Jordan at no charge. It was stressful and sometimes inconvenient, but it allowed me to gain the experience I needed in the courtroom and for preparing legal documents.

I had very little money at that time. I improvised a lot. When I ran out of black ink, I printed documents with the remaining color ink and made copies at the Community Legal Aid Office for free to create black and white documents. I built my caseload with Legal Aid cases, and after attending the required continuing legal education course, I received Guardian Ad Litem appointments from the court. I spent more time with my children. I was home when Jaylon left for and returned home from school, but it was a struggle financially. I needed to increase my income.

Based on a referral, I interviewed with a law firm in Akron. The interviewer wanted a letter from Judge Robert Horowitz and others that he knew in Stark County. I felt like I was on a scavenger hunt and had to run around getting requested items before the firm would consider me. Judge Horowitz and others wrote the reference letters, but I was not hired. Instead, the interviewer referred me to the Summit County Common Pleas Court to speak to Judge James Williams who was looking for a new Judicial Attorney. The interviewer from the law firm happened to be a former Judicial Attorney for Judge Williams and knew of the judge's search for a new Judicial Attorney. I sent my resume and followed up a couple of weeks later.

* * * * *

"Good afternoon, may I speak with Judge Williams," I said.

"May I tell him who is calling, please?" the pleasant voice on the other end responded.

"Corey Minor Smith," I said.

"Hold please," she said.

I listened to soft elevator music before hearing a slow gentle voice say, "You waited a long time to call, Mrs. Smith."

"Uhh, yes sir. I was providing time for you to review my resume."

"Well, you almost waited too late. When can you come to my office?" Judge Williams said back to me.

Holding back my excitement, I said, "At your earliest convenience, sir."

I met with Judge Williams later that week. He is well respected in the Summit County area. He invited me into his office to discuss opportunities in his court.

"You have an impressive resume, Mrs. Smith," he said as he sat down in his tall black leather chair behind a large dark mahogany wood desk covered with briefs and legal books. The whole office, including the chambers, seemed huge with high cathedral ceilings and wood trimmed doorways that stretched to the ceilings. He motioned me to sit in the chair in front of his desk as he started to tell me his expectations for his court.

At the end of the conversation he said, "Well, I hired someone else. I just wanted the opportunity to meet you in person and see if there is anything I can do for you."

I was stunned.

Why did he have me come here? Why did we just spend close to an hour talking as if I was being interviewed?

But Judge Williams did do something for me. A short time after my "interview" he discussed my credentials with the Administrative Judge. There was an open position for a Floating Judicial Attorney. The following week I went to meet with the Chief Magistrate and Administrative Judge. I got the job and started the following Monday.

* * * * *

By Monday morning I was a jumble of nerves. As a Floating Judicial Attorney, I was assigned to any Judge that needed legal research and writing, including visiting judges sitting by assignment from the Ohio Supreme Court. My first assignment was with Judge Jane Bond; a judge who did not believe that women should wear pants. She actually restricted female members of her staff from wearing pants to work.

The Judicial Attorney told me, "You can wear pants during the first week because the judge won't be here, but during the second week, you have to wear skirts or dresses."

I did not have enough skirts to wear for a week. I always wore pantsuits. I was nervous. It was my first assignment and I knew I did not have enough proper clothes for work; and I surely did not have money to buy dresses and skirts to wear.

I heard that the judge was very strict, stern, and demanding. My confidence was still in repair from the situation that led to my resignation from the Prosecutor's Office. I was scared I would not do well with my first assignment and that the judge would want me to resign. The assignment was to write the judge's decision for a malpractice case against a local attorney. I researched the issues, completed the decision, and submitted it to the judge. I waited a day. I waited another day. Finally, the judge responded with a sticky note on the copy sent back out to me.

"Good job."

She agreed with my written decision. The judge requested on the note that I finalize the order. I did as she instructed and she signed the order. The case was appealed to the Ninth District Court of Appeals and was affirmed. My first written opinion was affirmed on appeal. I was excited until the doubt set in. My doubt pointed out to me that it was an incarcerated criminal defendant that filed the malpractice complaint accusing his attorney of wrongdoing. He filed it *pro se*… meaning on his own.

The defendant accused the attorney of failing to file documents and not fully advising him of his rights. My doubt and lack of self-confidence led me to believe the case was clearly a slam-dunk for me as the attorney because an incarcerated defendant filed the case on his own. He was not an attorney. He had no legal background. Additionally, in many cases, courts will not reverse a case where a defendant clearly waived his rights and pled guilty. In that case, the defendant pled guilty. After going to prison, he blamed his attorney and filed a malpractice complaint.

My next and longest assignment was for Judge Brenda Unruh, a judge that was known to be tough. As we continued to work together, I participated in her Bible study sessions and shared my interest in speaking to young ladies about overcoming difficulties. During the assignment for that judge, I wrote a decision for one of the biggest cases I was ever involved in at that time…a double homicide with a third charge of attempted murder.

My first assignment with her court was during her Judicial Attorney's maternity leave. For my second assignment in her court, Magistrate

Shoemaker walked over to my desk to tell me about the assignment. As he stood standing over me, he looked down as though he tried to hold back his smile. He told me that Judge Unruh personally requested me to fulfill the duties of her bailiff during his paternity leave. I tried to hold back my smile hearing the news.

She personally requested me, I thought as he said, "I guess she thinks you did a pretty good job the last time."

At the end of my second assignment in her court, Judge Unruh stood at the open door and called me into her office. When I came in, she stood by the door with her hands behind her back. She asked me to close the door.

With her hands still behind her back, Judge Unruh said, "I really enjoyed your time in my court. You did a tremendous job with all the decisions. You were even able to manage all the responsibilities of being a bailiff… you have a strong work ethic."

As she brought her hands from behind her, Judge Unruh extended a beautiful pot of flowers in my direction. I took it in my hands and looked down in awe at the flowers.

"I want you to know that I appreciate you and wish you the best in your career," she finished as she reached to give me a hug. I smiled and held back tears of joy as Judge Unruh and I hugged. My work was appreciated. I felt a sense of confidence.

After that boost of confidence, each assignment with each judge and visiting judge gave me more and more confidence in my legal skills. I wrote more and more opinions. Each opinion approved and signed by a judge was another ounce of confidence added to my self-esteem. Each decision that I wrote that was affirmed on appeal was a gallon of confidence added to my self-esteem.

At the same time, the longer I worked for Summit County, the more I felt that I wanted to start my own law practice. For many months, I discussed the possibility of starting my own practice with other private practice attorneys. I researched the expenses, looked for office space, and learned how to get appointed cases. I watched other attorneys during criminal arraignments. I admired them as they completed their cases and moved on to the next court to complete other cases and completed other tasks in their own offices. Their time was their own. It was not necessary for them to sit at a desk all day, day in and day out.

I, on the other hand, felt like I was trapped in an office all day. I was tired of wondering, *What if?* I was tired of the limited income that I made. I wanted to be free to make my own decisions on case proceedings, free to represent clients, and free to be my own person.

How hard could it be? There are too many attorneys doing it for it not to be worthwhile, I thought to myself.

I was willing to take the chance. I read Johnnie Cochran's, *Journey to Justice* and Jock Smith's *Climbing Jacob's Ladder: A Trial Lawyer's Journey on Behalf of 'the Least of These.'* The autobiographies encouraged me even more to start my own law practice. Jock was my "cousin." Grandma Bluchelle's brother—Uncle Wade—was married to Jock's mother, Aunt Betty. Family members encouraged me to contact Jock when I was in law school. I sent him a letter and my resume when I graduated from law school. I called to follow-up. I did not hear from Jock. I thought that I would never hear from or meet Jock.

In 2005, I was in New York to see *The Color Purple* on Broadway with my best friend, Kim. I always call Uncle Wade when I am in New York. He told me that Jock was also in town and that they were going to have dinner while he was there. I told him that I would love to have the opportunity to meet Jock. To my surprise, the next evening Uncle Wade called to invite me to have dinner with them. It was very exciting to sit down at dinner, talk to Jock about his career, and hear how he built his practice. I was also excited to learn that his wife is also a member of Delta Sigma Theta Sorority, Incorporated. After that dinner, I knew I was making the right decision to start my own law practice.

However, I had to tell my supervisor, Magistrate John Shoemaker, that I was going to leave. I felt that it was not the right time because we were short staffed, but I had to make the move. The day I decided to give my resignation, I stayed after work and went into Magistrate Shoemaker's office. I stood in the doorway waiting to have his attention. Eventually, he looked in my direction.

Once we made eye contact, I said, "I'm going to start my own practice."

He did not respond. He stood behind his desk and looked back down at papers he shuffled in his hands. He started shaking his head and then put the papers down on his desk. Surprisingly, he extended his arms straight out. I realized he wanted a hug. I walked toward him and hugged him.

He said, "I knew it was coming. You're ambitious, and I know you will be successful."

His blessing gave me more confidence to start my new journey.

* * * * *

On my way

Hey Corey,

I wanted to say thank you again for breakfast. That was real cool. We have to continue to do things like that. We are truly on another level now. We're in our thirties. Maybe by the time we're forty, we'll be flying somewhere for breakfast. I was bragging on you yesterday to my pregnant/parenting group. I made copies of the newsletter and we read and discussed some things. It was a testimony for them to know that you persevered through a lot, even having a baby in college. It was eye opening for them. Thanks again for pushing and pressing through for others who you don't even know. I AM PROUD OF YOU, GIRL! Well, I guess we will talk sooner than later.

Have a blessed day,
Camela

You have knocked (prayed about it) and now the door is open. What are you waiting for?????? Go through it. Nothing good has ever come easy for you, but it ends up being good. Take this next challenge and roll with it...like you do. It is one of your heart's desires. Run with it and "make it do what it do."

Have a good one.
Camela

* * * * *

Camela

Camela sent me encouraging emails after I told her that I was going to start my own law office. Camela and I have been friends since second grade. From the cornbread sandwich in second grade at Madge Youtz, to being homecoming princesses and class officers at Timken Senior High School, to being roommates at Bowling Green State University, to being a part of each other's weddings, children being born, divorces, and careers... we are still friends today. Her words gave me more self-confidence. I left Summit County Court of Common Pleas on a Friday. On Monday, I was in the Law Office of Corey Minor Smith, LLC. It was great. I already had appointments from Summit County Courts and other cases from word-of-mouth referrals.

However, the confidence I gained did not seem to be enough to combat the insecurities I felt going back into the Stark County Domestic Relations Court to practice law for the first time in years. Even though I started my own law office, I was scared to go to the court the first time as a private attorney. My fears were based on my thoughts of wondering what others thought of me. I wondered if anyone knew why I left the Prosecutor's Office. I wondered if the new Assistant Prosecutors (AP) were told who I was and why I left. I thought one encounter with a new AP was horrible and confirmed my suspicions. She was rude, abrupt, and seemed to have a very nasty attitude when she spoke to me. I could not imagine that an attorney would act as she did to another attorney. Another AP seemed to become agitated when I questioned her theory of a case.

She yelled, "Just try the case then!" and walked away from me. I asked other defense attorneys about these two particular APs. I questioned whether they experienced the same type of behavior from the APs. They did. Although I tried not to take it personally, I did. I was insecure.

Perhaps it was their tactics for resolving cases. Perhaps it was their way of letting defense attorneys know that they were not going to easily negotiate cases and would "take it to trial" for each and every case without the possibility of any plea negotiations. Perhaps they were just a part of that small group of people that are considered, *difficult to work with*. I tried to explain it to myself, but instead, I took it personally. I was insecure and thought their behavior had to do with negative things they may have heard about me.

One day, I overheard an Intake and Pretrial Release Officer recommend me for a case as they opened the courtroom door and saw me waiting directly across the hall for my case to be called.

"Corey would be good for the case."

I began to smile and look in their direction. Then I heard, "Corey would be a great influence for the young lady defendants; especially this one. She heard Corey speak and..."

The magistrate hurriedly took them around the corner. The conversation became inaudible as the magistrate began to whisper.

They later told me that the magistrate told them that she was not authorized to assign cases to me. I tried to maintain my confidence and not allow my insecurities to build up. My smile left. I felt defeated for the moment. I did not know why cases could not be assigned to me. I completed the mandatory seminar and provided a letter of interest and my resume to the Administrative Judge as he suggested. When I did, the Administrative Judge told me that I would receive appointments. Whatever the issue, I tried hard not to let it fuel my insecurities. I had to overcome the recurring theme I created in my own head...*I'm not good enough.*

I thought of the pictures my cousin Larry gave me at the first Minor and Mitchell (M&M) family reunion I attended after graduating law school. The pictures are in the same styled frames as my high school diploma, Bachelor's, Master's, Juris Doctorate, and Supreme Court Admission. My degrees remained in the folders presented at each graduation. I kept them in a box with other memorabilia from my educational career. I did not take them out and frame them until I opened my private practice.

One picture was of Ollie Mae Cooper from Washington, DC poised with grace that exudes confidence larger than life. Cooper was the first black woman to start a law firm in the United States. The second picture, Jane Bolin. Bolin was Yale's first black female law graduate and became the Nation's first black female judge when she was appointed in 1939. Through this country's history of racism and sexism, these women prevailed. I thought about the images of the ladies in the pictures a lot. I began to think, *I, too, can prevail in my legal career despite any obstacles.*

My confidence increased with each case I completed. Even when another Intake Officer said, "Corey, I don't know why they don't like you," when he referred to staff members in the Domestic Relations Court. I did not bother to ask who, what, when, or why. Instead, I thought of Olle Mae and Jane, and I tried to maintain my confidence; refusing to allow my insecurities to build up. I focused on how Olle Mae and Jane succeeded in their careers in the midst of overt and extreme racism and sexism. I had to keep my head held high. I had to prove my ability to myself.

I continued to go to the Stark County Domestic Relations Court for cases. Some were appointed; perhaps only by the Administrative Judge since the magistrates were told not to assign cases to me, if that was the situation. I was retained by private clients for other cases. With appointments, the court paid for the legal services on behalf of defendants because they were deemed indigent and unable to afford to pay for legal representation themselves. With retained cases, my clients paid me directly. Since the cases in Stark County were limited, I pursued cases in other counties. I was determined to be involved in big, meaningful cases. I was determined to succeed.

My first big case on my own was a criminal case with several co-defendants. The other defendants had big name, high-profile criminal defense attorneys. My client had me; a new private practice attorney trying to build her self-confidence. I needed more confidence in my legal skills. I needed more confidence in myself. I was determined to do well on the case, but I was scared that I would mess up. I was afraid that I might miss something that I should have filed on my client's behalf.

I stayed up throughout the night, night after night, researching, and drafting any and every applicable motion. My client's case was reduced from a multiple felony drug case to a misdemeanor falsification case. The other defendants—with their high-priced attorneys, pled guilty. They were convicted of felony charges. My client fought it for as long as he had the energy. If my client was willing to go to trial, even a bench trial, things were in his favor for the case to be dismissed. However, he was tired and did not want to go on any further. Unfortunately, that is the case with many defendants. The legal system can be time consuming and exhausting. Some people enter a plea just to get the case over with. They just want to go back to their normal lives. That happened in this case, but my client walked away with a misdemeanor instead of multiple felonies.

To help increase my network in the legal field, I attended a National Bar Association (NBA) conference in Atlanta, Georgia. There, I had the opportunity to meet Attorney Willie E. Gary. I read about him in *Ebony Magazine*. His story inspired me. I did not want to pass up the opportunity to speak to him.

After introducing myself to him, I eventually got up the nerve to ask him if there would be any chance he would be willing to work with me on cases. To my surprise, he agreed to assist me with cases in Ohio. When I returned home, I took him up on his offer to help me with one of my pending personal injury cases. It was great to have Attorney Willie E. Gary, pro hac vice, on my filed documents. After working with him, I later used the skills I learned working with him to settle other cases on my own. I looked forward to the opportunity to try and get verdicts for multi-million dollar cases one day in the same manner that he and Jock did.

While reading the biography of the Honorable Thurgood Marshall, I learned the history of the NBA. I was honored to be a member of such a prestigious organization. I continued my membership with the NBA, attended the conference in Houston, Texas the next year, and again met up with Willie and my cousin Jock. Jock mentioned to me that he was going to pursue cases in Ohio due to the overwhelming number of individuals who lost their homes to foreclosure.

In *Climbing Jacob's Ladder*, Jock talks about a conversation with his wife. They discussed Jock wanting to work with Johnnie Cochran after meeting him and developing a social relationship. Jock's wife responded that she was sure Johnnie would call Jock again one day. After some time, Johnnie called Jock. Eventually, they created what is now Cochran Firm, USA. Like Jock waited for Johnnie to call him, I waited for Jock to call me. I finally got a call from Jock about a potential case in the Cleveland area. For me, that call was like the call Johnnie made to Jock. However, we were never able to work together. Jock died unexpectedly from a massive heart attack on January 8, 2012.

Since I already completed nine years of higher education and earned three degrees, I had another strategy to achieve success. At one point in my life, I felt that any celebrity that I met would move me closer to my dream job as a sports and entertainment attorney. However, meeting celebrities started to mean nothing more to me than merely a photo op. I no longer felt the excitement of believing that any of them would help me get into the world of entertainment and sports law.

In my first attempt to pursue a career in entertainment and sports law, I flew to L.A., during spring break of my second year in law school, to see if the entertainment industry was truly where I wanted to establish my career. Bright lights, the beautiful skyline, shopping, Rodeo Drive, big city life…I loved it. I just needed to establish my niche and determine exactly what type of legal work I wanted to do in L.A., if I decided to move there and start my career.

While in L.A., my cousin Rhonda and I had the opportunity to stay with Pro-Football Hall of Famer running back Jim Brown. He was a family friend and invited us to stay with him and his wife. During my stay in L.A., I asked Mr. Brown to come to my law school to speak. After a lot of tenacity, planning, and coordinating, the day finally came for me to pick him up from the airport and take him to the University of Toledo College of Law as a speaker for the lecture series. It was a great opportunity, but the relationship established with him did not lead to opportunities that I had hoped for. After the speech, communication was minimal. I was consumed with finishing law school, being a wife and mother, and working. And he... well, he is Jim Brown. That alone entails a busy schedule. I stopped pursing my dream job through him.

When I met Halle Berry, I was discouraged from attempting to network with her. Halle was the keynote speaker for the breakfast and led the breast cancer march sponsored by the Epsilon Omicron chapter of Delta Sigma Theta Sorority, Inc. My friend Terrie and I helped prepare the University President's guesthouse for her arrival. Halle was to be an overnight guest there. Terri and I cooked and cleaned, but Halle did not come and stay the night. Instead, she arrived the morning of the event and went directly to the event. I walked next to her holding the banner in support of breast cancer research and funding. I had the opportunity to talk to her one on one. It was probably the perfect opportunity to give her my resume and other information. She could have reviewed my information during her ride from Bowling Green back to Cleveland. But, I did not give her my packet. I was at a point of feeling it was fruitless especially after giving my packet to other actors, entertainers, and nothing came of it. I had even given my packet to Senator John Kerry when he ran for President, and nothing came of any of it. It seemed that there must have been some other steps that I should have taken to reach my goal. I needed the decision makers...not the talent, political figure, or athlete. I could not give up on my dream job.

At the same time, I learned the value of being prepared the day I met Les Brown. He is an international motivational speaker and author. Mr. Brown came to Canton to be the keynote for a program. I was the mistress of ceremony. After the program, I gave him my packet of information that included a cover letter, my resume, and copy of the local newspaper article that featured my story, *Canton Native Succeeds at Everything She Tries* written in August 2004 by Charita Goshay, a writer for *Canton Repository*.

Later that night, Les called me at home and told me, "You have a story for the world to hear."

He encouraged me to attend his motivational speakers' conference in Florida that spring. I was excited. At the time, I could not afford the conference, but I was interested in how he might be able to help me share my story with the world.

I stayed in contact with Les over the years. In 2006, after starting my private practice, I called Les and asked whether I could quote him in my advertisements. He told me, "I will do better than that. I will write the Forward to your book if you want me to."

My mouth dropped open and my eyes widened. Before I could say anything to show my excitement, he told me to send him the first two chapters of my book and five key ways that I thought he could help me. My excitement turned to dismay. I did not have the first two chapters of my book. The only thing I had was a joyful statement: "I'm writing a book!" In reality, I did not commit time to complete my book. Instead, I looked for every other thing I thought was an opportunity to reach "success."

I helped others in their established careers. As I continued to meet people with successful careers, fame, and fortune...I found myself looking at how I might be able to help them rather than pursue my own goals and reach my own success. I tapped into others' gifts and not my own. I needed to find out my gift. I needed to establish an action plan to reach my own success. I found guidance in the book *In Charge: Finding the Leader Within You.* In that book, Dr. Myles Munroe says:

"A leader is born when you discover your gift. Finding out what excites you and consumes you, discovering your passion, helps to determine your gift. This requires a process of self-discovery. How will you know what your gift is? Here are some clues: Your gift is fun. You enjoy it, you can do it all day, and people will even pay you to do what you like to do. It is your passion. You could do it without pay, 24/7 for 365 days of the year." (Page 7)

"Whatever your gift in life is, it is not for you to keep; it is for you to give to the world. God gave it to you. Pass it on. Servant leadership is serving your gift at every opportunity." (Page 10)

"No one can take your unique spot of gifting, and you cannot take anyone else's spot either...The Creator is preparing you for what he has prepared for you. Your position of leadership preceded your conception. You were built with spiritual, mental, and physical circuitry for your specific leadership gift." (Page 26)

"When people are out of their spot—gift, position, strength—life torments them. They are unfulfilled, angry, bitter, confused, frustrated, and sad." (Page 35)

Dr. Munroe also discusses the Mother of Zebedee's sons. Quoting from Matthew 20:23, Dr. Munroe shares the story of a mother going to Jesus to ask that her two sons have preferred positions among His following. But Jesus responded, "But to sit at my right or left is not for me to grant. These places belong to those for whom they have been prepared by my Father." Dr. Munroe suggests that "leadership requires preparation, and the preparation is part of the cost. You have to prepare yourself for that which is prepared for you." (Page 58)

During the time I worked for the Summit County Court of Common Pleas, I also worked for the James Family Foundation (LeBron James' charitable organization which is now called the LeBron James Family Foundation). Working for the Foundation, I hoped to establish my career in entertainment and sports like I focused on in law school. My "number one dream job" was to be an entertainment and sports attorney. Thinking of the sports agents that I read about in law school, I was grateful for the opportunities the Foundation gave me to coordinate events, review contracts for celebrity entertainment at events, and organize registration and promotion for the Foundation's annual King for Kids' Bike-a-Thon. It was a great opportunity for me. I truly believe that had I not worked for the organization, there would have been times that I would not have been able to put gas in my car. There I was, an attorney, and I could not afford to put gas in my car.

However, I often wondered why I subjected myself to menial tasks, stayed up late to complete projects, and spent so many hours away from home when I was not paid or paid very little. Then came the termination of the director which cut off the work of those who worked with the director; including me. I was not even told in person. I found out about it while reading the Foundation newsletter. The newsletter that once featured me giving out awards on behalf of the Foundation revealed that the annual King for Kids Bike-a-thon was not going to take place. From that, I knew my time with the Foundation was over. There was no more work for me to do. It was very unfortunate because I was in the middle of a program with Cleveland Municipal School District recognizing student athletes.

I was the named coordinator for the program. Despite whatever internal conflicts there were, I wanted to complete the program. I understood that I would complete it at my own expense. I would not be paid for my time or reimbursed for any expenses.

Although my time with the organization did not end well, I hold on to my fondest memories of passing out food to Northeast Ohio families during the holidays. Above all, I am humbled by the experience of coordinating the tractor-trailer deliveries to Mississippi, Louisiana, and Texas, and personally helping in Houston, Texas with the distribution of household necessities to families whose lives were rocked by Hurricane Katrina.

People who knew I worked for the Foundation thought I was successful because I was around LeBron James, one of the most successful and talented NBA players. But I did not feel successful. By that time in my life, I was around, and had the opportunity to mix and mingle, work, and even dine with the nation's leading attorneys and most famous celebrities…but I did not feel successful. I learned that success did not include the hours upon hours of my personal time campaigning for other people, working for people, and appearing on television and radio programs promoting other people. It was time to stop working to help others be more successful with their endeavors. It was not my spot. I wanted and needed to discover myself. I needed to find out what I was born to become. I did not want to be one of the "many people [who] die without manifesting [their] seed of greatness." In the words of Dr. Munroe, I did not want "to take [my] gift to the grave without using it." I did not want to "be buried with untapped treasure." *(In Charge*, Page 79) Instead, I was determined to discover my own gift and achieve my own success. It was time for me to commit the time and make the sacrifices necessary to achieve my own success.

During the first few months of working in the Law Office of Corey Minor Smith, LLC, I was not only the attorney, but I was the receptionist, the maintenance worker, and the runner. It was a bit overwhelming. However, I saw a lot of potential for my legal career. My goal was to be able to maintain my law office and household expenses without any undue burden on Craig. I thanked God I did it.

After successfully reaching my one-year anniversary, I was presented with another career opportunity. There was a big mayoral race in Canton that year and William J. Healy, II ran again after an unsuccessful attempt four years prior. After he won, he visited my law office. He brought with him a listing of all the available city positions. As he showed me the list, he wanted my thoughts on who would make a good fit for each vacant position. Eventually, it became apparent that he wanted me to work with him for the City of Canton. I appreciated the opportunity, but I had just started my office and did not want to leave it. I graciously declined without a second thought.

"I don't want to leave my office," I told him. I did not even discuss it with Craig. Instead, I recommended Craig for a position. I thought it would be great for him to be able to earn a higher income and advance his career. I continued to push for Craig to be hired rather than me. I wanted to stay in my private law firm. However, the new mayor apparently continued to think about having me work for the city. He let me know he wanted to appoint me as the Legal Compliance Director a number of times after the initial meeting in my office.

"Think about it...Fair Housing and EEO...I talked to the staff. They said it would be great if the person can speak Spanish. You speak Spanish, right?"

"Un poquito," I responded with a smile.

He continued, "Well, this position is just for you. I will combine compliance related programming...with your legal background and hard work, you will be perfect for the position."

I took time to think about it. Perhaps there was something I overlooked. Perhaps this was an opportunity that I should not pass up. Later that night, I discussed it with Craig. After talking with Craig, my mentor—Attorney Ed Smith, family members, friends, and city officials from other areas, I decided that I would strongly consider the opportunity. I contemplated how I could keep the office open and work for the City of Canton. For example, the biggest obstacle was who to have in my office while I was out of the office. I did not know who I could trust to be in my office. I was out of the office a lot in court in Akron, Barberton, Cincinnati, almost anywhere in Ohio.

I needed somebody that I could trust to handle things. I needed someone that I did not have to worry about stealing from me or not accurately taking messages or resolving issues while I was out. I was anxious. I prayed to God for help in selecting the right person and helping me to make the right decision about accepting the mayor's offer. A couple of weeks later,

Lenora called me to let me know of her interest. I smiled the whole time she talked. I knew that it would work out if I had her in my office. Lenora is Mom's friend from junior high school. They cheered together at Hartford Middle School in Canton and remained friends since. Lenora became my office manager and was a blessing to me, my family, and my office.

Before being asked to work for the City, I befriended an attorney from Canton who practiced in Cleveland but wanted to return to Canton. He needed office space. I asked him if he had any interest in moving into my office. There were a few things he had to work out before finalizing his move to Canton, but he was interested. Things were falling in place for me to accept the appointment. After more discussion with Craig, and getting a confirmation that the attorney would move into my office, I told Mayor Healy that I would accept the appointment and keep my office open. Shortly thereafter, I was appointed to a newly created position as the Compliance Director for the City of Canton. The name was changed from Legal Compliance Director to avoid any confusion with the Law Department. I did not act in my legal capacity during my time with the City of Canton. However, as the Compliance Director, I was introduced to a multitude of opportunities. I researched and drafted the first Project Labor Agreement for the City of Canton, worked to revise and update Executive Orders, and drafted the city's first Ethics Ordinance.

Action

Chapter Twenty-seven
#Me Too

Although my self-confidence continued to increase, it met another challenge when I worked with another member of the mayor's administration. I'll call him "the bully." Throughout our first year in office, I continued to hear of situations that I considered inappropriate workplace behavior involving the bully. I heard that he yelled at people, talked harshly to people about their weight, and demeaned others for minor typographical errors. It sounded like work place bullying to me.

Then, I had my personal experience with the bully. He assigned a case for me to "investigate" as a potential disciplinary matter. I was responsible for Equal Employment Opportunity Compliance (EEOC) claims, and I investigated issues throughout the city that might involve potential EEOC concerns. By the end of the week, the bully asked for a status update.

I was preparing to attend a weeklong conference in Washington, DC and intended to provide the report before I left. I went to his office to give him a verbal briefing along with my written report. He did not want a report. "You did not need to research the law on this counsel. You and I both know the law. I wanted your recommendation on what disciplinary action to take."

I responded, "Because of the details of this matter and the potential termination of the employee, there are EEOC implications and the City needs to be aware of how similar situations were addressed in order to move forward accordingly."

"Don't give me all that," he muttered. "What would you do, Ms. Smith? What is your recommendation for discipline?"

I shrugged my shoulders, "Give a write up, and a one or two day suspension."

"Now, you know I don't need your opinion to make a decision, right?"

"Yes, I know that," I said.

"Well, go tell her then," he taunted.

I became agitated as I thought of all the things I still needed to do before I left the office only to be faced with more work at home before I left for the conference. I got up and walked two doors down to the young lady's office only to find she was not there. I returned to his office with an attitude. I felt he was playing games. I did not have time for games. I appeared in his doorway to find him looking in his file cabinet.

"She's not here," I said feeling ridiculed.

"I know that," he said. "If you would have come earlier, you would have been able to tell her. I wanted to give you the opportunity to provide input on a disciplinary action and you wasted time investigating," he sneered with his hands imitating air quotes.

"I am not wasting time. I take my work seriously," I replied.

"I told you to stop giving your opinion," he snickered.

"I am not giving an opinion. I am stating facts," I snapped back, matter-of-factly.

I felt myself about to lose all professionalism and get straight South Vallejo on him as he returned to his desk from his file cabinet. I wanted to walk out and leave, but feared it would be considered insubordination and reflect badly on me. I sat down in the chair in front of his desk.

"I like you, but you get on my nerves," he said as he stared at me.

I stared back at him wondering, *what does this have to do with anything?*

We stared at each other for what seemed like an hour. I did not care how long we sat there and stared. All I knew was that I would not be the first to blink or look away. I would not allow that man to intimidate me. I could not let that man know that he was "pumping fear in my heart," as Da' Posse used to say whenever we talked about being intimidated.

I stared at him knowing that I was not going to turn away first. I started believing that if I turned away first, I would lose. He turned away and looked down toward the drawer of his desk. He opened the desk drawer, pulled out two miniature chocolate bars, and tossed them gently across the desk to me.

"No, thank you. I do not want chocolate bars."

I needed to get out of that office, finish my other work, get home to my family, and prepare to leave for the weeklong conference. Instead, I was in his office for no reason. From that day forward, I was determined to release any fear of him. Anytime he left a message on my voicemail, I went directly to his office to talk to him face to face instead of returning his call. I was ready at any moment to face him. I was ready to face any challenge head on rather than quiver, be nervous, or run away because someone thought that I did something wrong.

A different type of inappropriate workplace behavior tested my level of confidence. Thinking back on it all, I am reminded of Mom's attempt to protect me from, or prepare me for, the possibility of experiencing sexual abuse. She always told me, "Don't be all up in no man's face...don't sit on their laps...nothing." When I was older, I learned what could fall in the category of being "all up in a man's face." I translated "being all up in a man's face" as anything that I could do, did, or potentially would do, to entice a man to want me sexually.

As an adult, I am conservative in my speech, dress, and actions. I do not want to entice a man or lead any man to believe that I want to be involved with him in any way outside of a friendship or business. Being married was my biggest shield against enticing men. To me, being married put any other man on notice that I was not trying to be involved with him. However, in my own marriage, I learned that infidelity is real, that people do engage in it, and many people do not care about marriage or the sanctity of marriage. I now understand that it did not matter that I was married. It was not an automatic shield to block men from wanting more than a friendship or business relationship.

Many times, I do not give men hugs. It seemed those who know me well get offended when I extend my hand for a firm handshake instead of embracing them as they initiate a hug with extended arms. Some men have even pushed my extended hand away and reached for a hug as they say, "Awh girl, what you doin' trying to shake my hand like you don't know me." It's not that I do not know them. I just prefer to be professional and not entice, or even give the appearance of enticing them with a hug. For example, when I graduated from law school, I was excited. I reached up and gave my Dean a hug after he handed me my degree. Some people said it looked like I kissed him. That hug would probably fall in the category of "being all up in a man's face," according to Mom.

While I worked as a member of the mayor's cabinet, I started to relax and lay down my guard. I gave a few hugs. I once gave the mayor a hug after he introduced me on stage at an event. Some people thought it was inappropriate. Once, I gave a one-arm, side-to-side hug to an older public official who was extra nice that day, and who seemed so excited to see me. However, he did not just hug me, he left his arm around my waist, and his hand, ever so gently, just touching my butt.

"Your hand is too low," I said discretely.

"What do you mean my hand is too low?!" he said, moving away from me in disgust. "How are you gonna tell me my hand is too low?!" he said, getting louder as he walked away.

I shook my head as I thought, *if he did not intend for his hand to be where it was, why not just apologize?*

Just as my thought ended, he came back to where I was to make more smart aleck remarks before starting to walk off again in disgust. I cared not what he had to say, knowing that this time was one too many times of him *accidentally* touching me where he should not.

"Your hand was too low. You want to make a scene about it, go ahead. I'm just letting you know."

He, in turn, rolled his eyes and walked off.

Then, there is the hug where I was pulled back into another public official's arms after I began to release from the hug.

He pulled me back into the hug again and whispered in my ear, "You feel nice."

I was disgusted.

Equally upsetting was the person who boldly grabbed my butt and held on to it as we posed during a group photo. I tried to keep smiling for the picture, but I felt that my eyes were bulging out of my head in shock at the man's audacity to hold on to my butt.

Why me? What did I do to entice them? Was I 'all up in their faces'?

I wear pantsuits with blouses that cover my cleavage. I speak professionally and carry myself in such a way that I've been criticized as being "too professional," "stuck up," "think you're better than other people because you're a lawyer," and "you gotta stick up your ass." Then, I try to lighten up a bit and give a few hugs. Yet, inevitably, something happens that makes me question whether I was "all up in some man's face" that led to some unwelcomed advance—that somehow, I must have led him to believe I wanted him.

I learned that I cannot control what others do, say, or think. What I can control is my response. While I wanted to go "South Vallejo" on the men who took the hugs too far, it would have caused a scene and been embarrassing due to where we were at the time. Sometimes alcohol was involved, and I gave the benefit of the doubt that alcohol was the culprit. Whatever the reason, I did not blame myself. I clearly stated to the men that what they did was not acceptable, in person and face-to-face.

While they smiled as if I was playing around, I said, "I'm serious." After which the smiles left their faces. I sternly said, "It won't happen again."

I thought about grabbing the scrotum sack of the one who grabbed my butt. I wanted to squeeze it with all my might knowing that area is one, if not the most, sensitive areas on a man. I visualized squeezing his scrotum sack during our hug as I whispered angrily in his ear, "You bet' not evah' do that shit again."

Then I thought about the fact that he probably would have liked it, and I would have opened another can of worms.

You never know how you will respond until something happens to you. At that time, I was prepared to be diplomatic and verbalize my concerns about unwelcomed advances. I am no longer the scared little girl believing that she was "all up in some man's face" and caused the unwelcomed advances.

While working for the City of Canton, I also worked directly with my former supervisor from the Prosecutor's Office. Initially, I was scared to work with her. I was intimidated. All the while, I sought her approval. In my mind, I wanted to "make up" for whatever negative thoughts she had about me from the Prosecutor's Office. I needed her to say that I did a good job. I needed her to acknowledge my work ethic, work product, commitment, and dedication to my work. I needed her to agree with my decisions. I needed her approval. I wanted and needed it in order to feel like I was good enough. It was as though her approval would fully restore my self-confidence. The longer I worked with the City, the more I thought back to the end of my career at the Prosecutor's Office. I thought about what my supervisor must have believed when she questioned me about the cases.

Throughout my time since leaving the Prosecutor's Office, I have encountered many employees who "worked the system," "tried to get over," or just flat out "didn't want to work." Since leaving the Prosecutor's Office, I became cynical like Alisha. Alisha and I were in law school together. It seemed that during every class discussion, she had a cynical remark. I never understood why Alisha made so many cynical comments in class. It seemed as though some comments were just mean. She seemed to always criticize people and accuse them of having negative, self-serving motives in most any situation. I hated to think that my supervisor thought of me in a cynical way. At the same time, after dealing with issues involving employees doing self-serving things at work, and not wanting to be reprimanded for it, I understood where she was coming from if she felt that way about me.

Before I resigned from my position with the City, I heard my former supervisor's approval. I had an EEOC case that did not settle. When the mayor assigned me to take over the Department of Human Resources, another department took over the EEOC program. My former supervisor was the attorney assigned by the Canton Law Department to the board that reviewed the EEOC claims. She needed to review the file for the case that did not settle. As I handed the file to her, it felt like we morphed back in time to my final days at the Prosecutor's Office. I tried to control the tremors in my hand as I handed the file to her. I was scared that she would once again review the information and find something wrong. I was afraid that she would find something that she did not agree with, or that she thought was contrary to the law. My self-confidence was shaken, but it remained intact.

I kept reminding myself, *you are not back at the Prosecutor's Office. However she views this case, you will be fine.*

At that point, I was confident enough in my work and ready to defend it with confidence. I understood there were differences of opinion all the time. It's seems to be the nature of the legal system…the United States is a very litigious society. People file cases, win or lose cases, cases are appealed, reversed or dismissed…that is why there is an opposing counsel representing the other side. Bottom line, people disagree all the time.

With that in mind, I was prepared for whatever criticism my former supervisor may have had. However, after she reviewed the file, she let me know that she agreed with my analysis and suggestions for the case. I felt great. I felt redeemed. My resignation from the Prosecutor's Office no longer bothered me. I was young then. It was my first job as an attorney. I learned a lot; and I received a lot of recognition for my career achievements during and since the time I left the Prosecutor's Office. Little did I know, I was yet to face one of the worst blows to my self-confidence.

Chapter Twenty-eight
Is This the End?

I wanted to be married. I enjoyed the thought of being close, inseparable, and *together* with someone. I visualized my husband and me working together for the good of our family. I envisioned us being two people together with the love of God excelling through life's journey. I had a friend from elementary school whose sister married a member of a popular '80s R&B music group. She showed Da' Posse' the video of a cookout at her sister's house. It was a mansion. The sister's son had a Crayola crayon themed room. I admired the beautiful home they shared with a perfectly landscaped backyard and a pool. We discussed how our friend and her sister deserved that lifestyle because they had a very troubled home life. At the same time, I started to picture myself living the same type of lifestyle and being on the arm of a high-profile person.

I thought that I would marry a professional athlete. I thought I was attractive and confident enough to deal with the life of a professional athlete, and the many women that would want to grace the same arm. But, as I matured, I figured I would skip all the drama that seems to be automatically coupled with the life of a professional athlete.

Nope, I wanted Craig. He loved me. He wasn't a celebrity. He would not cheat on me. We were too busy trying to provide for our family to have time to cheat. Not Craig, I thought.

But, I am reminded of Eddie Murphy's live stand-up comedy show *Raw,* where he describes the situation of women not thinking that their men cheat on them.

"Yes, your man too!" he said to the women in the audience as if to slap them into reality.

I felt I had a good marriage, wonderful sons, a promising career, a beautiful home, and a dog...and it seems that I accomplished those things the right way, pretty much, until I was slapped into reality.

Craig once told me that my list of accomplishments had asterisks. For example: good grades - asterisk because I met to discuss my grades with professors when I did not agree with the grade I was given and my grade was changed. Asterisk because I pledged my sorority through the graduate chapter, not in undergrad. Asterisk because although I made it through law school and passed the bar the first time, I was not a "shark," "a go get 'em" attorney because I am "too nice."

He said that the asterisks meant that there was a footnote to explain each of my accomplishments. It was as if I was not fully worthy, did not earn my accomplishments with my own merit, or lacked the skills required to do so. His words hurt and intensified my feelings of not being good enough. Hearing those things weakened my self-confidence. Many of his comments made me feel that an asterisk would follow me forever. I felt that I would never be able to get rid of the asterisks in my life.

After reading a draft of my book, my mentor, Ed, told me that I had all that I wanted. But, as I went down the list, there are asterisks. Home* barely able to afford; 2.3 children* first pregnancy was at the same time as another woman—the children are only six weeks apart; dog* not ours—we dog sat for my friend for nearly a year. As far as marriage, that is the biggest asterisk. Nothing compares to me coming out of denial and acknowledging the reality of my marriage. Nothing...

Since the beginning, you were a blessing in my life
And on this day, I will become your wife.
Today, I pledge my love to you,
May together with the Lord,
we see all things through.
During stressful times,
I will be there for you,
In happiness, my love will shine through.
I pledge my commitment with any illness,
And may our health be strengthened with our every caress.
May our love not be distracted by money nor power.
Rather, as we become one,

we strengthen our faith
in the Lord Jesus Christ
as our sole Higher Power.
~I love you Craig Curtis Smith, Sr.~

And on this day, I pledge to give my hand in marriage
As a symbol of my dedication, commitment and sincerity.
As your wife, our union will be filled with God's security.
I pledge today to provide unconditional love
regardless of any strife.
May the Lord bless this lifetime union as you,
my husband,
and I,
your wife.

Those are the vows I said to Craig on June 6, 1998 at Deliverance Christian Church filled with our family and closest friends. I meant it from the bottom of my heart. I had no reason to doubt that he meant his personalized vows just as much.

After eleven years of birthdays and holidays, the best of times and some bad, I awoke one night after one of those bad moments and hurt feelings, and felt fear. I literally woke up in the middle of the night, and my mind started racing with thoughts that were sad. I thought of all the women, and a few men, that hired me to file for divorce on their behalf. During my initial consultations with them, they questioned whether they should file for divorce. Yet I always had my clients explain their situations, and the reasons why they wanted a divorce. It helped me develop the theory of the case and potential claims for the divorce complaint. At the same time, I tried to hold back my facial expressions and other non-verbal expressions as I wondered, *why are you staying?*

As I lay in bed that morning, I tried to go back to sleep, and wondered why I woke up in the first place. I thought about my marriage. I asked myself the same question, *why are you staying?*

I could not sleep. Craig usually woke up very early to go work out while I was still asleep. That morning, I was up when he came back into the room before he left for the gym.

"Why are you up? What's wrong?" he asked.

211

"I'm tired and overwhelmed with a lingering question about our finances; where is your money going…and, there are still too many unanswered questions. I've been to the doctor so much; I was told I do not need to get tested that much."

"You want a divorce?" he asked with a puzzled inflection in his voice.

"Yes," I said without hesitation.

I could not believe how fast it came out my mouth. Craig had, at least three times before in our marriage, brought up divorce because he was not happy about something I did. I always thought the discussion was unwarranted. That morning, and with the information that I would soon find out later, proved that the discussion was more than warranted. I had to face reality.

My reality tells me that our time together, our relationship, and unfortunately, our entire marriage were built on lies. With the lies, I created a false reality. Each incident rushed through my mind like a movie reel on fast forward with only a few scenes that slowed down slow enough for me to remember, all too clearly, what took place. The time he told me he would never cheat, the time I discussed my feelings about him talking to my friend…taking her fishing and taking her "storm-chasing," and the time he got mad and left because I was too tired to have sex. Or the weekend his sister visited us from Columbus and he did not come home all night. I thought it was awfully bold of him to not come home. He did not say a word when he came in either. He showed his arrogance and confidence in the fact that I was helpless to my dream of how I wanted a marriage and a family. His sister did not say anything. I did not say anything. It was as if it did not happen.

My reality is that he was not solely with me as a husband should be. After I told him I wanted a divorce, I lay in my bed at night unable to sleep night after night. I thought about my days ahead…being a single woman. I tried to face my reality; a reality that shattered my world like no other obstacle in my life.

My reality is that I went to the doctor way too much; not because of a towel, sharing clothes, touching a toilet seat, or anything else that he would use as an excuse. The truth is, I was with one man for fifteen years and his explanation, or lack thereof, was not the source.

Mom is mentally ill, that is my reality. Dad sold drugs, went to jail, and lost what seemed like everything. That is my reality. I wish Mom and Dad were there for me more, but they were not. That is my reality. I have come to realize that my marriage was only "picture perfect." Picture perfect is not reality.

I woke up and decided to stop allowing a *dream* of what I wanted in life to color my vision of what my life truly was. I realized that all along, I had been playing house, but I was not living in a home.

I started really seeing things for what they had actually been and realized that after Craig and I broke up during our junior year in college, we had a turbulent relationship. We remained involved with each other through a lot of mess during that time. However, in my mind there was another story. In my mind the relationship was "picture perfect." It was great while we dated. We had some trials once we broke up, but we matured, grew to love one another, and decided to get married. We were working together to build a life for our family.

As thoughts of divorce ran through my mind, I reflected on my marriage. It was a struggle in the beginning. I accepted struggle. We were in college, and apart often. The question that loomed in the beginning, and actually all the way through our marriage, was…where Craig was many times. He was absent way too many times for my comfort level. I recall fraternity parties, fraternity meetings, fraternity conferences, conventions, or annual gatherings of some sort or another. Trips with his guy friends, and boys' nights out were some other reasons for his time away. On any given night, Craig served as the dean of pledges and was always busy pledging candidates for membership in his fraternity. He worked, but his money was not used to take care of our family and our household expenses. Our finances never added up, he was always short, and I covered more than I should have; yet, it was our home, and making our home function was more important to me than not.

* * * * *

Flipping the script became a part of our marriage in what I later learned was his way of throwing me off his scent of finding out that he had other women. Craig had other relationships all along.

Toward the end of our marriage, he accused me of being with members of New Edition because I attended their concerts, hung out at the hotel after the concerts, and kept in touch with my favorite member—Ralph's uncle. I argued with Craig that I was always introduced as "a cousin"…I was treated with respect…I was far from being a groupie. I am just one of those people who truly admires a celebrity, music group, or an artist, and really likes to follow their careers.

I remember hearing Mom and her friends talk about women who threw their panties on stage for '70s R&B crooner, Teddy Pendergrass. I did not respond that way to New Edition. I truly and sincerely like New Edition as nothing more than a group whose music I had fallen in love with. Mom was the one who gave me my first New Edition album and I was in love with their music from that day on. Anyone who knows me knows that New Edition is my favorite group, Mickey Mouse is my favorite cartoon character, and hot fudge sundaes with whipped cream, nuts and a cherry on top is my favorite dessert. New Edition was just one of my favorite things in life. There was nothing sexual or over the top about my intentions. I would never throw myself at any man or have sex with him just because he's in a musical group or otherwise famous. Nevertheless, I accepted Craig's concerns because I sincerely considered both sides of the story and in his favor.

In 2009, I found the truth; it was in me all the time. Denial died. I lifted my head out of the fog of my dream of marriage and family. Craig did not have to say a word of the certainty.

Why did I believe so much dumb stuff? Damn, I'm a lawyer.

During our marriage, I thought about how Craig probably joked and laughed about me being so dumb. He probably got a kick out of me being naïve to have never questioned him about any of his time away from home.

Why would I not question those things?

Since I carried the load financially, I believed that he could not afford to pay for anything for other women. I also believed that even though he was not around a lot, he would "need even more time away from home" in order to have affairs. As we talked about divorce, he used excuses that he could not take care of things financially right then, or that child support had prevented him from helping to cover our household expenses.

My mind questioned that.

Did the other women cook for him? How many dinners or nights out did he pay for?

I made it clear during our talks about money, that even if it was a five dollar meal at McDonald's, that was five dollars that did not come into our house to help our family. I accepted his excuses for not being able to help financially and for being away instead of helping more with the children.

As we tried to lay all our cards out on the table concerning our marriage, I shared my concerns and I expressed how I felt; yet I still accepted his responses and took on the guilt he shifted my way.

According to him, child support for his older son was always a factor for us financially. I lowered my head, ashamed of how I felt, each time he mentioned child support. I loved his son. I loved him being in our home, and made his son a part of who we were as a family. To my sons, that was their brother; and I always made sure he was comfortable with me referring to him as my son when we were together because I never wanted him to think I was trying to replace his mom in any way. Today, I am willing to be as much a part of Craig Jr.'s and his son's life as he would like. Craig Jr. was part of a package deal that I accepted when I married Craig. We were a family; and together we were going to make it.

My reality is that I allowed myself to be used, manipulated, taken advantage of, deceived, bamboozled, run amuck and led astray…all in the name of love. I wanted desperately to believe Craig or to believe in love. I wanted to stay in my marriage. It was not until that morning when I awoke with my soul full of all the proof I needed, and I saw things for how they really were.

Why did I know that it was time to change?

Because I realized that until then, I had wanted marriage so badly that I was willing to die for each day I could be married; but it was a war that had to end because the truth was in me…and I had awakened. I was now woke…literally and figuratively.

I wrote Craig a letter.

> *I am not happy. I have not been happy. I think of our relationship and become frustrated. I am frustrated with all the situations that have taken place of which I voiced concerns that were not heard. I am frustrated that the load has been on me. I am frustrated that I have sacrificed all that I am. I am frustrated that I have been stressed, overwhelmed, undervalued, deceived, and manipulated.*
>
> *Is there anything left in me that wants to save this marriage? My answer is 'No.' I love my children with all my heart. It is only now that I become emotional because I don't know how my decision will affect them. Although I love them above all,*

*I have also come to love myself. I love myself enough to know
that it is OK to put myself first. I want peace of mind. I want
to go about my day without being distracted. I have allowed
too much to be overlooked. I have put up with too much. I
have nothing left to give this relationship. I have no emotional
connection to the relationship. I cannot connect with any joy in
this relationship outside of our children. I don't feel that I love
you as a wife should love her husband. I am not pleased with
our marriage. It hurts and I cannot take it anymore.*

The next morning, I gave Craig the letter. He read it. We talked. He
continued to tell me that he did not do anything.

He asked, "How can I admit to something that I did not do?"

I looked at him. He stared at me with tears in his eyes. I wanted to
believe him like I believed him every other time. He continued to say he
did not cheat on me. He continued to say that he did not do anything.

He then looked at me and asked, "Will you pray with me?"

*I cannot believe that this man is trying to use my relationship with God
against me,* I thought to myself.

Before I accused him of being totally manipulative and deceptive, I
thought of Grandma Bluchelle. I thought about how even though I was on a
punishment, she let me go to a revival with Camela at her dad's church. At
the time, she said, "I am not going to stand in the way of anyone's relationship
with God." With those words, she let me go; trusting and believing that I
was going to where I said I was going. I went to the revival at church, and I
came right home.

However, even with that flashback in my mind, it took everything in
me to fight off the feeling that Craig was manipulating me as he had done
in other ways. I believed he had ulterior motives. He never wanted to pray
with me about anything other than saying grace over our food. Yet, when
he made the request for me to pray with him that time, I knelt down on
my knees next to him. With our arms braced alongside the bed and hands
pressed against our foreheads, he began to pray. I listened. He did not pray
for us to stay together. He prayed for me to have peace.

I was done!

For weeks Craig remained in the house after I told him I wanted a
divorce. I continued to listen to him explain, rationalize and justify his actions

all the while denying that he cheated. He continued to talk. I continued to listen, but my brain finally faced reality. As an attorney, I have worked as a prosecutor and I have been a defense attorney. In both positions, I worked on cases involving defendants with overwhelming evidence against them. I visualized all the things that Craig did in our marriage. I knew all the emotional and physical harm he brought home with each woman. He committed crimes of infidelity; there were charges with overwhelming evidence against my spouse, the defendant. My brain was the prosecutor. My heart was the defense attorney:

My Brain: You could not have been with the same man for over fifteen years, and requested blood work and tests so much that your nurse told you that you do not need to be tested every time you go to the doctor. You have rationalized, justified, and minimized all of his deceit.

My Heart: But he said he hasn't done anything. He said he doesn't know why I feel this way.

My Brain: This is a trial where the defendant is lying. Remember the felonious cases where you sat second chair? The defendant's story changed throughout the case. There was evidence against the defendant. Remember all the jurors said 'guilty?' There was that one juror that held out. The question is…reasonable doubt. That juror held on to some kind of doubt, but that doubt was not reasonable…just like you are doing… you are holding on to unreasonable doubt. With everyone you have shared your story with…they knew without a doubt that he was lying before you even finished the story.

My Heart: But he said he did not do anything. He said he would never cheat on me. Why would he continue to lie when he sees how bad this is hurting me…when I've begged him to tell me the truth?

My Brain: You are that sole holdout juror. What are you holding out for? Your doubt is not reasonable when it is only grounded in his self-serving, false testimony. Remember when he said, "I did not do anything. How can I admit to something that I did not do?" He even looked you right in your eyes and said, "I did not cheat on you."

Those statements are not true.

217

I thought of another case where I wrote decisions on a double homicide, attempted murder case. Again, there was evidence presented that the defendant continued to change his story—all lies—but he held on to his story that he did not murder or attempt to murder anyone. Even as he was led away shackled at his ankles to a large group of inmates, he held on to his lies. He was the only one dressed in "trial clothes" (suit, regular clothes) while the other inmates wore the county orange jumpsuits. They were all chained together with him leading the pack. He had handcuffs around his wrists in front of him and shuffled his shackled feet as he tried to walk.

I visualized Craig leading the pack of other cheating husbands. He led them away from their homes with loving wives and children, to their adulterous lives with all the women, liquor, and easy living they wanted. My emotions were all over the place.

All I knew is that I wanted a family. I wanted stability. I thought I had a stable marriage, a stable family life, but I struggled all the same. I became angry at any given moment to think of all that happened during my time with Craig.

Did I work too much? Did I cause it, or lead him to it like he told me I did?

I thought about whether I should just "stick it out." I had conflicting thoughts

"Follow your heart," I remember hearing Bunny say when I asked her what she would tell her own daughter if she were in the same situation.

My heart and my brain were in a constant battle. I thought about how I worked for the benefit of our family when Craig did not. I did not want us to struggle like I did in my youth. I wanted my children to have lunch money, school supplies, clothes, and everything else they needed to be successful in life without any stress being put on them. I had to put things in perspective. I know that we all fall short of the glory of God. We all are sinners saved by God's grace; but Craig's actions, in my mind, were unconscionable. I needed to forgive as God forgives. However, I felt that even though God forgives us, it does not eliminate the consequences we must face for our wrongdoing.

I always pictured myself being a sort of June Cleaver mom. Before I had a family, I envisioned having after-school snacks readily available when my children came home from school. But, *Leave it to Beaver* is not reality.

From the time I made up my mind and told Craig I wanted a divorce, it was not pretty. We argued, and we had long days of mad silence. When we did talk, it was fire and ice conversations. He told more lies, denied telling me the truth, and he did not agree to a divorce—at least not the easy way. We stayed in the house together for some time in a very uncomfortable situation. I enlisted his family to help, but that did not work.

One day, I heard the doorbell ring and I wondered who was coming over to our house late at night. I went to the front door and opened it. To my surprise, it was my cousins Yvette and Michael.

"What are you doing here?" I asked.

"You are not letting him have Grandma's house," Yvette said as she walked past me and into the house.

Michael, always quiet and not knowing why he was there, came inside shrugged his shoulders and followed behind her.

That is all I need is for Craig to think that I called my cousins to come and intimidate him to leave, I thought to myself as I closed and locked the door.

I told Yvette, "You should not have come here" as I walked back to my room. I left them to find wherever Craig was in the house, and to say or find out whatever it was that they wanted to know from him.

After what seemed like hours, I texted Yvette to find out what they could possibly still be talking about. She responded that Craig was still talking.

"What's he sayin?" I texted back.

"A hol' bunch of stuff, but we still don't know what's going on," Yvette texted back. Eventually, she came back to the room to get me.

"He agreed to leave as long as you don't change the locks or security code."

"If that is all he wanted, that could have been done," I responded in anger. "He's putting me through all this unnecessary drama and emotional stress because he thinks I will lock him out? That's stupid!" I yelled.

Angry…I had every right to be angry with him as I had lived with Craig and his irresponsible and immature behavior over the years, and yet he was putting me through more drama. He is the one person that I have been with the longest out of my Mom, Dad, grandmas or anybody else. He is the one that I lived with for over twelve years. With our children, we were a family. He is the one that I trusted. He is the one that I married. He is the one that I loved. He was the one I thought loved me. But in the end, he was at his worst.

Craig moved out and I was alone in the house, finally. I went to church the next day. I simply wanted to sit in church and let my soul be still. I sat in the front pew with the "mothers" of the church. The church was full, and I figured I could sit wherever there was a seat. Although on any given Sunday, it seems that the front right row is reserved for the "mothers" of the church, I sat there anyway. I sat in church, like I wanted to do. The choir sang. It was an all-female choir wearing the colors of their age range as suggested at the Women's Day meeting. That Sunday was Women's Day. That Sunday I had my first spiritual experience. As the all-female choir began to sing *Praise Him* I stood with one of my arms outstretched high above my head. Then, I raised both arms high in the air with hands outstretched in total surrender to God. All of a sudden, I began screaming at the top of my lungs:

"Hallelujah!!! Thank you, Jesus!!!" I frantically began pulling back and forth on the pew in front of me. I thought I was going to pull it out from the bolts and out of the floor. It seemed I was in and out of consciousness. At some point, I briefly regained consciousness and wondered, *is someone gonna come to get me? No one came.*

Back out of consciousness, I whirled away from the pew stomping with both feet, squatting and springing back up, squatting and springing back up. I was conscious again.

Is somebody gonna come get me? No one came.

Back out of consciousness. All of a sudden, my squatting and springing up led me to the wall next to my pew. I leaned up against the wall with my arms outstretched against the wall, head hung low, and moving my head slowly left to right, left to right. It was amazing. It was like an out-of-body experience. It seemed as though I sat and watched it all. My body calmed down. I came to myself. I went to the door about four feet in front of me that led to the downstairs area. I went directly to the bathroom. I looked in the mirror. My tears made my mascara run all over my eyes.

One of the "mothers" of the church—the First Lady, Reverend Beverly Lewis, affectionately called "Reverend Bev"—and my cousin Rae came into the bathroom to find me still crying. They helped cool me off and calm me down. Reverend Bev told me that I experienced a "purging." I had never felt the Holy Spirit or "caught the Holy Ghost." I had often questioned whether it was real; especially when it seemed to be the same people that got it. They do the same routine of shouting and jumping and everybody just looks at them until they are done. This time, I felt it. I experienced it. It was real, and it happened to me.

I sensed God's presence many times in my life: at the birth of my children, when I married Craig, and at the times I tried to find a way to help my Mom and God came through; even before the bar exam results were released. I remained calm, cool, and collected since I had God leading my way.

I will never forget that spiritual experience during the Women's Day service. I know it was the Holy Spirit. I was not in control, even when I wanted somebody to come get me. The Holy Spirit was in control. God is amazing. I thank Him every day for the strength He gave me to make it through all of my obstacles.

* * * * *

I thought that when I was fifteen and had to decide where I would live after Mom left me in Houston, that it was the biggest decision I had to make in my life. When I made that decision, I thought I was over the obstacles in my life. But it turned out that the biggest decision I would have to face in my life was still ahead of me.

Was I going to stay in my marriage?

Although Craig was out of the house, I still had to see him every day when he brought the children home in the evenings after his time with them. He usually wanted to talk. He wanted to work things out. I struggled with whether I really wanted a divorce.

I remember a plane ride home from Las Vegas when I scanned the dark skies and looked for God in the dark. I knew God was there. He had been there many times when I did not think of Him, and He held me and helped me. During that time, my Lord, my God…He held me up at thirty thousand feet above the earth. I begged God to help me to remember my thoughts. Even though I was so tired that I did not feel like writing down my thoughts, I did. I believe God spoke to my soul in what happened next.

I sat between an elderly couple on the plane; feeling like a wedge between them, I asked the wife, "Would you like to sit together?"

She smiled and replied, "No. He likes the window. I like the aisle," she leaned her head to the right as if pointing to the center aisle of the plane.

They complimented each other. This was unlike me and Craig. Instead of complimenting each other, we criticized each other and argued because "You sleep with the TV on," I would say. "You always have books and files in the bed," he would say.

I continued to reflect on the couple. I enjoyed just looking at her and then him. As they wished, she sat to my right. He sat to my left.

Her outfit was perfectly coordinated. Her pink shirt matched the colorful design that trimmed the jacket she wore over it. Her fingernails were polished, and her hands looked soft. Her wedding ring was placed perfectly on her thin ring finger. He wore tan khaki pants and a button-down plaid shirt with a thin light cream jacket. He sat quietly and looked completely relaxed. Each read their books and seemed to turn the pages in sync with the other as if they were reading along together. They lived their lives in sync, unlike me and Craig.

As I thought about the couple, I listened to a song, "I Don't Want to Lose Your Love." Keyshia Cole sang as if she meant every word in the song. Whomever she was referring to in the song, she wanted him back.

I lost love. My divorce was not final, but no bone in my body had the desire to be back with Craig. Although I did not want to be with Craig, we had children together and had to share time during the week with our children. We alternated weekends. During the times without my children, I was overwhelmed with loneliness. As an only child, a latchkey kid who experienced having one parent, then the other parent, and sometimes having neither parent…I never felt as alone as I did on the nights I came home and my children were not there.

"I don't want to spend time with Mommy, I have more fun with you," I heard Jordan tell Craig when Craig returned the boys home one evening. He encouraged Jordan to stay.

What? Not my baby boy. What is this doing to the children?

For me to hear my baby boy talk that way hurt my feelings. He was only six, but he was my baby boy.

Chapter Twenty-nine
Rise Up

Filing for divorce was not the only stress I endured at that time. At one point, things seemed to accumulate to a point of breaking me down with no chance to return. The lawyer in my office left without paying the rent for that month. The money I generated from my law office cases was few and far between. I tried to maintain my law office and my household expenses with my City income. Unfortunately, as the executive team of the mayor's administration, the cabinet participated in voluntary furloughs which decreased my pay. Even though Craig was out of the house, he was still responsible for the gas, electric, and cable. He missed paying the gas bill. Consequently, the gas was cut off on a Friday. Craig went away for the weekend to help a female friend move. The children and I were left with no gas and no hot water. All the while, I was dealing with Mom being arrested and going in and out of the ER without being pink-slipped. Craig's suggested solution was for me and the boys to go to his mother's house until the gas was turned back on.

Legal fees, past due balances on the bills transferred over from Craig, and city, state and federal taxes owed, all put me in a financial bind that I did not know how to get out of. I tried to get other work from individuals, organizations…anyone. No one had anything at that time. There were only future opportunities for me to make more money. I called to have my student loans deferred…*again*. I was proud to have finally started paying them. Then, within the same year, I needed to return to deferment. I was not eligible. I also received acceleration notices for the mortgage because I was behind on my mortgage payments. As if it could not get worse, the "repo man" came for my car. He did not take the car because I was not home. Later, the cable man came to disconnect the cable. It seemed like insurmountable stress. I had sleepless nights, headaches, loss of appetite, irritability, and exhaustion. I was just plain worn out; yet, I wanted the divorce.

At the same time, I was going through an emotional and spiritual struggle. As a child, my feelings did not seem to matter so I ignored them, denied reality, and kept on doing what I had to do to finish school, graduate, and get a good job. After Mom attacked me, it seemed that counseling introduced me to feelings I did not want to feel, so I ignored them. The events that led to the separation from Craig, and ultimately the end of our marriage brought on a level of stress and feelings that I did not know what to do with. I could not ignore them. I could not try to deny they existed. I had to face them and deal with them.

On some days, I felt better. Things seemed calm, whole, and complete in my world. I thanked the Lord for a sense of peace when all things seemed like they should have been chaotic.

When I had peace, I enjoyed the days and nights that I felt full and complete appreciation of all that I had; not material things, but my family, my mental stability, my being, my faith, my growth and personal development. I sensed that I did not have all that I wanted, but I had what I needed. For that, I thanked God.

The sense of complete appreciation was quickly interrupted with agitation whenever Craig suggested that we could work things out. I felt that his words simplified the whole situation as if an "I'm sorry" erased all the hurt, shame, and feelings of worthlessness…and replaced them with feelings of us being together in happiness.

Then I would go back to feeling peace. I appreciated the times of not feeling overwhelmed by guilt or shame, and questioning myself, *what did I do wrong?* I appreciated all of the people who talked to me daily and helped me clarify my thoughts and emotions. Sometimes, out of the blue, things were on my mind. I usually sent out a text message to Kim; my sister-in-law, Gemel; Camela; and even my Aunt Doris and Aunt Shanie. I eagerly awaited the first response from any one of them. One day I sent Gemel this text message:

Can only do what I am doing…divorce. No need to cry over spilled milk, right?

Gemel's response was so profound. Her words still help me today:

Tears are a balm for a wounded soul, they help us to let go of the pain inflicted upon us. So yes, cry cuz; it ain't just spilled milk. It's a life and a dream that's been shattered, but not destroyed. Let out your pain, you may need to cry a whole lot more. Don't try to hold it in thinking you're being strong or forcing yourself to 'get over it.' You'll stop crying when you stop crying. Only your heart knows when that will be.

I truly appreciate all the time Gemel spent talking me through my thoughts, my emotions, and my unwavering sorrow. Gemel introduced me to so many relaxation techniques that helped me through my different emotional phases. She taught me journaling, listening to relaxing sounds, sitting quietly, and just allowing myself to feel the pain and not stay in it. I heard about the techniques before, but I considered them a waste of time. After practicing them, I found them to be invaluable. They helped me to reduce stress, gain peace of mind, and enhance my ability to relax, if only for a moment.

Counseling helped as well. I agreed to go to counseling with Craig in an effort to save our marriage. Time revealed that he continued to lie during the counseling sessions. I ended the marriage counseling and started individual counseling. I gained an open and positive mindset. I was determined to take the steps necessary to make it through.

One night, I did not see his car when I went to drop the children off at his parent's house where he lived. It was late and his car should have been at his parents' house where he stayed. I felt that he did not care where I was or what I was doing. He no longer had to answer to me, and I did not have to answer to him. Our only connection was the children. I called him and asked where he was. I told him that I brought the children back and he should have been there. He was at a pool party. I was hurt. He was having fun while I sat in the driveway of his parents' house heartbroken and crying. Nothing had changed whether he and I were together or not. Reality had come; it was time to start over.

I asked God, "Haven't I been through enough?"

At the same time, I knew with all the ups and downs in life, I asked for forgiveness each time that I felt that I thought ill of Craig. I hated the visions I had of him with other women while he was married to me and coming home to lay with me. I hated all that he did to cause me pain. Daily, I asked the Lord to forgive me and to help me to let it all go.

For the four years prior to that time, Camela, her sisters, and her friends all spent Mother's Day weekend in the Bahamas. Trying to deal with the divorce, I badly wanted to go and get away from all the emotions I felt at home. Even though I was overwhelmed with bills and debt, I used available balances on multiple credit cards to spend Mother's Day 2010 in the Bahamas at the Atlantis with Kim, Camela and her family. I tried to hold back my tears throughout the trip. Whenever my tears welled up, I would not allow them fall from my eyes. At the same time, it seemed that my tears, if they fell, would fall from my eyes like waterfalls. I stared at four giant conch shells chiseled out of concrete that adorned the interior of an opening over a pool of water in the Atlantis outdoor courtyard. I imagined that two of the conch shells represented my eyes.

If only I could let the tears fall from my eyes, the amount of tears would be like the water that fell from the conch shells. If I let the tears fall, the pressure would release, and the tears would fall like waterfalls from my eyes to the pool in my lap below as I sat on the side of my bed, in my car, at my desk at work or the middle of a meeting. As the waterfall of tears continued to fall, the pain would slowly release.

I wanted to let it all out. I wanted to release the pressure, but the overwhelming emotional images and thoughts always appeared when I thought it was not appropriate to cry. Therefore, I held back the tears and dealt with the pressure in my chest that spread to my head, neck, shoulders and back. My body was stiff and tense with emotional pressure.

I did not want my children to see me cry. I did not want to break down at work. I did not want to break down while I drove home from work. I did not want to break down during a meeting or while negotiating a case. Yet, I needed to release some of the pressure. The emotional pain was tremendous. My throat felt swollen as if I could not swallow. I struggled to swallow anyway. Each swallow added more pressure in my chest. Whether I cried or held my tears, I needed and wanted to cry, but the pain was too intense. I wanted to truly forgive in order not to deal with the reality of my marriage. I had to admit to myself that forgiving was difficult, when I sincerely felt that the person I loved and cared about had hurt me so deeply.

I reached a point where I accepted that change had come, and I had to move on. An email helped me. It was titled, "Forgive Everyone for Everything." It cited Luke 6:37: *Forgive and you will be forgiven.*

The email went on to say:

Everybody has had someone who has "done them wrong." When someone hurts us, we want to hurt them back. We live with anger and thoughts of revenge. We want to see them suffer. We want them to feel what we have felt. We want them to know they can't get away with what they did. But they did get away with it if your anger keeps you stuck in the situation. When the table turns, we make mistakes, we create pain for others, and we cannot understand why they do not and cannot forgive us. Perhaps it is because there is someone we need to forgive. Forgiveness frees us from the pain of the past and moves us beyond our mistakes in the future. What you give, you get. Forgiveness is for you.

I sent the email to Craig. It was difficult for me to express myself to him because it seemed that he minimized what I said, or because I made him feel bad. I thought that the email expressed how I felt in words I was not able to put together myself. I just wanted someone to love me. I wanted someone to care about me. I wanted someone to be there for me.

Thoughts continued to run rampant in my mind. I imagined how Mom must have felt to lose control over her thoughts when she was not on her medication. She continued to have thoughts of self-doubt, thoughts that her daughter did not love her, and thoughts that her family did not want her. She even had thoughts that someone stole the remote control when it fell off the couch and was under a pillow on the floor, and thoughts that her keys were forever gone when she forgot that she put them in her pants pocket.

I was determined to make it through.

One night, I watched Joyce Meyer of Joyce Meyer Ministries. I always find her messages encouraging and inspirational. During the sermon that night, she talked about how people should not compare their circumstances to other people's circumstances. She suggested that we become frustrated with life when we believe that another person is doing better than we are. We may compare ourselves to people who have more, who are able to do more, who are happier, and whose children are doing well in school while our children are failing in school and other comparisons about life situations in general. I took notes when she said we needed to "Praise God despite our circumstances. If you do not praise God during the wilderness, you will not praise God in the Promised Land."

Ms. Meyer encouraged her audience to have the mindset to go the extra mile, to be generous, and to give and do more than enough. What stuck out most for me was her explanation that God may give blessings to balance out the stuff we know nothing about in another person's life. She encouraged her audience not to compare their lives to the lives of others. She explained how others may look like they are more blessed, but may have more problems that no one may know anything about.

I feel that way about the circumstances in my life. People have told me over the years that they thought I was born with a silver spoon in my mouth. Others said I do not look like I have been through the things that I describe. I have been called stuck up, too good, even arrogant, because I have three degrees or because I am an attorney. People do not know all the loans I have and the drama, sweat, and tears I endured to make it through earning each of my degrees with a child and later a husband and another child. People do not know what I have experienced throughout my childhood with Mom's illness, Dad's rejection, and dealing with the ultimate betrayal of someone I loved and trusted.

I wanted to marry him…he married me. I wanted to divorce him… he got an attorney and filed for custody of our children, child support, and spousal support. I was angrier than ever before.

What am I gonna do? I thought to myself.

I finally realized that I strived for perfection to make up for the losses in my life. I was afraid to make mistakes, fail, and to have people upset with me; and sadly, I was afraid of not being wanted by others who were significant in my life. Reality is that I am not perfect.

* * * * *

On the day of our pre-trial hearing for the divorce, it took all I had within me not to "lose my religion" as my Aunt Geneva used to say.

Lord, help me, I thought to myself whenever I was in Craig's presence.

I just wanted to end the marriage so I could move forward. I knew that there was nothing I could do about the past.

Craig claimed that going through the divorce led him to develop a relationship with the Lord. He claimed to be a better person. He claimed to be in the best physical health of his life. It hurt to think of how much I went through for him to establish a relationship with the Lord, become saved, and to become a better person. I cannot question anyone's salvation, but I wondered why I had to suffer for him to become saved.

I thought Jesus made that sacrifice for all of us.

After the pre-trial hearing, there were so many things that I wish were said. I asked the Lord for forgiveness and to *please deal with my heart and the anger I feel.* I tried not to dislike Craig, but when he said he hoped that we could be friends, I really needed the Lord to help me.

I contained myself and replied, "Friends don't do friends like this. If a friend of mine did me like this, I would not be that person's friend anymore."

A friend to me, at that moment, seemed more valuable than a spouse. A friend is someone you can turn to when you are at odds with your spouse. Craig was not my friend, and soon he was not going to be my spouse.

As we stood outside the court building looking at each other and talking, it would be one of the last times we talked to each other as husband and wife. It was a beautiful August day—sunny with a nice breeze. The same beautiful couple that stood before a pastor and church full of people to exchange vows as husband and wife, now stood outside the court building that would end their marriage. A beautiful day and a beautiful couple; but still an ugly situation—a picture perfect couple, but the frame was taken from the wall and thrown to the ground. The glass shattered. The picture was ruined. Yet and still, during the days that led to the trial, I thought, *it's not over until the Judge strikes the gavel or the judgment entry is filed. Even then, it does not have to be over.*

I figured *if Jesus comes down and tells me not to do this,* I will not. However, the day of the trial, I lost it. I came out of myself and saw the whole thing like an out-of-body experience. Craig and I were in a conference room to discuss the final details of our separation. I wanted him to pay half of the children's medical expenses for the 2010 calendar year, including Jaylon's braces which Craig failed to pay half as he previously promised. Once Jaylon's braces were off, Craig refused to pay.

"It's not that I don't *want* to pay. The law says I don't *have* to pay," he stated as an excuse to go back on his promise.

"THE LAW!!! Who cares what the law says!" I jumped out my chair and started pounding on the conference table with my fists. There was no need for the Judge to strike the gavel, and there was no need for us to wait until the judgment entry was filed. There was definitely no need for Jesus to come down from heaven and tell me not to get divorced. It was over.

"What kind of man are you?!" I screamed. "You don't want to pay for your own children's medical expenses?! Your children! They are your children; not the law's children! They are your children!"

Every time I spoke, I hit the table with my fists. The veins in my neck and head throbbed. The more I screamed, the more they bulged out of my head and neck. I grabbed my briefcase and just as I snatched open the conference room door, a deputy had his hand on the knob to open the door. I did not realize how mad I was. I did not realize how loud I was. All I knew was at that very moment, the marriage was over.

Totally beside myself, I left the conference room. I went so far as to leave the court building entirely. I went and sat in my car in the parking lot across the street. I listened to the Fred Hammond CD that Camela gave me. Just when it reached my favorite part of my favorite song, my attorney called.

"Corey, where are you…what are you doing?"

"I'm in my car."

"Your car…what are you doing in your car? Get back in here. You know that is the type of stuff you get contempt of court for!"

Knowing full well he couldn't, I still said, "Can't you go on without me?"

"Corey…"

There was no need for him to say anymore. I listened to the song until it was over and went back into the court building. My attorney tried to convince me to just settle after Craig continued to refuse to pay for the children's medical expenses. I refused to settle.

"Take it to the Judge," I said with my arms crossed and pure anger all over my face. I paid for too much, struggled too much, and in my opinion…all unnecessarily. I knew I risked everything being split down the middle, but at that moment, I did not care. I was not giving in as I did throughout our marriage.

When we were in the courtroom, I ended up arguing my own case, especially when it came to the medical expenses. The Judge ruled in my favor. It was over. It was all over. So I thought. Eight years later he filed for sole custody of our youngest son, Jordan, along with child support.

According to Craig's report to the Guardian Ad Litem:

"Mother does not have the tools to set him up for future success. If you talk to Mother you would think she was a perfect kid and did all the things she has done on her own…

Mother can provide food and water, but she is neglectful in her relationship with [her son] and in [his] emotional well-being.

Father reported maternal grandmother had mental health issues, specifically schizophrenia.

Father reported maternal grandfather was not there for Mother. Father reported he believes this has impacted the type of mother she has become.

Father reported when cameras come on, Mother is there, but she is nonexistent for the daily grind."

According to the Guardian, "some witnesses, as well the records, report more involvement from Mother. Based on that, I disagree with Father that Mother is nonexistent for the daily grind."

Each word cut my soul as easy as paper slices a finger resulting in intense pain and instant, nonstop bleeding. Embroiled in a custody battle, I agonized over excruciating emotional hurt and pain to ultimately stop the bleeding. I offered to only see my son every other weekend and to provide support. I resolved the matter. I will continue to love my children with all my heart and soul. Along with their birthday gifts, I sent the following message to both of my sons:

"The source of my most excruciating, heart wrenching pain… and yet, my most exhilarating joy and happiness. I thank God for blessing me with the opportunity to bring forth life in you!

Happy Birthday!

I praise God that you are and will be a strong, independent and self-sufficient young man, living your best life."

Chapter Thirty

Continuously Motivated to Succeed

I feel that a lot of what I have experienced in life "just ain't right." However, I was, and continue to be, determined to change my thoughts from feeling dumb for choosing to believe and overlook irrational and blatant lies. I feel that I got played, but I had to move on. During one of my annual check-ups my nurse asked, "How are things going?"

"I got the divorce. It's over."

"Oh, okay," she said. "I know you talked about it the last time you were here. Are you dating anyone?"

"No, I am not quite comfortable with it right now."

We discussed my future involvement with other men. I described my concerns and inability to fully enjoy the possibilities of new experiences with male companions.

"I mean...he was my husband. If he treated me that way, what can I expect from any other man?"

All of a sudden, she put down her notepad and slammed her pen on top of it. She just glared at me with calmness in her eyes; along with a touch of irritation.

"You need to get past it. Perhaps you need to forgive him. You need to forgive yourself."

I turned my eyes away from her and looked down toward my lap. My back began to slouch from my upright position as I sat in the chair across from her, in front of her desk.

"You have to forgive yourself, Corey."

She was the same nurse that I spoke to each time I felt I should have a checkup because of Craig and all he was doing as a married man, but acting single when he was not home. She knew about my feelings; we discussed them at each appointment. She knew that I was devastated by it all.

After a bit of a pause and with a big smile, she said, "Now put that in your book!"

All the pain I felt seemed to erase with each word my nurse said. It was not my fault. I know that I am valuable. I love, appreciate, and respect myself. I expect nothing less from others. I often pray to God and remind Him of His Word that says, *whatever is bound on earth shall be bound in heaven, and whatever is loosed on earth, it shall be loosed in heaven.*

With that as support of my petition, I begged in my prayer that the Lord would help me free myself from negative relationships, feelings, thoughts, desires, and temptations. I prayed that He would release me from self-criticism, self-hatred, and any lack of self-love.

Heavenly Father, I trust and believe in you. I know you are the only one to see me through. Help me through the fear of the unknown, the fear of uncertainty, and the fear of insecurity. I am a child of God. I am blessed.

I realized that this is life. People feel what they feel, and do what they do, based on how they feel at the time. Losses are a regular part of life, and I spent many years hating myself for each and every one of my losses. As I learned from *Overcoming Crisis, The Secrets to Thriving in Challenging Times*, by Dr. Myles Munroe:

"No one is exempt from crisis, not even the most righteous believer in the Kingdom of God. But the Kingdom of God itself is never in crisis. As citizens of that Kingdom, we need to make it our business to tackle every crisis situation in faith, knowing that part of the reason God allows and even sends crises is to enable us to grow." (Page 236)

After some eye-opening experiences, my life's focus has been to be "successful." I want success so that my children will not have to go through the same struggles that I endured. Throughout my time working for others, and seeking their approval in hopes of them helping me to achieve my "success," I have come to realize that my success is defined by me. Success is what I make it for me. My success includes the many opportunities that I have to set goals, and continue to be motivated and determined to accomplish my goals.

Success is not a destination. Success is a continuous journey. As I continue to set goals, strive to achieve them, and actually reach them, I know that I will continue to be successful. Success is mine and success can be yours. Despite any undesirable circumstances, you can be Continuously Motivated to Succeed. The only limitation is you.

As Dr. Munroe says, "You must believe that you have the capacity to solve the problems you are facing. With faith in God, you know that He will supply you with anything you may be lacking. Your ability to solve problems stems from His unlimited ability to solve problems." *Overcoming Crisis, The Secrets to Thriving in Challenging Times.* (Page 224)

My way of solving problems was to engulf myself in a tidal wave of activities and achievements. After the divorce, I was forced to think of my life as a single woman with two young men that I wanted, with all my heart, to grow up to be independent self-sufficient men. For me, I needed to find my "spot." As that little girl so eager to go to court and wanting so badly to see how the court operated, I now was a brokenhearted attorney not knowing what to do with herself. After working with the City of Canton for three years, I felt stuck with no opportunity for growth. I intended to only serve one term whether the mayor won the next election or not.

But what to do, I did not know. My life was in rewind as I thought about me as a high school student who worked for Canton Municipal Court through the Job and Training Partnership Program. During that time, I learned the inner workings of the court which led to my vision of being an attorney. Subsequently, I graduated seventeenth in the Timken Senior High School class of 1992 and went on to earn a Bachelor's Degree of Arts in English. Many seemed to have given up on me when I became pregnant my senior year at Bowling Green State University. However, I graduated in four years and with Jaylon went on to earn a Master's Degree of Education in Guidance and Counseling from Bowling Green State University.

While earning my Juris Doctorate from the University of Toledo College of Law, I served as 2L Class Representative and as President of the Black Law Student Association. I was a member of the Student Bar Association and competed in the 15th Annual University of Minnesota Law School National Civil Rights Moot Court Competition entitled, *Breaking Up the Ghetto: The Barriers to Integrating Low Cost Housing and People of Color Into the Broader Community.* I also won first place in the American Society of Composers Artists and Publishers' Nathan Burkan Memorial Competition.

I then began my legal career as an Assistant Prosecutor with the leadership of Robert Horowitz. As a Judicial Attorney for the Summit County Court of Common Pleas, I authored decisions that were upheld by the 9th District Court of Appeals before establishing the Law Office of Corey Minor Smith, LLC. Soon after that, former Mayor William J. Healy, II handpicked me to serve as the Director of Compliance for the City of Canton. At that time, I was one of the youngest mayoral cabinet members in Canton's history.

As a member of the Ohio and Georgia Bars and licensed to practice before the United States District Court of the Northern District of Ohio, I now serve as General Counsel for Stark Metropolitan Housing Authority ("SMHA").

Yet, with all that, it was not enough. I wanted more.

Night after night, I could not sleep. I started praying, asking God, "What do you want me to do?"

Sleep deprivation started to weigh in. I was exhausted at work and could not sleep at night.

I'll do it tomorrow…I would say, and then the next day, *I'll do it tomorrow*…then the next day, *I'll do it tomorrow.*

Time and time again, I would tell myself, *I'll do it tomorrow* as I take a shower and fall in my bed from exhaustion. I struggled to fall asleep for at least an hour and a half as my mind juggled a thousand thoughts of what I forgot to do that day, and what I had to do the next day. Often, I think about how to organize my time to get the most things possible completed. It is as if I have a non-exhaustive list of "things to do."

Above all, I wanted to get my manuscript published. The thought of writing a book has been with me since I was sixteen. In 2012, I finally committed time to get my story written and developed a focus group to review the manuscript. Members of the group signed confidentiality agreements and were to have their suggestions for revisions to me by the end of February, 2013. The group met its deadline. I did not.

At that point in my life, I wanted more for my career, more than just being "an attorney." I struggled to fall asleep and to stay asleep each night. Each day at work I felt exhausted. After weeks of not sleeping well, I decided to investigate what it would take to pursue another career goal. In addition to being an attorney, I had goals of being an author, professional speaker, and a courtroom Judge.

On February 5, 2013, I inquired about local judgeship terms in an effort to organize next steps for my career. After making inquiries and accumulating information, I decided to run for Judge of Canton (Ohio) Municipal Court. But I faced an immediate challenge: the filing deadline for the election was the next day, February 6, 2013.

My mind began to race with thoughts, yet my body froze with anxiety... *You say you wanna be a Judge one day...it's here right now. What are you gonna do? You said you want it. What are you gonna do?*

I had less than twenty-four hours to make a decision. I gathered myself, shook off any remaining anxiety, and went to the Board of Elections to pull a petition. Ninety-nine signatures later, and with an hour to spare, I filed my petition as the first African American female candidate for Judge of the Canton Municipal Court.

On the eve of my campaign, a ruling was issued heavily critical of me as a hearing officer. Although it was brought up by those who chose not to support me, I did not take it personally, and I could not let it distract me.

It's a case with "buzz words" cited as a part of the analysis to meet the standard needed to reach the conclusion that justified reversing my administrative decision. "Buzz words" were what I was encouraged to focus on as an exam taking strategy to pass the bar. It's just like the cases we hear about all the time that are appealed; one court will agree and uphold a lower court's decision, or it will disagree and reverse a lower court's decision, I thought.

At the same time, I thought about how quotes from the decision could be used to tarnish my legal career and any chance of me winning an election or getting votes for that matter. However, I respect the judge's decision and the law. I went to training, improved my skills, and continue to address issues during administrative hearings prepared to defend my determinations whenever they may be challenged.

Additionally, as if the court's decision was not enough, SMHA was under fire with allegations that questioned my involvement in "stealing money" and drafting a confidentiality agreement that some considered overreaching. The local newspaper dedicated a weekly series of articles featuring the Office of Inspector General findings against SMHA. HUD named the agency a *Low Performer*. To make the matter worse, I was laid-off. Through it all, I know God protected me along the way. After a month, I was re-hired. I then worked to help SMHA satisfy the terms of a Recovery Plan and negotiate a Repayment Agreement with HUD.

With all the hard work of SMHA staff, ultimately SMHA improved its performance status with HUD.

After a whirlwind of events, fairs, parades, dinners, and programs, and as the first African American female to be a candidate for Judge in the Canton Municipal Court, I received thirty percent of the vote against a twenty-plus-year incumbent. It was an exciting venture for me. Fox News covered the story: *Local Candidate Hopes to Make History*. Subsequently, I received the most votes out of five candidates, and I was elected to the Canton City Schools Board of Education during a pivotal moment in the district's history.

At the start of my term, the last two high schools in Canton merged. My alma mater, Timken Senior High School, dissolved resulting in one Canton City high school, McKinley Senior High. It was a sad time for many, but it was an honor and privilege to be a part of the first combined Timken Senior High School and McKinley Senior High School graduation where both schools were fully recognized with colors, alma maters sung, and the top ten students recognized.

After both campaigns, I just wanted to breathe. I wanted to take a moment to "smell the roses" as many people have suggested that I do throughout my school and legal career. I was, and still am, elated at the opportunities I dared to take. Meanwhile, my manuscript—complete with revisions based on the suggestions of the anonymous focus group—continued to sit on the top shelf of my closet collecting dust. Children and demanding school/work and obligations in general, have controlled my life since I was a young adult. Time rolled by with the hour, minute, and second hands rapidly circling the clock as the seasons changed in fast forward. It seemed like I had forgotten about my manuscript.

Although I've been to speaking workshops, seminars, presentations, and I've even presented nationally and internationally...my manuscript still sat on the shelf. Years have come and gone since all comments were due back from the anonymous focus group that I tasked with reading my manuscript. The desire to publish my manuscript slowly diminished to just a thought.

Then I got this nudge: "Would you be a guest columnist for our newsletter?" An email from Dr. Tim framed the inquiry.

Dr. Tim and I initially met over the phone through a connection of a mutual friend. He asked that I send him random excerpts from my manuscript so that he could determine my writing style. Sometime later, we met in person when he and his wife were in Ohio visiting from Atlanta. By that time, Dr. Tim had read my excerpts.

During our meeting, Dr. Tim said, "You went from JD to JD."

I looked at him puzzled.

"Do you know what that means?" he continued.

"No…" I said.

"You were a juvenile delinquent of sorts, and you went on to earn your Juris Doctorate…you went from JD to JD."

Smiling as I nodded in agreement, and thought about how differently my life could have been, I said, "I guess I did."

Little did I know that on my forty-second birthday, I would receive a Facebook post from someone that experienced a part of my different life…

"Happy Birthday, Corey!! I am soooo proud of you! There was a day in South Vallejo that I will never forget! And now look at you, you grew up to be a very strong, and positive example to women all over!"

Oh my goodness…tears welled up in my eyes as I thought to myself. I felt my heart drop to the pit of my stomach as I immediately flashbacked to that same day in South Vallejo when we (Da Posse) jumped a girl with no one else there to help defend her. I too remembered that day in South Vallejo. I cannot imagine what mental scars we caused that will make her "never forget." Things we do in life can leave lasting impressions good and bad. From her Facebook post, there is some hope that she sees that people can change—I changed—to do things for the good.

In 2015, nearly five years after meeting Dr. Tim in Akron, I could not believe that Dr. Tim was still interested in working with me. After all, I let so much time pass, I started to wonder when I would ever get the manuscript published. My first joyful statement that I was going to write a book was at the age of sixteen. The day after my thirtieth birthday, I met Les Brown. Even though he showed an interest in my story then, it was six years later that I contacted him again. Even after I received the content of the Foreword, I still did not proceed with finishing my manuscript. Time continued to pass by, and I seemed to be satisfied with saying, "I have a book coming out soon" only for it not to come out yet.

How do I end it? Perhaps if I am elected to judge, that will be the grand ending with a significant meaning. It just doesn't seem like the story is good enough. I need a bang of an ending..."

Each thought seemed to translate into a decade of time passed.

But Dr. Tim was still interested in working with me despite all the time I allowed to pass. I accepted his offer and wrote an article titled, "Getting out of My Own Way." It was time for me to get out of my own way, grab the manuscript that had sat too long on the top shelf of my closet, wipe the dust off of it, and get the manuscript published. The manuscript was edited by an adjunct professor, and reviewed by an anonymous focus group and by Dr. Tim. Eventually, the manuscript developed into *#Driven*, a motivational memoir designed to be an example of how readers can overcome real life obstacles in order to reach their goals.

Thinking back over my life, I focused on my initials with the intent to create a statement that described me. I came up with Continuously Motivated to Succeed.

There's no other way to describe me, I thought to myself.

Through IT All, on my way to having IT ALL, I am Continuously Motivated to Succeed...CMS. From the acronym, I developed five principles to be CMS:

1. Faith – be encouraged by and have faith in your God-given ability to do anything you want to do in your life.

2. Motivation – despite undesirable circumstances, continuously connect with outside sources to reboot and enhance your desire to achieve the goals you establish for yourself.

3. Determination – maintain the driving force within you that no one can give you, or take away from you, and allow it to propel you toward your goals.

4. Preparation – do all that you can do to learn about available resources and to acquire the skills you need to be prepared to receive the help that is available for you to reach your goals.

5. Action – write down your goals and take the steps necessary to reach your goals in life because dreaming, wishing, and hoping, will not develop into anything without action.

Life is not about a big grand ending. It is a journey with ups, downs, obstacles, and undesirable circumstances. Those things do not magically stop when "you've made it." Success comes with being able to…as my best friend Kim says, and like the spelling of her name…"Keep It Moving."

By sharing the intimate details of my personal challenges, I hope that you know how, even when faced with what appears to be impossible undesirable circumstances, to hold fast to your hopes and dreams. You have to believe in yourself, as you K.I.M. during your journey to making your goals reality. You are the only one that can prevent you from reaching your goals.

REMEMBER: Don't allow undesirable circumstances to be excuses for you to fail, but allow them to be reasons for you to excel.

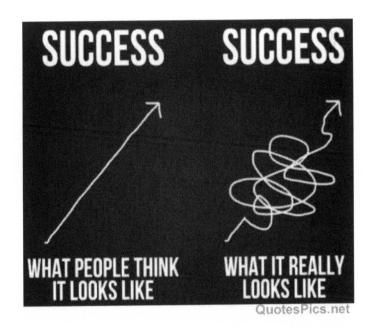

Epilogue

History with a Twist

E lection Day, November 7, 2017, is a day that history was made in Canton, Ohio. I received the most votes in a six-candidate race, and I am the first African American to be elected to Canton City Council at Large. The journey was spectacular with the assistance of committed volunteers that dedicated time and resources to complete traditional campaign strategies and more. However, the campaign was all but traditional.

According to CantonRep.com Special Projects Editor, Todd Porter, "The odds would say to bet against her. The odds would be wrong." Other candidates had long-term name recognition from their own extended time dedicated to public service, or that of their parents. Me, I attended fourteen different schools, lived in three states, and in eight different households. Some believe that I have accomplished great things despite adversity. However, many do not know about the on-going, traumatic, and emotional adversity that I experience as a daughter with a mother that has mental illness.

My mother was diagnosed with manic depression/schizophrenia when was I about thirteen years old. When I was fifteen, she attacked me. A No Contact Order was issued by the court, and I was placed with my paternal grandmother. As an adult, I still have fear of my Mom because of the day of the attack, and other days that followed. Yet, during the campaign, I experienced incomparable fear when I received a call from a public employee in another jurisdiction that found my Mom staying in a vacant house with no utilities. Along with my family, I worked with local mental health and law enforcement agencies to help my Mom. She was hospitalized, received treatment, eventually released to live on her own, and...the cycle continues. It's a constant battle.

I have learned to name and own every last bit of my story through prayer and faith in God. It has resulted in an explosion of grace and healing from the most unimaginable experiences that haunt me. When a person is living with a serious mental illness, family and friends may also be impacted.

Here are five suggestions that can help family and friends with loved ones that have mental illness:

1. Pray.

2. Educate yourself about the illness/illnesses and have realistic expectations.

3. Maintain current contact information for local mental health and law enforcement resources.

4. Reach out for support, even for yourself—It's ok to go to counseling.

5. Work closely with your loved one's treatment team.

If you or someone you know would like more information, contact organizations like the National Alliance on Mental Illness (NAMI):

Text: NAMI to 741741
Call: 1-800-950-6264
Visit: NAMI.ORG

You can also research other local mental health resources in your community.

Acknowledgments

I give all thanks to God for the opportunity to progress through my experiences and transform my undesirable circumstances into the highest quality life that I can possibly obtain. I once said that I want to be successful so badly that it hurt. My family and friends have been a tremendous support system for me, and have eased my pain as I journeyed on my path to success. In no way can I name each and every person that has made a positive impact in my life. Many have played significant roles during my journey, and I thank you all for fulfilling your role to the fullest.

Mom and Dad
Bluchelle Scott McDonald
Wanetta "Ms. Vickie" Minor
Aunt Doris and Uncle Etheridge Smoots
Aunt Nambi Angaza
Aunt Shanie Minor
Aunt Melody Roberts
Kimberly Askew-Webb
Camela Chavers Douglass
Gemel Thomas and Marlon Smith
The Minor and Mitchell Family (M&M)
The Scott Family
Veronica Bannister and Family
Jeanne "Mummy" and Frances McGraw
Linda and Rock Ferguson and Family
Eric and Roxanne Nance
The Smith Family
Walida Gibson
Monica Heflin
Kinta and Tiffany Mitchell
Nycole Daniels
Tara Flakes
Wanda Lash
Andrea Perry
Athena and Joe Ostrowske

Christine and Scott Ridgway
Jumana Selah
Virginia Jeffries
Beverly Gainer
Christine "Chris" Smith
Raymond Strain
Myra Watkins and Young Life
The Honorable James R. Williams
Attorney Edward Parms
Attorney Lewis Adkins
Attorney Edward T. Smith
Attorney Edward L. Gilbert
Attorney E. Mark Young
Patricia Coia
Pastor Walter and Darlene Moss
Fonda and Pam Williams
William J. Healy, II and Family
"Uncle Kim" Perez
Bill and Randi Smuckler
Aimee Schlernitzauer
Michael Kanam and Family
Alvin L. A. Horn
Lorraine Elzia
Curtis A. Perry, III
Patricia Henderson and The Reporter
Robin Kratzer/Jobs and Training Partnership (JTP)
Bowling Green State University
University of Toledo College of Law
Black Law Student Association
Delta Sigma Theta Sorority, Incorporated
National Alliance on Mental Illness, Stark County
The Honorable Ira G. Turpin Scholars Committee
Akron-Canton Barristers Association
Canton City School District
Stark County Community Action Agency
And to all those who have loved me,
prayed for me,
cared for me,
supported me,
and voted for me,
THANK YOU!!!

About the Author

Corey Minor Smith was born in Canton, Ohio and graduated from Timken Senior High School. She earned a Bachelor's Degree of Arts in English and a Master's Degree of Education in Guidance and Counseling from Bowling Green State University.

She is a member of the Ohio and Georgia bars and licensed to practice before the United States District Court of the Northern District of Ohio. She began her legal career as an Assistant Prosecutor and later served as a Judicial Attorney authoring decisions that were upheld by the 9th District Court of Appeals before establishing the Law Office of Corey Minor Smith, LLC. Currently, as General Counsel for Stark Metropolitan Housing Authority (SMHA), Corey represents SMHA in civil and administrative proceedings and guides the Executive Director and SMHA staff on an array of complex legal, labor relations, and contract matters. Nationally, Corey was a panelist at the Housing and Development Law Institute conference in Washington DC. Internationally, Corey presented in Cape Town, South Africa during the Southern African Housing Foundation Conference as a delegate of the United States.

The Canton Oldtimers Ladies Auxiliary Club honored Corey with its Phenomenal Woman Award, she was named one of Stark County's Twenty Under 40! and an ATHENA International Women's Leadership Finalist. The Boy Scouts of America Buckeye Council also honored Corey with the Spirit of Scouting Award and she was inducted into the YWCA Women's Hall of Fame, Class of 2016. Her current community activities include being a motivational speaker, a member of the Honorable Judge Ira Turpin Scholars Recognition Committee and the Akron-Canton Barristers Association. In addition, she is a proud member of the Stark County Alumnae Chapter of Delta Sigma Theta Sorority, Incorporated. Among her accomplishments, Corey was the first African American female to be a candidate for Judge in the Canton Municipal Court and received 30% of the vote against a twenty-plus-year incumbent. Subsequently, Corey was elected to the Canton City Schools Board of Education after receiving the most votes out of five candidates. Corey now serves as an at-large member of Canton City Council after receiving the most votes out of six candidates. She is the first African American to ever be elected to a citywide race in Canton, Ohio.

Book Corey for your next event!
Corey Empowers
330-452-9937
cms@coreyempowers.com

Corey
EMPOWERS | AUTHOR
| & TRANSFORMATIONAL
| SPEAKER

Made in the USA
Columbia, SC
02 February 2019